Alva Ixtlilxochitl's Native Archive and the Circulation of Knowledge in Colonial Mexico

Amber Brian

Vanderbilt University Press
NASHVILLE

This book is printed on acid-free paper.
Manufactured in the United States of America

Library of Congress Cataloging-in-Publication Data

LC control number 2015014603
LC classification number F1219.3.H56B73 2016
Dewey class number 972'.01—dc23

ISBN 978-0-8265-2097-5 (hardcover)
ISBN 978-0-8265-2099-9 (ebook)

For Brian, Mira, and Silas

CONTENTS

ACKNOWLEDGMENTS

W ORK ON *ALVA IXTLILXOCHITL'S NATIVE ARCHIVE* has spanned many
years and many communities of friends, colleagues, and mentors. Along
the way I have accrued countless debts. My work on don Fernando de
Alva Ixtlilxochitl and don Carlos de Sigüenza y Góngora began in graduate school during classes I took, serendipitously in the same semester,
with Margarita Zamora and Steve Stern. In those early research papers, I
began to see underexplored connections between the two Mexican intellectuals. Though that work took place many moons ago and the project
has taken numerous turns since, I owe the origins of this book to their
foundational guidance. A travel grant from the University of Wisconsin-
Madison allowed for an early trip to see the manuscripts—then housed
at Cambridge University—that are central to this study. I am grateful to
Margarita and Steve whose continued support and careful direction were
instrumental to my initial thinking and writing about Alva Ixtlilxochitl
and Sigüenza. I also thank Steve Hutchinson and Guido Podestá. Course-
work and conversations with these professors provided the intellectual
foundations for *Alva Ixtlilxochitl's Native Archive.*

A residential fellowship at the Newberry Library in the summer of 2007
came as I was beginning to reimagine the earlier iteration of the project
as a book. I am especially grateful to Andrew Laird who orchestrated the
seminar that was the capstone to my invigorating months-long stay in
the reading room at the Newberry, where I was able to work with important manuscript copies of Alva Ixtlilxochitl's works. The framework and the
speakers who participated in the workshop, "European and New World
Forms of Knowledge in Colonial Spanish America, ca. 1520–1800," proved

to be extraordinarily stimulating for my own thinking about Alva Ixtlilxo-chitl and Sigüenza. I am particularly grateful to Andrew, David Boruchoff, Cristián Roa-de-la-Carrera, and Lisa Voigt for their encouragement and advice as I was developing this project. During that summer I also had the good fortune to meet Susan Schroeder in the Newberry reading room. I owe a tremendous debt of gratitude to Susan for her early and enduring support for my work, as well as her strategic guidance throughout.

At the University of Iowa, I have benefitted from enriching conver-sations and sustained encouragement from colleagues and friends, par-ticularly Denise Filios, Claire Fox, Lisa Gardinier, Cathy Komisaruk, Kathleen Newman, Mercedes Niño-Murcia, Phillip Round, and Chris-tine Shea. I also thank Daniel Balderston, who extended enthusiastic and crucial support for my project while he was at the University of Iowa. I would like to acknowledge the University of Iowa's Arts and Humanities Initiative award, which allowed me to travel to Mexico City and conduct critical research at the Archivo General de la Nación.

I am indebted to many colleagues and friends who have offered feed-back at conferences and other gatherings. I am especially grateful to Rolena Adorno, Galen Brokaw, Jongsoo Lee, Tatiana Seijas, David Tavárez, and Camilla Townsend, who each at various moments asked key questions and made probing comments as I worked through the contours of my analysis. My work on this book has coincided with two other collaborative projects related to Alva Ixtlilxochitl, which have been thoroughly stimulating and nourishing. I thank Bradley Benton, Pablo García Loaeza, and Peter Villella for their countless hours of effort and conversation, as we toil over transla-tions of Alva Ixtlilxochitl's writings. I am grateful to Wayne Ruwet for gen-erously sharing his deep knowledge and keen interest in the topic. This book would be unimaginable without his finding of the original Alva Ixtlilxochitl manuscripts decades ago. Mónica Díaz, my dear friend and interlocutor, has been a steady source of encouragement and insight. I am forever grateful to her for her unstinting confidence in the value of this project and my ability to complete it effectively. I claim as my own all flaws and errors contained within the following pages, but any insights found here are indebted to ongoing dialogue with these and other esteemed colleagues.

I am truly fortunate to have been able to publish *Alva Ixtlilxochitl's Native Archive* with Vanderbilt University Press. Eli Bortz expressed early and sustained interest in the project. He, as many can attest, is a delight to work with—smart, curious, extraordinarily attentive, and always encouraging. Joell Smith-Borne oversaw every aspect of production with a keen and impeccable eye. I am very appreciative of the extremely conscientious efforts of Peg Duthie, who undertook the copyediting with meticulous care. I am most grateful to the anonymous readers whose incisive and insightful comments made this a better book. I would like to thank *Colonial Latin American Review* for permission to publish in Chapter 1, in revised form, portions of my article "Alva Ixtlilxochitl's Original Manuscripts," *CLAR* 23 (1): 84–101 (*www.tandfonline.com*). Portions of Chapter 4 were prepared as the essay "Alva Ixtlilxochitl and the Guadalupe Legend: The Question of Authorship," which I contributed to a volume that is forthcoming from University of Arizona Press.

My parents, Michael and Suzanne Brian, have eagerly awaited the conclusion of this book. I thank them for the jovial support they have extended during its many years of incubation. I also thank my beloved siblings and their families and my dear in-laws for their support. Though my mother-in-law, Doris Gollnick, did not live to see the completion of this project, I would like to remember her enduring support here. Mira and Silas Gollnick, my bright shining stars, came into the world as this book was getting underway. Each stage of my research and writing was marked by new joys and feats in their young lives. As I complete this project, they are developing their own passions and beginning their own adventures in reading. To Brian Gollnick, my life partner and cherished intellectual companion, I owe more debts and gratitude than I can fully express here. He has supported and encouraged me at each stage, both as an enthusiastic interlocutor and an ever-present partner in parenting. His love and support have made for the bedrock of this book.

INTRODUCTION

Giving and Receiving

A gift has both economic and spiritual content, is personal and reciprocal, and depends on a relationship that endures over time.
— Anne Carson, *Economy of the Unlost*

ALVA IXTLILXOCHITL'S NATIVE ARCHIVE FOCUSES ON the production and circulation of Native American knowledge within and beyond the indigenous communities of colonial Mexico. I begin with a gift, passed materially and symbolically from a family with deep roots in Mexico's pre-Columbian past to a son of recent Spanish immigrants. In the 1680s, don Juan de Alva Cortés, a son of the mestizo chronicler don Fernando de Alva Ixtlilxochitl (ca. 1578–1650), gave his father's collection of native alphabetic and pictorial texts to the creole intellectual don Carlos de Sigüenza y Góngora (1645–1700).[1] This collection became one of the most important archives on pre-Columbian and conquest-era Mexico, and the cultural significance attached to its transfer as a gift has far-reaching relevance. Scholars have long viewed Sigüenza's inheritance of the Alva Ixtlilxochitl materials as a key event in the emergence of patriotic Mexican history (Brading 1991, 366–67; 371). My study enhances that appreciation by examining the complex circumstances and tangled relationships that provide a background to the moment when Alva Ixtlilxochitl's archive passed to Sigüenza, and so from the control of a native-identified family to that of a European-descended scholar.

The transfer of Alva Ixtlilxochitl's collection to Sigüenza has sometimes been interpreted as a gesture of gratitude from the native family to the creole, for his aid in fending off aggressive advances by the viceregal government against their holdings and privileges (Leonard 1929, 10; Keen 1971, 190), and sometimes as an act of thievery by a greedy creole who coveted indigenous historical materials (Rabasa 2010, 211). This book complicates the context of this exchange. Indeed, in the spirit of the epigraph above, I see the gift the Alva Ixtlilxochitl family bequeathed to Sigüenza as the outgrowth of an enduring connection between two very different intellectuals, a creole and a descendant of native lords, both with deep and abiding loyalties to the land in which both were born. While framing her own analysis of two poets from dissimilar historical moments and cultural contexts (Paul Celan and Simonides), Anne Carson synthesizes an argument about gift economies (1999, 12), which Marcel Mauss originally emphasized as the fundamentally *reciprocal* nature of giving (1967).[2] Like Mauss, I see the gift as a window into human relationships bound in the moment of exchange through a preceding history of service and gratitude. For Mauss, the gift is characterized by three linked actions or obligations: giving, receiving, and repaying.[3] These obligations spring from the past relationship between givers and receivers, and understanding the gift economy demands attention to those preceding contexts. By probing the interwoven series of exchanges between individuals, families, and communities that came before Sigüenza took possession of Alva Ixtlilxochitl's collection, we are able to gain a fuller understanding of the context, motivations, and consequences of this paradigmatic example of native knowledge circulating in New Spain.

It is commonplace to say that indigenous culture has been a touchstone in the making of Mexican national history. Writers from the seventeenth century on relied on Aztec—or, more precisely, Nahua—culture to define New Spain as distinct from Old Spain. Jacques Lafaye, Enrique Florescano, David Brading, and Jorge Cañizares-Esguerra are just a few of the influential scholars who have looked at how creole intellectuals drew from native culture to forge a nationalistic narrative of Mexican society.[4] Alva Ixtlilxochitl's collection figures prominently in the studies of how native knowledge and customs influenced creole patriotism. In fact, Brading ascribes more importance to Alva Ixtlilxochitl's collection of native materials than to the histories Alva Ixtlilxochitl wrote or even those of Sigüenza.[5] For Brading, these pictorial and alphabetic texts became instrumental to historians from the eighteenth century, including Lorenzo

Boturini Benaduci, Francisco Javier Clavijero, and Mariano Fernández de Echeverría y Veytia. This is a powerful line of inquiry, but I want to avoid its teleological tendency to read the archive of native knowledge amassed by Alva Ixtlilxochitl only in terms of its impact on later Mexican history. My intention is not to see native knowledge as ceding, inevitably, to national histories. I prefer to focus on what the gift of Alva Ixtlilxo-chitl's collection of native texts reveals about the connections between indigenous communities and the wider intellectual sphere in colonial Mexico. Through these relationships we can gain significant insight into how historical memory in Mexico was created among many actors.

Michel de Certeau opens *The Writing of History* (1975) by comment-ing on Jan Van der Straet's sixteenth-century drawing "America," with its iconic image of a conquistador's landing in the New World, featuring a fully clothed man standing, flag in hand, next to a nude woman reclining on a hammock. The drawing was widely reproduced as an engraving and the fact that it is a representation of Amerigo Vespucci became a mere detail; the man could be Christopher Columbus, or Hernando Cortés or, by allegorical turn, European colonialism writ large. For de Certeau, historiography emerges from the European encounter with the unknown other, and the Van der Straet image communicates what de Certeau calls "a colonization of the body by the discourse of power" (1988 [1975], xxv). "This," he says, "is writing that conquers. It will use the New World as if it were a blank, 'savage' page on which Western desire will be written" (xxv).[6] De Certeau's work relies on an impression of the Indian as defeated; he takes for granted the image of the supine and therefore subordinate native. The term *indio* (Indian) has long been burdened by this connotation of loss, even within Spanish America, leaving us with a situation ripe for contention by scholars and activists.

Prominent among those contesting the image of a passive Indian was the Mexican anthropologist Guillermo Bonfil Batalla (1935–1991), who famously said that the concept embodied in the term "Indian" is inher-ently colonial. According to Bonfil Batalla, the most important factor in subsuming the many and diverse groups of natives under the single cate-gory of "Indian" is not race, ethnicity, or class, but their lesser position in colonial society (1972). In the four decades since Bonfil Batalla articulated this position, scholars in the fields of history, art history, literature, and anthropology have done groundbreaking work on Indians. Though quite different in their approaches, James Lockhart's work on Nahuatl documents, Elizabeth Hill Boone's work on Mesoamerican pictorials, Rolena Adorno's work on the Andean indigenous intellectual Felipe Guaman Poma de Ayala, and Frank Salomon's work on the Huarochirí Manuscript and *khipus*, Andean knotted cord record-keeping devices, have opened new paths for understanding the complexity and diversity of native cultures and their struggles against subordination.[7] "Indian," as a homogenizing term, does not accurately connote the variety of languages, histories, and cultural practices of peoples placed in that category; however, the relationship between Indians and the colonial social and political structure was not one-dimensional or uni-directional either, and subordination does not work terribly well as a common ground for thinking about indigenous communities.

The decline of the indigenous population after the arrival of the Spaniards was, and still is, shocking. In their monumental study, Sherburne F. Cook and Woodrow Borah estimated that the native population in central Mexico in 1519, the time of Hernando Cortés's arrival, was 25.2 million (Borah and Cook 1963, 88).[8] A half century later, in 1568, that population had dropped precipitously to approximately 2.65 million (Cook and Borah 1960, 47). Understandably, influential scholarship on the conquest has focused on demographic and cultural collapse as a starting place to understand how vast and sophisticated societies succumbed to external domination so quickly (León-Portilla 2008 [1959]; Ricard 1966 [1933]). However, a trend that contradicts the image of the subordinated and vanquished Indian is found in recent work on "Indian conquistadors," emphasizing the uneasy line between Europeans as agents of colonization and natives as victims. As we approach the quincentenary of the Spanish invasion of Mexico in 1519, the conquest itself and its repercussions have emerged as topics of great scholarly interest. The so-called New Conquest History has reframed analysis and discussion of the Spanish military conquest of Mexico by complicating our understanding of the nature and impact of the conquest of Mesoamerica, particularly by recognizing the active involvement of native groups. Matthew Restall, Laura Matthew, Michel Oudijk, and Florine Asselbergs are just a few of the scholars who have demonstrated how Spaniards relied on native allies in their subjugation of Tenochtitlan and the conquest campaigns into the northern and southern reaches of Mesoamerica.[9] In her overview of trends in conquest studies, Susan Schroeder has suggested that "the old stereotype of abject and muted Indians [has been] permanently erased and the canon debunked" (2007, 23). More broadly, since the 1980s, scholars of colonial Spanish America have focused intently on the ways in which native traditions and knowledge persisted under the impact of European conquest and colonization. Recent and significant publications on indigenous intellectual activities and creative production are part of this trend.[10]

New Conquest History and indigenous studies thus provide momentum for us to look at native peoples as agents of their own realities. This perspective can also benefit our approach to the study of mestizos and creoles. In part we have learned from this new trend in studies of the conquest and the lives and cultures of native peoples in its aftermath that binary categories, such as victor and vanquished or colonizer and colonized, should not be viewed as hardened and inflexible. Rather, both during the course of the conquest campaigns and in the colonial period that followed, Indians acted from a variety of motives, including ambition, coercion, and micro-patriotism (that is, the intense loyalties to their home cities or towns that carried over from pre-conquest times). These more complicated and nuanced studies can serve as models, informing a new approach to the relationship between native, mestizo, and creole intellectuals.

The works of creole and mestizo authors have traditionally been studied as distinct bodies. Scholars have tended to trace the works of Indian and mestizo historians of New Spain, such as don Hernando de Alvarado Tezozomoc, Diego Muñoz Camargo, don Domingo de San Antón Muñón Chimalpahin Quauhtlehuanitzin, and don Fernando de Alva Ixtlilxochitl, as part of a marginalized and contestatory tradition—a vision of the vanquished.[11] Meanwhile, creoles are viewed along a different trajectory, one tied to cultural nationalism and ultimately involved in the fight for political independence from Spain. The personal and intellectual connections between Sigüenza and the Alva Ixtlilxochitl family force us to look at ways in which these two segments of colonial society were intertwined. Though he was of mixed blood, Alva Ixtlilxochitl's authority, both in his histories and his working life, rested on his being part of the native elite.

He identified as a descendant of the illustrious pre-Columbian ruling class from Tetzcoco (also known as Texcoco), which included the famed leaders Nezahualcoyotl and Nezahualpilli. Alva Ixtlilxochitl was a member of the República de indios, as the administrative and legal domain governing Mexico's native groups was known. Born in Mexico City to Spanish parents, Sigüenza was undoubtedly part of the República de españoles, the corresponding set of institutions that the European and European-descended population inhabited. Sigüenza worked and wrote in that environment, but Sigüenza the creole and Alva Ixtlilxochitl the mestizo both bridged the cultural and discursive distance between the Spanish and Indian communities. Though not historical contemporaries, they were involved in parallel projects: Sigüenza drew from indigenous pictorial and alphabetic texts in his formulations on Mexican history; Alva Ixtlilxochitl relied on European historiographical traditions in his rearticulations of the Tetzcoca past. These cultural borrowings and exchanges were crucial to each writer's works and suggest an approach to colonial Mexico's intellectual life not rooted in inflexible separations.

By studying Sigüenza and Alva Ixtlilxochitl within a context of exchange, we are forced to engage with and test the scholarly discussions of *criollismo* and *mestizaje* in seventeenth-century New Spain. Both writers were colonial subjects whose writings were mediated by imperial ideology. Neither was deemed rebellious or subversive and both participated actively in the governing functions of the viceroyalty. Sigüenza was an engineer, a chaplain, a mathematics professor, a geographer, and a scholar of the native past. Alva Ixtlilxochitl was a great collector of Nahua pictorial and alphabetic texts, a governor in the República de indios, an interpreter in the General Indian Court (Juzgado de Indios), a representative of an important Indian family, and a chronicler of the native past. The creole idealized the Mexica and adopted them as his cultural ancestors. The mestizo engaged with European history and drew attention to the Tetzcoca as key allies of the Spanish conquerors. Both authors were familiar not only with their own literary, cultural, and historical traditions but also with the other's. Versed in European language, ideological and discursive traditions, Alva Ixtlilxochitl attempted to articulate the Tetzcoca history and experience in terms amenable to Spanish norms. Sigüenza, trained in Nahuatl and well studied in native writing traditions, sought to incorporate that knowledge into his writings wherever he could. To understand the gift of Alva Ixtlilxochitl's archive to Sigüenza we must make sense of the intellectual and social contexts in which each lived and the relationships that rooted them in those historical moments.

The long-held separation of creole from native and mestizo traditions became powerfully ensconced through Ángel Rama's study *The Lettered City* (*La ciudad letrada*; 1984), in which he synthesized how education and literacy marked a highly asymmetrical social division between the "lettered city" and the "real city." Rama offered an influential articulation of the essential role of letters and knowledge in the colonial system of domination.[12] But his notion of the lettered city is closed and does not account for the presence of educated Indians who participated in elite culture. Working within a dichotomous theory, Rama described a society in which the colonial city is organized as a series of rings where the lettered city is at the center of administrative and official power and is inhabited by "a group of religious, administrators, educators, professionals, notaries, religious personnel, and other wielders of pen and paper" (1996 [1984], 18). According to Rama's discussion, this inner ring of power was surrounded by two "enemy" rings: the first being that of the plebes—primarily *castas*, or people of mixed race—and the second, outer ring comprised the Indian communities in Mexico City and the countryside (32).

This model presents a relationship between the intellectuals of the lettered city and the inhabitants of the two outer rings of the colonial society as antagonistic. By relegating Indian intellectuals to an "enemy territory" separated from the white, creole elite, Rama neglects the position of elite Indians who, like Alva Ixtlilxochitl, negotiated their place vis-à-vis the centers of power and privilege in the viceregal administration. In a 1987 article, "La *ciudad letrada* y los discursos coloniales" (published just three years after *La ciudad letrada*), Rolena Adorno suggested ways to extend Rama's analysis of the lettered city and the *letrado*, or colonial intellectual, beyond the European dominated *traza* (city center). In a dramatic and insightful suggestion, she expands Rama's scheme to include dominated subpopulations of Moriscos within Spain as well as Indian populations in the Americas. By focusing on a Morisco, Francisco Núñez Muley, and a native Andean, Felipe Guaman Poma de Ayala, Adorno ultimately confirms Rama's basic thesis on the connection between power and language in the Spanish colonial milieu. However, she complicates the dominion of the lettered city by pushing its boundaries beyond the limits of the European and creole elite. Adorno suggests that "the lettered city is a labyrinth of relations—of dominations, of subordinations, and also collaborations—both external and internal" [la *ciudad letrada* es un laberinto de relaciones—de dominaciones, de subordinaciones y también de colaboraciones—tanto externas como internas] (23).[13] Following Adorno's analysis, which extends Rama's own, I want to propose that the lettered city is founded on an exchange and dialogue between those who occupied the centers of power and those who existed at the margins. As such, the lettered city should be appreciated as a manifestation of various sorts of relationships and collaborations rather than a dichotomy.

Alva Ixtlilxochitl and Sigüenza embody the kinds of *letrados* whose works can be studied as outcomes of the dominations, subordinations, and collaborations Adorno describes. A Nahua *letrado*, Alva Ixtlilxochitl was engaged with multiple discourses associated with power and knowledge in seventeenth-century Mexico and commonly understood as aspects of the lettered city. As a governor of Indian towns, he negotiated the colonial administrative discourse, and as a litigant, he represented his family's interests in the viceregal courts through legal discourse. His work as a historian reflects both his knowledge of European and Nahua historiographical traditions and cultural traditions. Sigüenza is more traditionally understood as a *letrado* and Rama cites him as an example of creole privilege (1996 [1984], 18). But Sigüenza was hardly a person of great influence. In reality he was unable to maintain a steady or important position within the viceregal government. His fascination with pre-Columbian Nahua culture and history was central to his own scholarly investigations, but he struggled to incorporate this learning when writing on other topics, generally on commission.

Just three years before his death, Sigüenza invited Giovanni Francesco Gemelli Careri, a Neapolitan traveler who passed through colonial Mexico in 1697, to view his library.[14] This itinerant student of the New World and the Old was one of the last scholars to see the collection intact before it was transferred to the Jesuit College of Saint Peter and Saint Paul [Colegio de la Compañía de Jesús de San Pedro y San Pablo] upon Sigüenza's death in 1700. Gemelli Careri copied numerous images of pre-Columbian figures from the pictorial texts in Sigüenza's possession and incorporated them into his own book, *Giro del mondo* (Tour of the world) (1699). The Neapolitan scholar affirms that his own representation of native antiquities was deeply indebted to Sigüenza and his collection (Gemelli Careri 1955, 80). Gemelli Careri also points out that Sigüenza came into possession of these images through his friend don Juan de Alva Cortés, who was, Gemelli Careri writes, "head of the *cacicazgo* [family estate] of San Juan Teotihuacan, who preserved the antiquities after having inherited them from his ancestors the kings of Tetzcoco, from whom he descended by direct and mixed line" [señor del cacicazgo de San Juan Teotihuacán, que las conservaba por haberlas heredado de sus antepasados los reyes de Texcoco, de quienes descendía por línea recta mezclada] (1955, 80). In fact, the texts Sigüenza inherited from the Alva Ixtlilxochitl family formed the centerpiece of his collection, which was to have a profound influence on succeeding generations of historians and antiquarians. Gemelli Careri's engagement with this collection of native materials is just one example of how influential Alva Ixtlilxochitl's archive became after passing into Sigüenza's possession. The circulation of Alva Ixtlilxochitl's manuscripts, maps, and pictorials within and beyond the native community highlights the important need to rethink core relations at stake in influential models like Rama's lettered city. Where Rama projects a one-way process within clear power hierarchies, figures like Alva Ixtlilxochitl and Sigüenza point to the ambiguities of lived social relations.

My work to rethink a well-established paradigm like Rama's comes in dialogue with recent historical scholarship that has complicated the study of broader dynamics between colonizer and colonized. Frederick Cooper, for example, has suggested that "colonizer and colonized are themselves far from immutable constructs, and such categories had to be reproduced by specific actions" (2005, 17). Cooper's attention to concrete circumstances rather than generalized observations reminds us that, as he and Ann Laura Stoler have noted, "colonial regimes were neither monolithic nor omnipotent. Closer investigation reveals competing agendas for using power, competing strategies for maintaining control, and doubts about the legitimacy of the venture" (1997, 6). As Stoler and Cooper further state, "it does us no service to reify a colonial moment of binary oppositions so that we can enjoy the postcolonial confidence that our world today is infinitely more complicated, more fragmented and more blurred" than societies of the past (9). The context of early modern Spanish rule in the Americas needs to be studied as a set of dynamic cultural relations, and studying such dynamics suggests starting from a fluid set of metaphors or organizing schemes. Stephen Greenblatt's recent work on the concept of cultural mobility would be one example (2010). But a concept like mobility can also be tied too closely to our present context of rapid movement and globalization and thus erase historical realities just as easily as binary oppositions between dominators and their helpless victims. Perhaps the best way to keep at least one foot strongly set in the past is to retain archival research as a central element of cultural analysis.

The fact of Sigüenza's possession of the Ixtlilxochitl archive is well known. What scholars have little understood is how and why a creole intellectual came to hold such an important collection of native materials. Through a combination of historical, archival, and textual research, I shed considerable light on the relationship between Sigüenza and the Ixtlilxochitl family. The exchanges I trace can be seen as emblematic of colonial Mexico's wider intellectual community.[15] I call these kinds of interactions "the colonial economy of letters" in order to emphasize a mutuality of debt, benefit, and obligation that embraced everyone involved, rather than the one-way appropriation often attributed to figures like Sigüenza in their relationship to the indigenous past. What emerges from my research is a more nuanced and vibrant image of colonial intellectual life in Mexico.

My study takes into consideration a host of primary materials, principally historical studies—published and unpublished during their lifetimes—by Alva Ixtlilxochitl and Sigüenza. Alva Ixtlilxochitl wrote five distinct texts: *Sumaria relación de todas las cosas que han sucedido en la Nueva España* (Summary account of all the things that have happened in New Spain), *Relación sucinta en forma de memorial de la historia de Nueva España* (Succinct account of the history of New Spain in the form of a petition), *Compendio histórico del reino de Tetzcoco* (Historical compendium of the kingdom of Tetzcoco), *Sumaria relación de la historia general de esta Nueva España* (Summary account of the general history of this New Spain), and *Historia de la nación chichimeca* (History of the Chichimeca nation).[16] The *Compendio histórico* is divided into thirteen relations; the "Thirteenth

Relation" is one of his most widely circulated and read texts, as it addresses the conquest of Mexico. The *Historia de la nación chichimeca* is generally considered to be Alva Ixtlilxochitl's magnum opus. Sigüenza's corpus is diverse, and my focus in this study is on his works that directly engage with native history, including *Teatro de virtudes políticas* (Theater of political virtues) (1680), *Parayso occidental* (Western paradise) (1684), *Piedad heroyca de don Fernando Cortés* (Heroic piety of don Hernando Cortés) (ca. 1689), and *Alboroto y motín de los indios* (published in English translation as "Letter to Admiral Pez") (1692).

Chapter 1, "Creoles, Mestizos, and the Native Archive," explores the nature of the native archive possessed by Alva Ixtlilxochitl and then Sigüenza, both in terms of its content and its significance. This archive of native manuscripts and codices offers an example of the physical genealogy of knowledge about the pre-Hispanic and colonial world in New Spain, but it also works as a point of convergence to elaborate on the structures of knowledge in seventeenth-century Mexico.

Chapter 2, "Land, Law, and Lineage: The Cacicazgo of San Juan Teotihuacan," addresses Alva Ixtlilxochitl's and Sigüenza's historiographical projects against the background of the family legal battles over inheritance and land possession. It is in this context of lawsuits and land claims that Sigüenza came into possession of the trove of native manuscripts and codices collected by Alva Ixtlilxochitl. These legal materials represent an underutilized resource for studying the context in which the native elite wrote histories and creole intellectuals investigated the indigenous past. Alva Ixtlilxochitl's historiographical project was motivated in part by the family's need to justify their rights to the cacicazgo. Sigüenza's writings about pre-Columbian Indian history are greatly indebted to the resources provided in the Alva Ixtlilxochitl collection. It also becomes clear that through his position as an advocate, Sigüenza became intimately familiar with a wide spectrum of experiences in the native community.

Chapter 3, "Configuring Native Knowledge: Seventeenth-Century Mestizo Historiography," focuses on the process and methodology employed by Alva Ixtlilxochitl in his historical writings. Examining the five texts he wrote and the materials he is known to have drawn from, this chapter looks at the ways in which Alva Ixtlilxochitl collected source information from elders in the native communities and textual sources produced by earlier generations of native scholars and intellectuals and then incorporated those materials into his own historical narrative. The chapter concludes with a close analysis of his representation of an esteemed ancestor, the renowned poet-king Nezahualcoyotl. I pay particular attention to the ways in which Alva Ixtlilxochitl incorporated European historiographical models and native histories to craft a representation of this pre-Hispanic ideal prince.

In the fourth chapter, "Circulating Native Knowledge: Creole Historiography," I complicate our understanding of creole discourse by highlighting how Sigüenza's historical writings are the product of multiple levels of collaboration and personal relationships among and between the creole, mestizo, and native intelligentsias. I look specifically at Sigüenza's association with the emergence of the Virgin of Guadalupe legend. Often viewed as part of a paradigmatic moment of creoles appropriating the native past, early writings on Guadalupe presumed an intimate relationship with native knowledge and native intellectuals, including Alva Ixtlilxochitl. This chapter puts Sigüenza's writings on the topic in dialogue with other texts by creole clerics, as well as the works of Alva Ixtlilxochitl and other native scholars.

I conclude with an epilogue, "Native Knowledge and Colonial Networks." Throughout the book, there is an implicit emphasis on the social webs that undergird intellectual production in colonial Mexico. The epilogue makes the case that to understand mestizo and creole texts better, we need to situate them both within the context of their production and in association with the diverse networks of intellectuals who informed them. As we examine Alva Ixtlilxochitl's and Sigüenza's social networks, we not only gain insight into the various connections and sources that influence their works but are also able to reevaluate the relationships between indigenous, mestizo, and creole intellectual spheres in colonial Mexico. In the process we gain a richer and more complete sense of the real structures of power and influence in this society.

CHAPTER I

Creoles, Mestizos, and the Native Archive

O<small>N</small> M<small>AY</small> 21, 2014, <small>THREE VOLUMES</small> of manuscripts that had belonged to don Carlos de Sigüenza y Góngora centuries ago were to be auctioned by Christie's in London. Known as Bible Society Manuscripts 374 (BSMS 374), the first and second volumes contain the original manuscripts of don Fernando de Alva Ixtlilxochitl's five historical works, while the third volume contains don Domingo de San Antón Muñón Chimalpahin Quauhtlehuanitzin's *Historia, o chronica mexicana*.[1] There are additional texts interspersed throughout all three volumes. The day before the sale, the set was removed from the auction list and sold privately. On September 17, 2014, press releases and subsequent news stories revealed that Mexico's Instituto Nacional de Antropología e Historia (INAH) had purchased the three volumes for one million dollars.[2] In celebration of the seventy-fifth anniversary of INAH and the fiftieth anniversary of the Museo Nacional de Antropología, the three volumes were reintroduced to the Mexican public with the new title of "Códice Chimalpahin," highlighting one author of the manuscripts' contents.[3]

In a press release titled "The Mexican Government Recovers the Códice Chimalpahin" [El gobierno de México recupera el Códice Chimalpahin], INAH announced these details:

> These invaluable documents were acquired by INAH, last
> May 20th, from the Bible Society in London, which had held
> them since the nineteenth century. Their acquisition builds

the Mexican bibliographical patrimony and represents the first
repatriation of a foundational document for the nation, an
example of the country's historical and cultural patrimony.

[Estos documentos invaluables fueron adquiridos por el INAH,
el pasado 20 de mayo, a la Sociedad Bíblica de Londres, que
los poseía desde el siglo XIX. Su adquisición incrementa el
patriomonio bibliográfico mexicano y representa la primera
repatriación de un documento fundacional de la nación,
patrimonio histórico y cultural del país.] (INAH 2014)

Scholars and politicians alike have now recognized the importance of
these three volumes to Mexican historiography and cultural identity by
ensuring their return to a Mexican institution. In this sense, the repatriation of the "Códice Chimalpahin" foregrounds the foundational role of
these materials in the Mexican cultural archive.

In many ways, the *archivo* (archive) has maintained the resonance of
its etymological roots in the Greek *arkheion* (residency of the magistrates)
by bringing to mind a building that houses public records in the service of
government (Corominas 1961, 59).[4] Joan Corominas, the great philologist
of Spanish, indicated that the term entered Castilian vocabulary in 1490,
serendipitously just two years before Columbus's first voyage. The introduction of "archive" as a term and a process into the language of the Catholic
monarchs would become intimately connected with the reality of governing
the distant territories they and their heirs came to possess. The state archives,
first at Simancas and then later in Seville, were established to house the
mountains of papers produced in the governance of the vast Spanish Empire.
Record-keeping was both a product of empire and a factor in its governance.

Of course, grand state institutions were not the only archives during
the period of Spain's rule over the Americas. There were also local archives, in small towns and cities throughout the viceroyalties of New
Spain and Peru. This chapter addresses an archive on yet a smaller scale,
though tremendously significant nonetheless: Alva Ixtlilxochitl's native
archive. By "native archive," I refer to the knowledge native communities
collected in an effort to preserve their connection to the pre-Hispanic
past in the context of European domination. Just as Corominas links the

archive to public power and office holders, the native archive contained knowledge preserved by the power-holders of the native communities as links between oral and written traditions both before and after the arrival of the Spaniards.

Alva Ixtlilxochitl's archive of native pictorial and alphabetic texts offers an example of the physical genealogy of knowledge about the pre-Columbian world in Mexico. In that sense this archive also works as a theoretically potent image for thinking about the archive as an institution and an intellectual endeavor. The concept of the archive has been a touchstone for influential work on colonial Spanish American literature (González Echevarría 1998 [1990]; Higgins 2000; More 2013).[5] While commenting on Corominas's entry for "archive," mentioned above, Roberto González Echevarría condenses the central argument of *Myth and Archive*: "Power, secrecy and law stand at the origin of the Archive" (1998 [1990], 31). Anna More (2013) focuses on the formation and articulation of what she calls a "creole archive" in the works of don Carlos de Sigüenza y Góngora, where Sigüenza positions himself as a privileged interpreter of material history related to the native past and thus a founding voice in patriotic Mexican history. Antony Higgins is also interested in the role of native knowledge in creole writings; in his study of Juan José de Eguiara y Eguren (1696–1763) and another neo-Latin poet, Rafael Landívar (1731–1793), he posits that "creole intellectuals constitute a body of knowledge as a theoretical ground for their claims to authority and power" and that this body of knowledge emphasizes the history of the native inhabitants as a means of differentiating the creoles from the Spaniards (2000, ix–x). In the case of Eguiara y Eguren, Sigüenza's collection of native writings was central to the eighteenth-century writer's scholarly authority.

In these studies, the power associated with the archive is aligned with the European elite. My invocation of "archive" here attempts to pull the embedded discussion of power and authority away from a strictly creole or European social and discursive context. Approaching Alva Ixtlilxochitl's collection of Indian texts as a "native archive" places the emphasis on the ways in which the native community and a native scholar established not only a corpus of materials that would become foundational to Mexican historiography, but also a means of interpreting those materials and giving them meaning and authority in colonial Mexico. During his lifetime, Alva Ixtlilxochitl amassed a large collection of pictorial and alphabetic texts. He also consulted with elders from native communities and documented the stories they possessed from pre-Hispanic and conquest-era Mexico. This collection offers us an example not of an archive directly generated by viceregal power but one that represented the perspective and concerns of the native landed elite as they engaged with the institutions of authority that kept the great public records of New Spain. As this native archive was formed and kept by Alva Ixtlilxochitl and then circulated among and studied by creole and European scholars, its significance was reformulated and its import redrawn. Throughout the centuries, however, it remained a source of information and authority for each writer who engaged with it.

"Códice Chimalpahin": Forming and Circulating the Native Archive

Upon his death in 1700, Sigüenza left the bulk of his large collection of books and manuscripts to the Jesuit College of Saint Peter and Saint Paul in Mexico City. Sigüenza's lengthy will, drafted on August 9, 1700, enumerates in eighty items how he wished his earthly belongings to be dispersed upon his death. Though the will does not offer a catalog of his library, Sigüenza does give broad descriptions of the books, manuscripts, and other materials he wanted to leave to the college, including studies of mathematics and books related to the Indies—a list encompassing both general histories of the region and specific studies of nature, medicine, and great men (Pérez Salazar 1928, 169–70). In paragraphs 37 and 38, Sigüenza provides explicit instructions for the care of his precious collection of manuscripts—in Spanish and Nahuatl—and of pictorial texts, which in pre-Columbian times were called *texamatl* or *amoxtli*, he says (170). He instructs that they be stored separately and in a cedar box to preserve them from bookworms (171). Sigüenza proudly announced in an earlier publication that he possessed all of don Fernando de Alva Ixtlilxochitl's papers (Sigüenza 1960 [ca. 1689], 65). The manuscripts and pictorial texts collected and written by Alva Ixtlilxochitl would have represented a significant portion of Sigüenza's library of Indian materials.

Sigüenza designated his nephew Gabriel López de Sigüenza as the executor of his estate and entrusted him with the care and transfer of his library. Just months after Sigüenza's death, López de Sigüenza published *Oriental planeta evangélico: Epopeya sacro panegyrica al apostol grande de las Indias, S. Francisco Xavier* (Evangelical eastern planet: Sacred and panegyric epic to the great apostol to the Indies, Saint Francis Xavier) (1700), an epic poem written by his uncle in his youth.[6] In a prefatory letter to Antonio de Aunzibai, the canon of the Mexico City cathedral, the nephew comments on the large collection of texts his uncle charged him with distributing:

> Among the 470 books that [Carlos de Sigüenza y Góngora]
> left to the Jesuit College of Saint Peter and Saint Paul, there
> were 28 manuscripts—12 folios and 16 quartos—very lengthy,
> and some of the most exquisite there are or will be, containing
> some of his things and some from others, all originals.

> [Entre cuatrocientos y setenta libros que dejó al Colegio de la
> Compañía de Jesús de San Pedro y San Pablo, fueron veinte y ocho
> manuscritos, doce de a folio y diez y seis de a cuarto, voluminosos,
> de los más exquisitos que hay ni habrá, así de cosas suyas como de
> otros, todos originales.] (Sigüenza 2008 [1700], 85)[7]

López de Sigüenza informs Aunzibai that while he kept some of the volumes in his own possession and gave away others, he did pass the great majority along to the Jesuits in accordance with his uncle's will (2008 [1700], 84–85).

In the end, 460 of Sigüenza's books were deposited at the Jesuit College of Saint Peter and Saint Paul. Among those were twenty-eight volumes of manuscripts. By the early nineteenth century, some parts of Sigüenza's collection had been moved to the library of the Jesuit College of San Idelfonso, also in Mexico City. In the entry for "D. Fernando de Alva" in *Biblioteca Hispano Americana Septentrional* (1883), José Mariano Beristáin y Souza summarizes the course of Alva Ixtlilxochitl's original manuscripts up to his day. Beristáin, who completed his study in 1816, cites a volume in the San Ildefonso collection that is titled "Fracmentos [*sic*] de Historia

Mexicana" (1:58–59). This title matches the label on the spine of the first volume of the "Códice Chimalpahin," strongly confirming the trail of Alva Ixtlilxochitl's texts up to this point.

However, shortly after this notice to the whereabouts of Alva Ixtlilxochitl's work, another critical gift exchange happened, this one mirroring in some ways the transfer to Sigüenza 150 years earlier but in other ways more representative of how indigenous historical materials were appropriated to other ends. A Mexican secular priest, Father José Luis de Mora, was the giver this time. Mora was a librarian at San Ildefonso and would have had ready access to the school's collection. In 1827, he presented three bound volumes to James Thomson, the representative for the Bible Society in Mexico (Schroeder 1994, 379).[8] Founded in 1804, the London-based British and Foreign Bible Society charged its members with distributing Protestant Bibles and collecting Bible-related materials in such faraway places as Tibet, Ethiopia, and Mexico. During their travels, agents from the Bible Society acquired over 500 manuscripts, written in more than 180 different languages. Their collection was moved from London to the library at Cambridge University in 1982 (Jesson 1982, v–vi; Schroeder 1997, 3). Though Mora was a secular Catholic priest and Thomson a Protestant Bible merchant, they shared a passion for educational reform and, as Schroeder explains, they collaborated on ways to distribute Bibles in the newly independent Mexico (1994). Thomson took the manuscripts back to England, where they passed into a century and a half of obscurity.

Though copies of Alva Ixtlilxochitl's corpus circulated widely in manuscript form during the eighteenth century, none of his writings were published until 1829, when Carlos María de Bustamante offered the "Thirteenth Relation" of Alva Ixtlilxochitl's *Compendio histórico* as supplemental material to an edition of Bernardino de Sahagún's *Historia general de las cosas de Nueva España* (General history of the things of New Spain). Bustamante gave Alva Ixtlilxochitl's seventy-page account of the conquest his own provocative title: *Horribles crueldades de los conquistadores de México*, or *Horrible Cruelties of the Conquerors of Mexico*. Two decades later, the eccentric Anglo-Irish nobleman Lord Kingsborough published all five of Alva Ixtlilxochitl's works in the ninth volume of his massive compendium, *Antiquities of Mexico* (1848); as with subsequent editions, this first one was based on eighteenth-century transcriptions of the originals. Several decades later, at the end of the nineteenth century, the Mexican historian and archaeologist Alfredo Chavero published *Obras históricas de don Fernando de Alva Ixtlilxóchitl* (1891–1892) as the first stand-alone edition of the author's writings. Most recently, Edmundo O'Gorman, a prolific Mexican intellectual, produced a remarkable edition of Alva Ixtlilxochitl's works, *Obras históricas: Fernando de Alva Ixtlilxóchitl* (1975–1977). Published in two volumes, the O'Gorman edition provides not only an exhaustively researched presentation of the primary texts but also a useful apparatus of commentary and additional materials, all of which have added greatly to our understanding of Alva Ixtlilxochitl.

But despite an achievement like O'Gorman's work, few of the scholars interested in Alva Ixtlilxochitl's legacy were able to consult his original manuscripts, which were consigned to archival limbo when given to Thomson. Scholars generally lamented the loss of these materials and made do with eighteenth-century transcriptions of the originals by Lorenzo Boturini Benaduci (1702–1755). A native of Milan, Boturini spent several years in Mexico collecting, studying, and transcribing documents related to the natives. In 1742, legal proceedings were brought against him, and within a year he was deported and his papers were seized by the viceregal authorities in New Spain.[9] Boturini's papers and transcriptions were then consulted, and sometimes recopied, by Mexican scholars from later generations, such as Mariano de Echevarría y Veytia, Francisco Javier Clavijero, Antonio de León y Gama, and Juan José de Eguiara y Eguren.[10] Boturini indicated in his transcriptions that they were taken directly from the originals written in Alva Ixtlilxochitl's own hand, which he had consulted at the Jesuit College of Saint Peter and Saint Paul.[11] By and large, Boturini rendered faithful copies of the content of the original texts, as he took great care to follow the cross-outs and marginal emendations found in the original seventeenth-century manuscripts. In fact, given the loss of the material from Sigüenza's library, Boturini's transcriptions served for two centuries as an ersatz original. That would change when, shortly after the publication of O'Gorman's *Obras históricas*, the original Alva Ixtlilxochitl manuscripts ended their long exile from historical memory, in part thanks to the assiduous bibliographic work of Wayne Ruwet, an independent scholar associated with the library at the University of California, Los Angeles.

In 1982, in the course of pursuing a long-standing interest in the sixteenth-century Franciscan friar Bernardino de Sahagún, Ruwet fortuitously rediscovered the three lost volumes of native writings. While scouring manuscript catalogs for leads on Sahagún manuscripts, Ruwet found mention of a possible text held in the British and Foreign Bible Society collection (personal communication, October 1, 2012). Ruwet contacted Alan Jesson, the Bible Society's librarian, to make further inquiries. Serendipitously, Jesson had just published *Historical Catalogue of the Manuscripts of Bible House Library* (1982), in which he lists, under the heading of Nahuatl texts, "Historical works by Ferdinando [*sic*] de Alva Ixtlilxochitl and other historical material" (189).[12] With this catalog note, Fernando de Alva Ixtlilxochitl's writings returned to the public light where, with the recent purchase of these materials by the Mexican government, it seems they will remain. Though the three volumes meant little to Jesson, Ruwet immediately recognized their importance. Ruwet passed this information along to Susan Schroeder, a historian and Chimalpahin scholar. Schroeder eventually teamed with noted Nahuatl scholar Arthur Anderson to create a translation and scholarly edition of the third volume of manuscripts, including Chimalpahin's *Chronica mexicana*, which they titled *Codex Chimalpahin* (1997).[13]

In the collection of manuscripts, now repatriated and renamed "Códice Chimalpahin," one of the vellum-bound volumes is inscribed on the front cover with the phrase "This book comes from the famous collection of don Carlos de Sigüenza y Góngora" [Este libro es de la famosa coleccion de D. Carlos de Sigüenza y Góngora] (Figure 1).

Containing a variety of manuscripts produced by members of the native community in the sixteenth and seventeenth centuries, the three volumes appear to have been bound by Sigüenza himself, after initially being collected by Alva Ixtlilxochitl. The first two volumes contain the autograph originals of *Historia de la nación chichimeca* and the four other historical relations written by Alva Ixtlilxochitl.[14] We also find extraneous materials intercalated between the lengthier histories, and an occasional odd folio within the texts themselves. For example, between folios 162 and 163 of the *Sumaria relación de la historia general de esta Nueva España*, there is a note in Sigüenza's hand dealing with the chronology of certain events related to the *cabildo* (town council) in Mexico City.[15]

Figure 1. Front cover, volume 1 of "Códice Chimalpahin." Courtesy of the Instituto Nacional de Antropología e Historia, Mexico City.

Sigüenza's distinctive handwriting is present in another set of unfoliated notes inserted between folios 92 and 93 of Diego Muñoz Camargo's *Suma y epíloga de toda la descripción de Tlaxcala* (Summary and compendium of all the descriptions of Tlaxcala).[16] Those jottings, like the notes found among the *Sumaria relación*, are unrelated to the texts to which they are added, but they are a part of the collection of manuscripts and in this sense force us to reckon with a diverse set of documents that were brought together in a specific time and place and passed on through agencies other than those of the original authors. They represent specific evidence pointing to the material construction of knowledge.

For example, the appearance of disparate texts in the same bound volumes prompts us to wonder who collected them. Ruwet has suggested "that the volumes were compiled or at least bound, by don Carlos de Sigüenza y Góngora" (1997, 17). Though it would seem that Sigüenza bound the volumes, my sense is that Alva Ixtlilxochitl was the principal collector of the materials held within. Most of the miscellaneous documents are related to legal and administrative matters concerning the elite Indian population in New Spain. Though not obviously related to Alva Ixtlilxochitl's historical project, these materials would have been part of the context in which Alva Ixtlilxochitl worked and lived as a court interpreter, a colonial administrator, and a member of the native elite. Diego Muñoz Camargo's *Suma y epíloga de toda la descripción de Tlaxcala* is found in volume 2 in its entirety (CC, volume 2, folios 84–152). There are also three extraneous documents that have been included in volume 2: (1) "Relación de la jornada que hiso don Francisco de Sandoval Acaxitli" (folios 153–59); (2) a testimony concerning the conduct of Nuño de Guzmán in the torture and execution of the Calzonci, the ruler of Michoacan (folios 187–91); and (3) documents related to lands belonging to Isabel Moteucçoma (folios 192–204). The first transcriptions of Alva Ixtlilxochitl's historical relations, on which later eighteenth-century transcriptions and nineteenth-century publications were based, included the three documents found in volume 2 of the "Códice Chimalpahin," though not the Muñoz Camargo text.

Thus, after their extraordinary historical hiatus, the Alva Ixtlilxochitl manuscripts now give us an opportunity to consult, and confirm or correct, the content of the texts based on the seventeenth-century holographs rather than eighteenth-century copies. Studying the volumes themselves and the materials they contain can also shed light on Alva Ixtlilxochitl's historiographical project and process, as well as embodying, in their very peripatetic journey, the changing intellectual conditions that have marked both their creation and our reception of them across nearly four centuries. More specifically, the "Códice Chimalpahin" gives us insight into the processes through which Alva Ixtlilxochitl drafted and compiled his historical works. The manuscripts are in that sense of high interest, showing us parts of the writing process Alva Ixtlilxochitl used to compose his histories. In the introduction to *The Writing of History*, Michel de Certeau asks whether historiography is not "an activity that recommences from the point of a new time, which is separated from the ancients, and which takes charge of the construction of a rationality within this new time?" (1988 [1975], 5). As a tangible example of Alva Ixtlilxochitl's historiographical process, "Códice Chimalpahin" allows us to define this "new time" in which he wrote about what were his own ancients, his pre-Columbian ancestors. For him, the new time of the present was circumscribed by struggle, as the native elites tried to maintain their privileged status and make sense of their patrimony within the viceregal state of New Spain, especially as the stories of the Indian past were fading from living memory.

Alva Ixtlilxochitl and the Native Archive

We cannot know for certain what was in Fernando de Alva Ixtlilxochitl's own collection of historical materials related to the Indian past—that is, what materials his nephew passed along to Sigüenza in the gift exchange described earlier. What we can understand is how Alva Ixtlilxochitl tried to position himself in relationship to the indigenous archive he amassed and how he used that material as a source of authority for what he wanted to say about the history of New Spain and about his family's ancestral community of Tetzcoco.

Throughout his historical writings, Alva Ixtlilxochitl foregrounds the archives in Tetzcoco, the *altepetl* (ethnic state) from which his esteemed ancestors hailed.[17] In this passage from the prologue of his lengthiest and most polished text, the *Historia de la nación chichimeca*, Alva Ixtlilxochitl highlights these archives as emblematic of civilization:

> The royal archives of all the writings referred to here were in
> the city of Tetzcoco, as it was the center of all learning and
> cultured practices, since the kings from the city were proud of
> this legacy and they were the law makers of this new world.

> [En la ciudad de Tetzcoco estaban los archivos reales de
> todas las cosas referidas, por haber sido la metrópoli
> de todas las ciencias, usos y buenas costumbres, porque los
> reyes que fueron de ella se preciaron de esto y fueron los
> legisladores de este nuevo mundo.] (1975–1977, 1:527)

As Alva Ixtlilxochitl describes it, the treasured Tetzcoca library and the knowledge it contained were nearly lost in the Spanish friars' efforts to destroy any remnant of idolatrous beliefs. The author himself, he relates, inherited what materials survived the fires and used them as the basis for his own historical texts (1975–1977, 1:527). Alva Ixtlilxochitl's project is in part an effort to reestablish this fragmented memory. Here, and throughout his writings, he presents himself as a mediator and translator between the pre-Columbian world and the colonial regime by emphasizing his role as a material keeper of the historical record.

We can be certain that the material history he had access to included pictorial items such as codices and maps, and that these were an important part of Alva Ixtlilxochitl's archive. Generations of scholars have noted three key pictorial texts that formed part of his collection and were used as source material for his writings: the Codex Xolotl, Mapa Quinatzin, and Mapa Tlotzin (Gibson 1975, 316–17; Gibson and Glass 1975, 338; Offner 1983, 18–19; Lee 2008, 50–54; Douglas 2010). All three of these texts emerged out of postconquest Tetzcoco (Boone 2000, 182–94; Douglas 2010, 8). Eduardo Douglas cautions that the pictorial texts should not be viewed as a transparent representation of the pre-Hispanic past of central Mexico (2010, 13). The pictorial texts were instead mediated sources, influenced as any others would be by the time and place in which they were written. As such, they were foundational to the "pictorial archive" from Tetzcoco that would in turn influence the writings of later authors associated with the city and region, including Alva Ixtlilxochitl (Douglas 2010, 8).

Elizabeth Hill Boone has commented that these kinds of pictorial materials were often taken by chroniclers as the "original histories" and that "the textual histories are [then] oral explanations of the paintings, transcribed alphabetically," such that "the chroniclers know they are merely copying and filling in" from this earlier record (1998, 193). Alva Ixtlilxochitl often makes reference to this same idea of "original history," a term that O'Gorman takes (more expansively than Boone) to mean "the reports from the elderly and notable Indians with whom he consulted and the interpretation he made, with their aid, of the codices and ancient manuscripts" [los informes de los indios ancianos y principales que consultó y la interpretación que, con el auxilio de éstos, dio a los códices y manuscritos antiguos] (1975–1977, 1:201). Regardless of how Alva Ixtlilxochitl employs the phrase "original histories," we know that Alva Ixtlilxochitl's archive and sources were not limited to pictorial material.

The indigenous archive that Alva Ixtlilxochitl assembled included as well a tradition of alphabetic writing. Scholars have noted that he himself transcribed various alphabetic texts that became part of his collection and also served as sources for his writings. The Benson Library at the University of Texas at Austin, for example, holds Alva Ixtlilxochitl's copy of Juan Bautista Pomar's *Relación de Tetzcoco*, which is now the only extant copy of that text. Attached to the manuscript copy of Pomar's *Relación*, we also find—in Alva Ixtlilxochitl's hand as well—the Nahuatl song collection *Romances de los señores de la Nueva España* (*Ballads of the Lords of New Spain*; Bierhorst 2009).[18] Both texts center on Tetzcoco's illustrious figures and history and it is evident that Alva Ixtlilxochitl consulted both works as he wrote his own histories. These sources strongly indicate that Alva Ixtlilxochitl drew on the diversity of record-keeping forms available to the indigenous communities in New Spain and that he was actively involved in their preservation, down to the level of copying texts to ensure their presence in his library.

We can also glean some of the contents of Alva Ixtlilxochitl's archive from his own writings and from the "Códice Chimalpahin" itself. In the first two volumes, interspersed between the primary texts, we find numerous documents related to legal proceedings in the hand of Alva Ixtlilxochitl. The only common thread they have is that they address cases related to noble Indians. We find, for example, a Spanish translation of the historical relation written in Nahuatl about don Francisco de Sandoval Acaxitli, a cacique from Tlalmanalco, and his participation in the conquest of the Chichimecs from Xuchipila. Additionally we find a document addressing the death of the last native leader from Michoacan, Tangaxoan, that is immediately followed by a cédula (decree) signed by Philip II, returning lands belonging to Isabel Moteucçoma in reply to her second appeal from 1579. These materials bear directly on Alva Ixtlilxochitl's personal involvement in the colonial administration, where he served as an interpreter in the courts, and they reflect his engagement with the interests of his family's own social class in the form of the native leadership or indigenous elites.

Finally, we can surmise that Alva Ixtlilxochitl used multiple methods to collect material for his historical accounts, including oral histories gathered from living people. At times he cites these sources in an emotional tone that speaks to the contexts in which he collected certain stories. For example, in the *Sumaria relación de las cosas que han sucedido en la Nueva España*, after discussing the death of his ancestor Ixtlilxochitl I (r. 1409–1418), Alva Ixtlilxochitl explains that "this story about Ixtlilxochitl is told by elder notables, his descendants, who remember his great travails and persecutions and his great valor with not a few tears" [esta historia de Ixtlilxúchitl cuéntanla los viejos principales sus descendientes no con pocas lágrimas, acordándose de sus grandes trabajos y persecuciones y su gran valor] (1975–1977, 1:342). Ixtlilxochitl I was killed after a prolonged series of battles against the *altepetl* of Azcapotzalco, which was led by its *tlatoani* (ruler; plural, *tlatoque*), Tezozomoc. A key part of the story is that Ixtlilxochitl's son, the future famed leader Nezahualcoyotl, hid in a tree and watched as his father was murdered in an open field, his body riddled with "countless stab wounds" [innumerables puñaladas] (1:341). The scene left a deep and lasting impression on the son, who also stood by and witnessed his father's loyal aides and servants preparing the body for burial. At the conclusion of the description of this scene, Alva Ixtlilxochitl announces that the stories about Ixtlilxochitl's death differ in their account of the condition of his body: "Many elderly and notable natives, especially don Gabriel de Segovia, notable from Tetzcoco, descendant of these lords, say that they cut off Ixtlilxochitl's head . . . but in the original history it appears in the way I have described" [Dicen muchos naturales antiguos y principales, especialmente don Gabriel de Segovia, principal de Tezcuco, descendiente de estos señores, que Ixtlilxúchitl que le quitaron la cabeza . . . pero en la original historia parece de la manera que lo tengo declarado] (1:341). This passage offers us three important bits of information about Alva Ixtlilxochitl, his access to sources, and his documentation of the stories he found in them. First, he makes clear that he had spoken with many natives about these events. Second, he names a specific source from Tetzcoco, don Gabriel de Segovia. And, third, he mentions a point of contradiction between what he had heard from don Gabriel and what he had read in the "original history."

In this sense, Alva Ixtlilxochitl saw himself as a point of convergence between what remained of indigenous documentation and extant oral traditions. The latter were not a priori favored, and the version of history that Alva Ixtlilxochitl offers aspires to be a definitive balance among the available accounts. Only a person in the position of Alva Ixtlilxochitl, able to consult with the full gamut of sources, could base a new written account on this form of authority. Moreover, his reference to an "original history" meant more than just the authority of the oldest materials. It meant his desire to communicate a more definitive version of events than those offered by other sources. Alva Ixtlilxochitl thereby ties the construction of historical authority to his work as an archivist, and that activity becomes integral to his writing of history. For him, custody of the native archive meant credibility, such that material authority over the documentation of the past was a crucial aspect to his self-construction as a reliable author who was also engaged with the historical memory of his contemporaries, even when he considered it to be less than accurate.

In fact, we have some evidence that consultation with the indigenous elders in his own time was also important for Alva Ixtlilxochitl's project. At the conclusion of his *Compendio histórico del reino de Tetzcoco*, thirteen relations that narrate the history of Tetzcoco from its earliest days until the time of the conquest, we find an endorsement by local notables. Leaders from the province of Otumba and the town of San Salvador Quauht-lacinco, located near Tetzcoco, provide testimonials in support of Alva Ixtlilxochitl's historical studies of the natives of New Spain.[19] Located to the northeast of Tetzcoco, Otumba was a satellite of that state, though in pre-Hispanic times it maintained its own *tlatoani* (Gerhard 1993, 207). On November 18, 1608, the native leaders gathered together in their town's council headquarters to sign their names to a document attesting to their approval of Alva Ixtlilxochitl's rendering of native history. Only the Spanish translation from Nahuatl, prepared by Francisco Rodríguez, has survived. In it the leaders testify to their knowledge of what Alva Ixtlilxo-chitl had presented as history in his writings:

> We have seen and read the history that don Fernando de Alva
> Ixtlilxochitl has written, which is very certain and true and
> agrees with our ancient histories, those which we have to this
> day, just as it agrees with what we have heard said by our fathers
> and grandfathers. For this reason we approve and confirm it.

[Hemos visto y leído la historia que tiene escrita don Fernando
de Alva Ixtlilxuchitl, la cual es muy cierta y verdadera y
conforme con nuestras antiguas historias las que el día de hoy
tenemos, y asimismo es conforme se lo oímos decir a nuestros
padres y abuelos, por cuya cause nosotros la aprobamos y
confirmamos] (Alva Ixtlilxochitl 1975–1977, 1:520)

The native authorities were convinced by Alva Ixtlilxochitl's research and
documentation of native history and, significantly, his results aligned with
the stories they knew from their fathers and grandfathers. Approved by
local leaders, then, Alva Ixtlilxochitl's historical writings sought to record
the local history of native towns, particularly in the region formerly controlled from Tetzcoco, his own ancestral *altepetl.*

Creating this kind of authority for himself as an indigenous historian
addressed multiple pressures in Alva Ixtlilxochitl's life—pressures that
continue to impact how his writings are understood. Because he was
the child of a mestiza mother and a Spanish father, Alva Ixtlilxochitl's
identification with the Indian community was questioned in his own day,
and it remains a point of controversy. Enrique Florescano, for instance,
has asserted that Alva Ixtlilxochitl, along with Juan Bautista Pomar and
Muñoz Camargo, "assumed the position of noble Indians before the
Spaniards, but culturally they were not nor did they feel Indian. . . . Their
histories, written in Spanish, were not directed to the Indian population,
but rather to the conquerors" [Juan Bautista Pomar, Diego Muñoz Camargo y Fernando de Alva Ixtlilxochitl asumieron ante los españoles la
sangre india que corría por sus venas, cuidando de señalar que era sangre
noble. Pero culturalmente no eran ni se sentían indios. . . . Sus historias,
escritas en español, no estaban dirigidas a la población indígena sino a
los conquistadores] (1994, 382–83). The question of identity and alle-
giances is complex, but unfortunately Florescano's approach forecloses
the possibility of understanding Alva Ixtlilxochitl's work as the product
of dialogues with diverse members of the Indian community in New
Spain. The miscellaneous documents contained in the "Códice Chimalpahin" point to a network of Indian intellectuals (and litigants) who
sought to retain their family's histories and maintain their precarious
positions of power in colonial Mexico. The traces of these connections

are faint but apparent, and deserve further attention for us to understand more fully the context in which Alva Ixtlilxochitl researched and wrote. One trace of these concerns can be found, somewhat unexpectedly, in materials unrelated to Tetzcoco, specifically in materials related to the conquest of Michoacan and the concerns of the Purépecha (commonly known as Tarascan) elite.

In the second volume of the "Códice Chimalpahin" we find a document concerning the criminal trial of Nuño de Guzmán for his brutal torture of Tangaxoan, the last leader of the Purépecha, during Guzmán's conquest of Michoacan. The document appears between Alva Ixtlilxochitl's *Relación sucinta en forma de memorial de la historia de Nueva España* (Succinct account of the history of New Spain in the form of a petition) and the above-mentioned cédula signed by Philip II concerning the lands of Isabel Moteuççoma. The folios seem to be a seventeenth-century copy of part of the judicial process brought against Guzmán, in which Tagaxoan is referred to as the *caçolçi* (Calzonci) throughout.[20] In the third volume of the "Códice Chimalpahin" numerous documents appear related to various legal petitions by don Constantino Bravo Huitzimengari (ca. 1540–ca. 1614), a descendant of the Calzonci. Though illegitimate, Huitzimengari inherited the cacicazgo of Michoacan and was also appointed to various administrative posts within the viceregal government. To a certain extent, his professional life mirrors Alva Ixtlilxochitl's: both men were skilled at negotiating the colonial administrative and legal system, and both were interested in preserving the histories of their respective communities. Boturini tells us that Huitzimengari prepared a map and a history of Michoacan [Mapa en lienzo de Algodon pintado el año 1589 y Memorias del Reino de Michoacan] (Beristáin 1883, 2:99), though they are now lost. Like Alva Ixtlilxochitl, Huitzimengari was a lettered man, active in the administration of Indian cities in New Spain. His father, don Antonio Huitzimengari, was known to have amassed an impressive private library in the sixteenth century, which included numerous works in Latin; *La lengua de Erasmo* (The language of Erasmo), a Spanish edition of the scholar's writings; and a dictionary by Antonio de Nebrija (Jiménez 2002, 142–54).

We can be certain that the two men knew each other because Alva Ixtlilxochitl mentions Huitzimengari in *Historia de la nación chichimeca*. In the final sentence of chapter 91, after describing events related to the conquest Michoacan, Alva Ixtlilxochitl states that "all of this written here was taken from histories and paintings about the kingdom of Michoacan, and I heard these things told many times by Constantino Huitzimengari, the grandson of this king [Tangajuan], who was cacique and lord of that province" [todo esto que aquí se ha escrito fue sacado de las relaciones y pinturas del reino de Michoacan, y se lo oí contar muchas veces a don Constantino Huitzimengari, nieto de este rey, que era cacique y señor de aquella provincia] (1975–1977, 2:245). As Alva Ixtlilxochitl himself announces in the dedication to *Historia de al nación chichimeca*, he relied on oral tradition, pictorial texts, and other Indian intellectuals as he wrote his histories (2:525). Huitzimengari offers one specifically named example of what would have been many such sources.

Moreover, the trajectory of the two men's public lives and the importance that Alva Ixtlilxochitl grants to Huitzimengari by mentioning his contributions hint at the context in which the two men would have met and shared stories. Alva Ixtlilxochitl was appointed governor of multiple *altepetl* in the second decade of the seventeenth century—Tetzcoco in 1612, Tlalmanalco in 1616, and Chalco in 1619 (Alva Ixtlilxochitl 1975–1977, 1:25–26). In 1607, Huitzimengari was elected governor of Coyoacán and in 1609 he was elected governor of Xochimilco (López Sarrelangue 1999 [1965], 214–15). They were also both active litigants in the court system, as they were both interested parties in maintaining wealth and privileges associated with the native elite. A series of documents in the third volume of the "Códice Chimalpahin" reveals the concerns of Constantino Huitzimengari in confirming his family's inherited rights to certain lands in Michoacan (volume 3, folios 102r–127r). The relationship between Alva Ixtlilxochtil and Huitzimengari, based on common interests and social positions, suggests a genuine case of friendship and collaboration. This relationship points us toward a critical factor at work in the originating context of Alva Ixtlilxochitl's native archive. Alva Ixtlilxochitl was not an isolated figure and not necessarily an exceptional figure except in the assiduousness of his collecting and writing and the serendipitous survival of both original manuscripts and transcriptions. His relationship and reliance on a collaborator like Huitzimengari suggests that in all of these activities, Fernando de Alva Ixtlilxochitl was but one member—an exemplary member, perhaps, but not a singular member—of an alternate lettered city with strong ties to the provincial countryside and the native communities.

Both Alva Ixtlilxochitl and Huitzimengari were, in fact, part of a network of Indian intellectuals who were interested in capturing and documenting the native past. At the end of Alva Ixtlilxochitl's *Sumaria relación de las cosas de la Nueva España*, the author mentions the names and vital information about other informants he consulted in researching the text. Many were quite elderly men from Tetzcoco who provided a link to the pre-Hispanic past through their knowledge of the Tetzcoca archives (Alva Ixtlilxochitl 1975–1977, 1:285–86). But Alva Ixtlilxochitl did not limit himself to elders from Tetzcoco. For example, don Alfonso Izhuezcatocatzin, also known as Axayacatzin, was a native of Iztapalapa, on the southern shores of Lake Tetzcoco, but he served as governor of the city of Tetzcoco and during that time he gathered stories from the elders and the famed royal archives (Alva Ixtlilxochitl 1975–1977, 1:286). Alva Ixtlilxochitl relates that Axayacatzin's daughter doña Bartola inherited parts of her father's collection and wrote a history of her own in Nahuatl and Spanish. Though her text is lost and our knowledge of her work is secondhand, it is significant that Alva Ixtlilxochitl declares he had that text in his possession and consulted it in writing his own history (1975–1977, 1:286).[21] Alva Ixtlilxochitl's network of sources and interlocutors encompassed several generations of native intellectuals from a variety of Indian cities, all of whom were eager to preserve the history of pre-Columbian New Spain. The native archive, in whose construction Alva Ixtlilxochitl played such an important role, was thus by no means a solitary project, and there are many indications internal to the "Códice Chimalpahin" that the project of preserving indigenous historical memory was more widely spread and collaborative than many scholars up until now have supposed.

Sigüenza and the Native Archive

Carlos de Sigüenza y Góngora drafted one of the earliest complete and geographically accurate maps of New Spain. As is the case with so many of Sigüenza's works, the original hand-drawn copy, which was never published, has been lost. The map, originally titled "Mapa general de Nueva España" (General map of New Spain) became part of the famed collection of colonial Mexican texts accumulated by the Italian scholar Lorenzo Boturini Benaduci. In the mid-eighteenth century, Boturini was forced to leave New Spain and leave behind his important library, which other intellectuals from the viceroyalty frequently consulted. Sigüenza's map— like other texts from the collection—appears to have been copied and circulated around Mexico City throughout the eighteenth century.[22] José Antonio Alzate, one of the most respected eighteenth-century Mexican mapmakers, studied Sigüenza's "Mapa general" as well as a number of his other geographical treatises and maps. In 1793, inspired by these documents, Alzate wrote the following in the periodical *Gacetas de literatura* (Literary gazettes):

> Finding myself in possession of the ranges and paths that
> the learned don Carlos de Sigüenza y Góngora laid out in the
> previous century, I share them here because even though they
> are not a geographical description at least the reader will know
> a little bit, more or less, on what route or at what distance a
> certain place is from the metropolis, Mexico City.

> [Hallándome en posesión de las cordilleras o derroteros que
> dispuso en el siglo pasado el sabio D. Carlos de Sigüenza
> las comunico, porque aunque no sean una descripción
> geográfica, por los menos el lector sabrá poco más o menos a
> que rumbo o a que distancia se halla tal o tal lugar respecto
> a la Metropolí Mexico.] (cited in Trabulse 1988, 72)

As Alzate suggests, for Sigüenza the whole of the viceroyalty existed in relationship to the capital. Though the seventeenth-century creole's geographical interests roamed widely, his curiosity about other parts of New Spain was always superseded by his loyalty to Mexico City.

Sigüenza's "Mapa general de Nueva España" was commissioned of him in his capacity as royal cosmographer. This position, which he apparently held from 1680 until his death twenty years later, encompassed the duties of "astronomer, surveyor, and map-maker" (Leonard 1929, 75). In those decades Sigüenza immersed himself in the history of Mexico, particularly its native history. Understanding Sigüenza as an intellectual figure in his own time first requires understanding how accidents of history and the formative power of the archive itself intervened in his textual production.

As Elías Trabulse has shown in his study *Los manuscritos perdidos de Sigüenza y Góngora* (The lost manuscripts of Sigüenza y Góngora; 1988), the simple matter of identifying what Sigüenza wrote and which of his texts were published is a challenge.[23] Trabulse notes that there is discord among scholars who have studied the corpus of Sigüenza's published and unpublished works. Irving Leonard has found that fifteen of Sigüenza's texts were published in his lifetime, while twenty works were left in manuscript form and another eleven letters and accounts were left unpublished. Meanwhile Jaime Delgado counts fifteen texts published during Sigüenza's life, six texts published posthumously, eleven unedited, and another eleven that Sigüenza thought of writing but did not (Trabulse 1988, 25). These conflicting numbers are indicative of the difficulties involved with evaluating the nature and content of Sigüenza's corpus. Whatever the exact number of texts published or left unpublished by the seventeenth-century author may have been, it is clear that Sigüenza aspired to a wider circulation of his works than what he was able to achieve.

Sigüenza laments the fact that he was unable to publish many of his own texts in part because he lacked the economic resources to do so. In the prologue to his history of the Royal Convent of Jesús María, *Parayso occidental* (1684), Sigüenza informs the reader that if he had more financial support, he would publish different sorts of books: "If there were someone in New Spain to finance these printings (just as the Royal Convent of Jesús María has done here), there is no doubt that I would bring to light many different works, which have been inspired by the great love I have for my country" [Si huviera quien costeara en la Nueva España las impressiones (como lo ha hecho aora el Convento Real de JESUS MARIA) no ay duda sino que sacara Yo à luz diferentes obras, à cuya composicion me ha estimulado el sumo amor que à mi Patria tengo] (1995 [1684], c2). He goes on to say that among those unpublished manuscripts he has been working on, the one he prizes most deals with "the Chichimeca, whom today we call Mexica" [los *Chichimecas*, que oy llamamos *Mexicanos*] (c2). He announces plaintively his fear that these writings "will probably die with me (since I shall never have the means to print them because of my great poverty)" [probablemente morirán conmigo (pues jamas tendrè con que poder imprimirlos por mi gran pobreza)] (c2). In terms of its scope and its topic, this unpublished and presumably lost manuscript about the ancient inhabitants of New Spain is reminiscent of Alva Ixtlilxochitl's historical writings, and we must consider that the text Sigüenza mentions is one he was reworking based on his access to and use of Alva Ixtlilxochitl's five histories.

Sigüenza mentions at various points in his published writings that he had inherited Alva Ixtlilxochitl's collection of native texts and he relies on that material for his own work. Yet, as Sigüenza makes clear in the prologue to *Parayso occidental*, there was a disjuncture between Sigüenza's own intellectual interests and scholarly research and his ability to publish and circulate his studies in seventeenth-century New Spain. Though Sigüenza's fascination with pre-Hispanic Nahua culture and history was key to his own investigations, he struggled to insert this element of his work into his publications. He does, however, hint at his scholarly passions in the historical works that were commissioned of him. In *Parayso occidental*, he proudly displays the fact that his knowledge of pre-Hispanic Anahuac was garnered from the manuscripts given to him by the Alva Ixtlilxochitl family. Specifically, in this text he cites a passage "that is found among those that were conserved from the mouths of the ancients by the Cicero of Nahuatl, don Fernando de Alva" [que se halla entre las que de boca de los Antiguos conservò es sus Manuscritos el Ciceron de la lengua Mexicana D. Fernando de Alva] (2).

Piedad heroyca de don Fernando Cortés (ca. 1689) also illustrates Sigüenza's struggles to confine the breadth of his interests and knowledge to the limits placed on him as a hired pen. *Piedad heroyca* offers a history of the Hospital Amor de Dios, which Cortés founded in Mexico City. As with *Parayso occidental*, Sigüenza was asked to write the history of the hospital for the colonial institution itself. As Sigüenza notes in the opening lines, he strained to keep the scope of this work to the requisite length of the compendio, a brief historical narrative: "It requires constant effort for me to reduce to a compendio what I want to write" [Oblíganmen ocupaciones continuas reducir a compendio en lo que quiero escribir] (1960 [ca. 1689], 1). As scholars have noticed and as Sigüenza himself recognizes here, his texts are brimming with erudition that does not always have a direct bearing on their topics. Though this could be construed as an example of baroque narrative, it is also a sign of the difficulties Sigüenza had in incorporating all of his diverse interests into the histories assigned to him to write and, perhaps more importantly, in making his erudition appealing to the readers. In a frequently cited passage in the text, Sigüenza claims that he has all of Alva Ixtlilxochitl's writings in his possession: "I say, and I swear, that I found this Relation among don Fernando de Alva's papers, of which I have all" [Digo, y juro, que esta Relacion hallé entre los papeles de D. Fernando de Alva, que tengo todos] (64).

We know that the three volumes now known collectively as the "Códice Chimalpahin," which contain Alva Ixtlilxochitl's original writings, were part of Sigüenza's collection, and we have hints as to some of the other native materials pertaining to Sigüenza. On the spine of one of these volumes we find the label "Fracmentos de Historia Mexicana" in a boldly penned gothic script. Along the spine of a Benson Library acquisition with a very similar vellum binding, we find the label "Pomar Relacíon de Tezcuco" in the same script (Pomar, *Relación*). It is clear that the Pomar text had belonged to Alva Ixtlilxochitl and, we may assume, that it was then transferred to Sigüenza with the remaining pieces of Alva Ixtlilxochitl's collection. These volumes appear to have been bound and labeled at the same time, most likely by Sigüenza. A third volume that gives every indication of having been part of Sigüenza's collection is the *Códice Ixtlilxochitl* (also known as the *Codex Ixtlilxochitl*), which is now housed at the Bibliothèque Nationale de France in Paris. The *Códice Ixtlilxochitl* consists of three parts, including a series of paintings of the *tlatoque* from Tetzcoco, Nezahualcoyotl and Nezahualpilli. In her discussion of the provenance of the volume of three bound documents, relying on previous scholarship by John Glass, Elizabeth Hill Boone mentions that "Sigüenza y Góngora owned all three parts of the Codex Ixtlilxochitl, bound with other material in a folio-size volume titled 'Fragmentos de Historia Mexicana'" (1983, 108).[24]

Having traveled around the globe, these three examples of native materials that belonged to Sigüenza—the "Códice Chimalpahin," Pomar's *Relación*, and the *Códice Ixtlilxochitl*—are now respectively housed in Mexico City (by way of Cambridge, England), Austin, and Paris. This is one indication of the impact and influence that Alva Ixtlilxochitl's native archive has had on scholarship of ancient Mexico by historians located in Europe and the Americas. Francisco Javier Clavijero (1731–1787),

the eighteenth-century Mexican Jesuit exiled to Italy, compiled a study
of ancient Mexico using Spanish and Indian sources from the sixteenth,
seventeenth, and eighteenth centuries, including the publications of
chroniclers such as Francisco López de Gómara and lesser-known authors such as Chimalpahin. Written in the last decade of Clavijero's life,
Storia antica del Messico [*Historia antigua de México*; Ancient history of
Mexico] relied on these earlier texts to build an analysis of pre-Columbian
New Spain that emphasized the civility and humanity of early cultures.[25]
The text was intended to counter the image of a savage and uncivilized
pre-Hispanic Mexico propounded by European Enlightenment writers
such as Corneille de Pauw, Georges-Louis Leclerc (Comte de Buffon),
and William Robertson.[26] To bolster his own credentials, Clavijero enumerates and describes his sources in a prologue. The list of texts, which
precedes Clavijero's own, demonstrates for the European reading public
a tradition of Mexican scholarship into which the exiled Jesuit inserts
himself. By offering a brief critical summary of over a dozen works on
pre-Hispanic Anahuac, Clavijero demonstrates a depth of knowledge that
his European contemporaries are not able to match. This is not meant to
say that Clavijero always agreed with his predecessors; in fact, he openly
criticizes some who appear in the bibliography. For example, according to
Clavijero, Gómara's work suffers from "errors that stem from the scant ac-
curacy of his primary sources" [errores originados de la poca exactitud de
los primeros informes] (1964 [1780], xxxvi). In contrast, what Clavijero
admired most in the studies of Alva Ixtlilxochitl and Sigüenza was their
knowledge of native sources—that is, their access to the native archive.

Clavijero describes Alva Ixtlilxochitl as a "noble Indian, exceptionally
knowledgeable about the antiquity of his nation" [noble indio, versadí-
simo en las antigüedades de su nación], who was the author of four books
that the Jesuit had consulted and who, perhaps more importantly, was the
guardian of a set of pre-Hispanic codices inherited from his ancestors. As
we have seen, Alva Ixtlilxochitl's codices came to Sigüenza, who left them
to the Jesuit College of Saint Peter and Saint Paul in Mexico City. It was
there that Clavijero studied these materials in the 1750s. Described in
Clavijero's bibliography as a "noted Mexican" [célebre mexicano]—unlike
most of the other authors, who were categorized as *indios* or *españoles*—
Sigüenza surely served as an important model whom Clavijero hoped

himself to emulate: like Clavijero, Sigüenza had been born in New Spain and had sought to understand and document pre-Hispanic Anahuac while incorporating the stories and myths of the ancient native populations into a patriotic narrative of contemporary New Spain. Sadly for Clavijero, Sigüenza was unable to preserve for posterity much of his research. After listing four texts by Sigüenza that addressed Nahua history and culture, the exiled Jesuit bemoans the loss of each work: "All of the extraordinarily erudite manuscripts, which could serve as a great help to my History, were lost through negligence by the inheritors of that learned author" [Todos estos eruditísimos manuscritos, los cuales podrían prestar un grande auxilio a mi Historia, se perdieron por descuido de los herederos de aquel docto autor] (xxxi).

From the beginning, the native pictorial and alphabetic manuscripts were the most noteworthy aspect of Sigüenza's library, and interest in this collection grew stronger during the century after his death. Eighteenth-century scholar Lorenzo Boturini Benaduci consulted extensively with the Sigüenza papers at the library of Saint Peter and Saint Paul, and John Glass has attempted to reconstruct the list of texts collected and copied by this one figure (1979, 1981). These copies were then consulted by Mexican scholars from later generations, such as Mariano Fernández de Echeverría y Veytia, Antonio León y Gama, and Juan José de Eguiara y Eguren. Sigüenza's bequest to the College of Saint Peter and Saint Paul thus projected Alva Ixtlilxochitl's library into an international framework, as it became a seemingly obligatory consultation for men who would become highly influential and cosmopolitan figures in Mexican historiography. It was via Sigüenza, in essence, that Alva Ixtlilxochitl's collection attained a new function not just as *one* native archive or as *one* part of a broader and collective project of indigenous memory, but as *the* native archive—the one of greatest importance for many generations of scholars working on central Mexico. The authority imbued in the material archive left by Alva Ixtlilxochitl and Sigüenza attained an ideological potency for the creole projects of these eighteenth-century historians. However, to appreciate the significance of Alva Ixtlilxochitl's and Sigüenza's work as archivists and writers, we must disentangle these seventeenth-century intellectuals from the way they have been constructed and portrayed by eighteenth-century scholars and locate them in their own cultural and social time and place.

Conclusion

The archive, as represented by Michel Foucault in *Archaeology of Knowledge* (1972), does not correspond to a material archive comprising papers and documents; it is an image that addresses the nature of study and how systems of knowledge function and generate their own objects of analysis. As a system that generates discourse, the archive is an agent in the production of information and not, as it would be in a conventional sense, the repository of data generated elsewhere. Foucault emphasizes that there are multiple discursive formations overlapping and crisscrossing at any particular moment. Foucault's discussion of discursive formations offers a means of positing the significance of Alva Ixtlilxochitl's and Sigüenza's seventeenth-century archives: understanding their work is not a question of resuscitating native history or of condemning unilaterally the appropriation of one people's past for the (often much later) benefit of another set of actors; rather it is a question of understanding how different people engage with broader social discourses at a particular epistemic moment.

We could suggest here that Indian culture, as an object of study, did not exist until the conquest generated a series of distinctions between European and Indian civilizations: Christian versus idolatrous, civilized versus barbarous, and so on.[27] If we follow this logic further, we can assert that Sigüenza's and Alva Ixtlilxochitl's object of study was not the same as that of the eighteenth-century scholars such as Clavijero and Eguiara y Eguren, in the sense that each group of intellectuals was working within a discursive formation that defined the position of the Indian differently. To the extent that discursive formations generate objects of analysis and do not simply apprehend them, there was a fundamental discontinuity from one historical period to the next. The notions of creole nationalism or even Indian culture are not static; they are constructed by the discursive formations operating at a given moment. The Indian past is inflected by the colonial present in Alva Ixtlilxochitl's and Sigüenza's texts. In this way the archive of native materials collected by Alva Ixtlilxochitl and then studied by the seventeenth-century and eighteenth-century intellectuals served a different function, as each scholar responded to a distinct array of discourses.

Emphasizing the tension between past and present in the writing of history, de Certeau cites Lucien Febvre, one of the founders of the Annales School, who wrote that "the Past is a reconstitution of societies and human beings engaged in the network of human realities of today" (de Certeau 1988, 11). The creation, circulation, and influence of Alva Ixtlilxochitl's native archive encourages us to remember these "network of human realities." Alva Ixtlilxochitl was part of a context in which networks of Indian intellectuals collected and reproduced knowledge of their pre-Columbian forebears, and we must turn next to the pressures that led Alva Ixtlilxochtil to create the kinds of collections and historical narratives he did in order to understand his project within the terms of its own epistemological moment.

CHAPTER 2

Land, Law, and Lineage

THE CACICAZGO OF SAN JUAN TEOTIHUACAN

The skull of the Venerable Mother Marina de la Cruz occupied a box—behind glass and taffeta—lined with brocade with a cover of crimson velvet and very carefully studded with golden tacks; I made the box myself using the assets of don Juan de Alva Cortés, her relative, for whom I was executor.

[Ocupando la [calavera] de la V. M. *Marina de la Cruz* entre tafetanes, y vidrieras, una caxa aforrada de brocado con cubierta de terciopelo carmesi y tachonada curiosissimamente con clavazon dorada, la qual hize yo de los bienes de *D. Juan de Alva Cortés* su pariente, de quien fuy Albacea.]

—Carlos de Sigüenza y Góngora, *Parayso occidental*

WHEN DON JUAN DE ALVA CORTÉS died in 1682, he entrusted his will and the transfer of the *cacicazgo* (family estate) in San Juan Teotihuacan to his dear friend don Carlos de Sigüenza y Góngora.[1] Alva Cortés was the unmarried and childless elder son of don Fernando de Alva Ixtlilxochitl and he had inherited his father's archive of native materials. After a lengthy legal battle, he had also inherited the title of cacique. Among the many requests and favors don Juan asked of don Carlos, which were registered within the forty items listed in the will, was that Sigüenza would write a *vida* (religious life story) of Alva Cortés's great-great-aunt, Mother Marina de la Cruz, and also that Sigüenza would make a box for her head

(Alva Ixtlilxochitl 1975–1977, 2:393). Born in a small town in Granada, Spain, Marina de la Cruz had traveled to Mexico with her husband, and after his death she entered the Royal Convent of Jesús María. Her life and impact were, in Sigüenza's telling, worthy of emulation and at times even miraculous in nature. It was in that light that after she died her skull had been preserved by a devotee as a relic of the saint-like deeds that Sigüenza chronicled in the *vida*, which he presents as book 2 of *Parayso occidental* (1684).

True to the trust of his friend, Sigüenza also created a lavish box to contain the skull, which had been hidden away in a sacristy drawer from 1621 until 1674, when it was rediscovered (1995 [1684], 128r). Don Juan de Alva Cortés must have gained interest in his great-great aunt soon after this point, since his will makes it clear that he wanted Sigüenza to garner a larger audience for her deeds by publishing her *vida* and securing a more ornate box to house her relic. In *Parayso occidental*, Sigüenza effusively expressed gratitude for "the affection and favors" [los cariños y beneficios] granted to himself by Alva Cortés (1995 [1684], 128r). These passages, along with other documents to be discussed in this chapter, amply illustrate a powerful personal bond between Sigüenza and don Fernando de Alva Ixtlilxochitl's son.

The intimate relationship between Juan de Alva Cortés and Carlos de Sigüenza y Góngora created an enduring legacy for Mexican national history, since it was Alva Cortés who bequeathed to Sigüenza the collection of indigenous pictorial texts and alphabetic manuscripts gathered by his father. In fact, the creole scholar's connections to the Ixtlilxochitl family reached well beyond that gift. After Alva Cortés's death, Sigüenza not only served as his executor but also assumed the role of *podatario* (legal representative) for don Juan's younger brother, don Diego de Alva Cortés, who eventually took on the title of cacique after many interventions by Sigüenza. In that context, Sigüenza maintained close relationships with both of Alva Ixtlilxochitl's sons during the final decades of the seventeenth century.

Intriguingly, there is a clear parallel between Sigüenza and Alva Ixtlilxochitl in terms of their intellectual pursuits and social contexts. Alva Ixtlilxochitl used his collection of native texts to bolster his mother's rights to the cacicazgo of their community, and a generation later Sigüenza used the same materials to defend Alva Ixtlilxochitl's younger son's claims to the same title of cacique. This chapter will explore the many ways in which land, law, and lineage, as supported by the native archive, underlie the personal and intellectual connections between the Alva Ixtlilxochitl family and Sigüenza. The legal struggles surrounding the cacicazgo of San Juan Teotihuacan heavily influenced Alva Ixtlilxochitl's writings and, perhaps surprisingly, Sigüenza's as well.

The Cacicazgo of San Juan Teotihuacan

On February 25, 1639, doña Ana Cortés Ixtlilxochitl, the mother of don Fernando de Alva Ixtlilxochtil, dictated her last will and testament in Mexico City. Among the seventeen paragraphs that explained how her assets and debts should be handled, she made two significant declarations: (1) that she was the *señora natural* of San Juan Teotihuacan, and (2) that her authority over the cacicazgo of this town was founded on her descent from an indigenous noble and lord:[2]

> *Item*. I declare that I am the natural ruler of the town of San Juan Teotihuacan. . . .
> *Item*. I declare that I am a legitimate descendant of the kings from Tetzcoco and its provinces, as I am the great-granddaughter of don Hernando Ixtlilxochitl, lord of the said city of Tetzcoco.
>
> [*Item*. Declaro que soy señora natural del pueblo de San Juan Teotihuacan. . . .
> *Item*. Declaro que soy descendiente legítima de los reyes que fueron de Tezcuco y sus provincias, como bisnieta que soy de don Hernando Ixtlilxóchitl, señor que fue de la dicha ciudad de Tezcuco.] (Munch 1976, 49–50)[3]

Cacique, and its female variation, *cacica*, are derived from the Caribbean indigenous language Arawak. In the Antilles, *cacique* broadly meant "leader," but in the sixteenth century the Spanish Crown ordered that it be used throughout its viceroyalties in association with the colonial practice of giving grants of land to Indians who would have represented the ruling class in pre-Columbian times.[4] As entailed estates granted to elite Indians by the Crown, the cacicazgos were at the same time a central marker of Indian power and authority in the colonial period, a site of conflict among Indian groups and even families, and an object of envy by land-hungry Spanish settlers. Additionally, as John Chance has noted, "Caciques acted as political and economic intermediaries between Spaniards and Indian commoners" (1994, 50). It is especially in this latter sense that the question of San Juan Teotihuacan is relevant to the question of indigenous and creole archival projects.

In her work on legal history and colonialism, Lauren Benton has described the position of intermediaries in a way that is enlightening for the discussion of the cacicazgo of San Juan Teotihuacan. Cultural and legal intermediaries, Benton says, emerged in the first moments of colonial encounters as "individuals and groups were identified right away to act as interlocutors and intermediaries" and cultural change was concentrated in the cultural transformation of these individuals. "Within a historically short space of time—, certainly less than a generation—we observe cultural practices that are products of neither 'dominant' nor 'subordinate' culture, but of the interaction. Further, the interpretation of these new cultural forms is not easy and cannot be deduced from a simple algebra of domination and subordination" (2002, 16).

The history of the cacicazgo of San Juan Teotihuacan illustrates just how intertwined the relations were between an elite native family and the Spanish conquistadors and settlers. Doña Ana Cortés Ixtlilxochitl's great-grandfather from Tetzcoco, don Hernando Cortés Ixtlilxochitl, served as a native intermediary during the military conquest of central Mexico and in the years following.[5] For generations afterward, Ixtlilxochitl's descendants continued to invoke his contributions to the conquest as they made their own requests of the Crown. Doña Ana's great-grandfather from Teotihuacan, don Francisco Verdugo Quetzalmamalitzin Huetzin (ca. 1518–1563), was a young child when the Spaniards arrived, but there is evidence that he participated in conquest expeditions to the northern reaches of New Spain in the 1530s.[6] As recognition of his family's noble lineage and for his contributions to the conquest of the north, don Francisco was named as the first cacique of San Juan Teotihuacan in 1533 (Alva Ixtlilxochitl 1975–1977, 1:10; Munch 1976,

10). Don Hernando Cortés Ixtlilxochitl and don Francisco Verdugo Quetzalmamalitzin Huetzin thus are recognized as founding figures in the extensive documentation related to multiple legal disputes over the cacicazgo held by their progeny.

Scholars have observed that the colonial legal system was one social space in which Indians asserted themselves, defined themselves, and fought for their rights and positions.[7] Here I use the term "Indian" intentionally, as it calls forth the legal category ascribed to and at times strategically deployed by the many and diverse native groups in the New World.[8] Indians in New Spain quickly became so adept at pursuing complaints against Spaniards and fellow Indians that a distinct trend of "indigenous litigiousness" [pleitismo indígena] emerged.[9] In her study of the colonial legal system and native culture in Mexico, Susan Kellogg has highlighted the role of law and the courts as "an arena of cultural conflict and accommodation and as a catalyst of cultural change and adaptation" (1995, xxii). The legal disputes around the cacicazgo of San Juan Teotihuacan illustrate a range of conflicts, accommodations, changes, and adaptations in relation to the litigants and their advocates.

In the Archivo General de la Nación (AGN) in Mexico City, inserted among layers of archival documents related to centuries of legal claims over the cacicazgo of San Juan Teotihuacan, we find a simple line drawing of "Dᵃ Ana Ystlil" (Figure 2).[10] Doña Ana Cortés Ixtlilxochitl is frequently cited in the volumes of legal documents related to the cacicazgo both as an example of a cacica—and thus a female rather than male leader—and as a means of connecting the Alva Ixtlilxochitl family to the pre-Hispanic ruling class.[11] Staring assertively ahead, she wears a distinctive necklace and earrings. These pieces of jewelry were likely inherited from doña Ana's mother, doña Francisca Cristina Verdugo, who bequeathed to her two daughters several "womanly trinkets" [menudencias de mujeres], including "a few chalchihuite stones" [ciertas piedras chalchihuites] (Alva Ixtlilxochitl 1975–1977, 2:289). In Nahuatl, *chalchihuitl* denotes a "precious green stone; turquoise" (Karttunen 1992, 45). That these items should appear in this simple portrait points to their importance for doña Ana's sense of identity and to the connection they establish with a distinctly indigenous lineage. This is a rare portrait of a powerful native

Figure 2. Ink drawing of doña Ana Cortés Ixtlilxochitl (unknown artist, seventeenth century). AGN-V volume 233, folio 10. Courtesy of the Archivo General de la Nación, Mexico City.

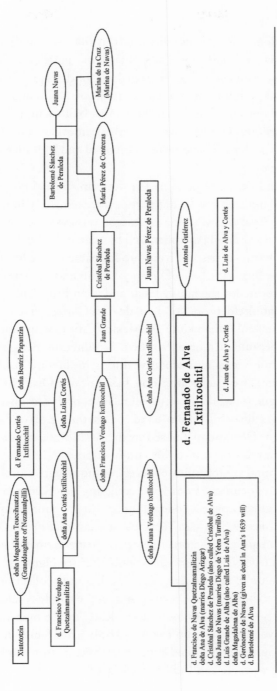

Figure 3. Genealogical chart of don Fernando de Alva Ixtlilxochitl's family, including his Indian and Spanish ancestral lines.

woman. But doña Ana was not alone in this role—certainly not in her family. As doña Ana's father was a Spaniard, her position as cacica of a native town was founded on her maternal line of descent.[12] In fact, both her mother and grandmother served as cacicas of San Juan Teotihuacan. Doña Ana and her son, don Fernando de Alva Ixtlilxochitl, came from a decidedly matrilineal family in which, perhaps unexpectedly, the family's connections to power and land were maintained and legitimated through the female line of descent.

Don Fernando was not doña Ana's eldest son and did not inherit the role of cacique himself, but he did participate extensively in the defense of his mother's legal claims to the cacicazgo, as these were regularly contested both by other family members and by Spaniards.[13] In both his legal and historical writings, descent from pre-Hispanic native leaders via the matriarchal line forms the base of his social status and validates his claims both as an advocate for the family lands and as an historian.

Don Fernando's elder son, don Juan de Alva Cortés, served as an interpreter in the General Indian Court in Mexico City, like his father. Unlike his father, he became cacique of San Juan Teotihuacan. Alva Ixtlilxochitl acted as the family's legal representative during his lifetime, and Sigüenza worked in a similar capacity after don Juan's death. Over the course of many years, Sigüenza worked to fend off relatives of the deceased don Fernando de Alva Ixtlilxochitl who tried to contest the claims of the younger son, don Diego. Documents housed in the AGN indicate the extent to which Sigüenza was drawn into this family dispute.[14]

Amid the hundreds of folios concerning the struggles over the cacicazgo, we find a document from 1684 certifying that Sigüenza has taken possession of "certain papers concerning San Juan Teotihuacan" [ciertos papeles concernientes San Juan Teotihuacán] and that he asks that these "manuscripts, maps, and pictorial materials" [papeles, mapas y pinturas] be inventoried (AGN-V volume 232, folio 232; see Figure 4). It is thus clear that Sigüenza took custody of Alva Ixtlilxochitl's collection of documents in order to bolster don Diego's claim on the family's cacicazgo. This part of the story allows us to look more closely at the movement of an archive of native materials from the Alva Ixtlilxochitl family to Sigüenza as part of a long-standing friendship, which asks us to rethink the relationship between creole and Indian intellectuals.

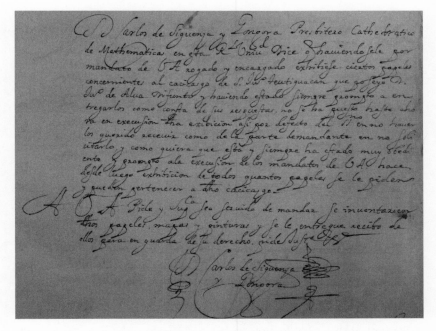

Figure 4. Document in the hand of don Carlos de Sigüenza y Góngora. AGN-V volume 232, folio 232. Courtesy of the Archivo General de la Nación, Mexico City.

Dual Republics and Legal Intermediaries

In seventeenth-century New Spain, *indio* and *español* represented the decisive social cleavage—that is, the place at which individual identities achieved juridical and institutional status as collective entities. Divided into two republics—the República de indios and the República de españoles—New Spain maintained a bipartite system that excluded peoples of mixed race and Africans. The laws guiding these segregated communities arose from a series of royal dispositions issued at particular moments for individual purposes and it was not until the late seventeenth century that these edicts were collected and systematized in the *Recopilación de las leyes de los reynos de las Indias* (Code of laws of the kingdoms of the Indies) (1681). During the first stage of racial separation, in 1536 and 1563, there were prohibitions enacted against non-indigenous vagrants living among the Indians. The systematic exclusion of mestizos, mulattoes, and those of African descent from native communities followed in 1578 (Mörner 1967, 45–48). Though the tradition of two republics emerged because of concerns by Catholic leaders about the corrupting influence of non-Indians on new Christians, the system affected the wider legal and political sectors of colonial society as well.

Of course, the lines between the two republics were never fixed. In fact, the impact of the República de indios and the República de españoles has been described recently as an "abstraction" and "more theoretical than real" (Fisher and O'Hara 2009b, 4; Mumford 2009, 53). María Elena Martínez observes how there was a transformation of "native notions of genealogy and the past" because of the Crown's policies, as there was increased scrutiny of both familial dynastic history and individual "'blood mixture' and 'race'" (2008, 112). Legal positions and claims by those associated with the República de indios were established based on the petitioner's status as a "pure Indian."[15] The cacicazgos granted to the native elite of New Spain became the battleground for numerous legal conflicts that point to the social fissures within and between the República de indios and the República de españoles. Martínez recognizes that "although efforts to maintain a strict segregation between the two republics failed, the dual model of social organization had long-term social consequences" (92). In particular, she highlights how the two republics promoted a discourse of purity of blood and an attendant emphasis on genealogy, especially where the concerns of elite Indians were at stake.[16]

Laws collected and published in the 1681 *Recopilación* shed light on some of the expectations of caciques and issues surrounding their rule.[17] The rationale for the Crown's establishing the position of cacique is articulated in a law from 1557 that states, "During pre-Christian times, some natives from the Indies were leaders of their towns, and after their conversion to our Catholic faith it is just that they maintain their rights and that their coming under our rule not lower their status" [Algunos naturales de las Indias eran en tiempo de su infidelidad Caciques, y Señores de Pueblos, y porque despues de su conversion a nuestra Santa Fe Catolica, es justo que conserven sus derechos y el haver venido a nuestra obediencia no los haga de peor condicion] (2:219v). Colonial officials were prohibited from reassigning the position of cacique, as it was intended to be passed, following "ancient law and custom" [antiguo derecho y costumbre], from father to son (2:219v). The title of cacique was intended only for Indians; mestizos were explicitly excluded from assuming that role (2:220r). As an inherited title that was restricted to Indians with ties to the pre-Hispanic ruling class, caciques were associated with a specific ethnic and racial position in colonial society that explicitly differentiated them from non-Indians and nonelite Indians alike.

The laws also hint at attempts to regulate relations between caciques and the Indians who were under their rule. Caciques were not to request an excessive amount of tribute or tax from the Indians within the cacicazgo. They were expected to pay Indians who worked in their fields. And, caciques were not to use or sell Indians as slaves (2:220r–220v; 2:195r). These laws demonstrate that the relationship between cacique and subordinate Indians within a cacicazgo was indeed meant to mirror that of pre-Hispanic leaders and the nonelite natives under their rule—or, in central Mexico more specifically, the relationship between *tlatoque* and *macehualtin* (commoners). To further emphasize the continuation of social relations among the natives in the postconquest period, certain laws point to holdover practices from pre-Hispanic times. For example, there was a prohibition against requesting daughters of Indians as a form of tribute. Moreover, colonial officials were instructed to be on the lookout for the sacrifice of Indians who were to be buried with a deceased cacique (2:220v). The cacicazgo was thus a legal structure based on continuity with the past, but its implementation created a new site of struggle over what historical practices could or could not be part of contemporary definitions of being Indian. The law was at the center of how the Crown and the native communities negotiated and struggled over these complex realities.

Defying what we might expect in the form of fixed dominant and subordinate roles for their participants, the legal disputes over the cacicazgo of San Juan Teotihuacan involved varying sets of litigants and advocates throughout the seventeenth century. At times the conflicts were intrafamilial, while on other occasions there were struggles between the Indian caciques and Spaniards, and between the caciques and nonelite Indians. Don Fernando de Alva Ixtlilxochitl and don Carlos de Sigüenza y Góngora were heavily involved in all such legal processes. In petitions,

Alva Ixtlilxochitl advocated for doña Ana's rights to the cacicazgo and Sigüenza advocated for don Diego's, both by emphasizing genealogy and noble lineage. The line of descent was very important for families who claimed connections to pre-Columbian nobility and who thus enjoyed special titles and privileges based on those historical relations.

In Alva Ixtlilxochitl's own family history, the separation between Spaniards and Indians was never complete, just as the exclusion of mixed-race members of the community was never absolute. His father, Juan Pérez de Peraleda, was a Spaniard, as was his maternal grandfather, Juan Grande. Strictly speaking, Alva Ixtlilxochitl was a *castizo*—that is, his mother was mestiza and his father Spanish. Though the seventeenth-century historian clearly identified with the native community and his mother was a cacica, the family's mixed ancestry proved to be a complication for their claims to the cacicazgo. For example, in 1643 a group of Spaniards who wanted to delegitimize doña Ana's claim to the cacicazgo wrote a petition asking that she demonstrate proper title. They described her as *española* and her children as *españoles* (Alva Ixtlilxochitl 1975–1977, 2:358). Doña Ana maintained her claim to the cacicazgo from this outside threat, but after her death the entailed estate became subject to a series of intrafamilial claims and counterclaims, which were also carried out and thus preserved in the historical record through legal documents.

From 1563 until 1641, the cacicazgo of San Juan Teotihuacan was controlled by three generations of female leaders: doña Ana Ixtlilxochitl (d. 1580), doña Francisca Cristina Verdugo Ixtlilxochitl (d. 1596), and doña Ana Cortés Ixtlilxochitl (died ca. 1645). Normally cacicazgos were inherited through male heirs, according to the Spanish customs of primogeniture and patrilineage. Yet, they were also to stay within the hands of natives, so when there was no son and no indigenous husband the cacicazgo could be inherited by a wife or a daughter. Since don Francisco Verdugo Quetzalmamalitzin Huetzin had no sons, upon his death in 1563 the estate went to his wife, doña Ana Ixtlilxochitl, who was the daughter of don Hernando Cortés Ixtlilxochitl and the first cacica of San Juan Teotihuacan. In the following two generations, the only surviving heirs were daughters, so the cacicazgo remained in the hands of cacicas until the death of doña Ana Cortés Ixtlilxochitl around 1645. For the better part of a century, San Juan Teotihuacan was a matrilineal enclave.

After the death of don Francisco de Navas y Peraleda—doña Ana's eldest son and successor—a bitter dispute over the cacicazgo would go on for decades, as detailed later in this chapter.

Don Juan de Alva Cortés and don Carlos de Sigüenza y Góngora were close friends—"amigos íntimos" (AGN-V volume 232, folio 265). Alva Cortés had fought for his right to inherit the cacicazgo of San Juan Teotihuacan and he was concerned that his younger brother, don Diego de Alva, would have difficulties acceding to the position as the rightful heir to the family's estate. Indeed, the cousin of don Juan and don Diego, don Felipe de Alva, contested don Diego's right of inheritance and Sigüenza stepped in to aid him in his legal battles. Sigüenza did not intervene on behalf of his Indian friends who were fending off a predatory colonial government or greedy Spanish settlers. Much more intriguingly, Sigüenza acted out of loyal friendship. Instead of revealing a patrician, exploitative relationship between creole and mestizo, as some have claimed, the legal documents surrounding the San Juan Teotihuacan cacicazgo demonstrate the close relationships between a creole *letrado* and members of a native landholding family possessed of its own intellectual tradition. These relationships crossed the racial and ethnic barriers of the seventeenth-century New Spanish dual republics. The complexities of this dispute—who counted as an Indian, who could claim legitimate inheritance, and so on—also show in microcosm how vexed the apparently fixed division between Indians and non-Indians could be as questions of lived social practice.

Magnus Mörner traced the gradual decline of the República de españoles and the República de indios and pointed to different factors that worked to dissolve this political and social separation, such as incursions onto Indian lands by Spaniards, creoles, and mestizo settlers and the exponential population growth of the *castas* (people of mixed, nonelite families), along with the simultaneous decline in the native population (1967, 98–99).[18] Racial and ethnic categories were, with increasing frequency, challenged by this rise in the number of the *castas* (Cope 1994).[19] The growth of the *castas* population and their sense of unity as a group signals the demise of the racial and ethnic segregation in favor of a consolidation of social groups formed more around class-based identities. The status and privilege that the elite Indians enjoyed under the dual republic system was increasingly fragile in this context, and the lawsuits brought against Alva Ixtlilxochitl and his family indicate the degree to which they were forced to defend their special privileges and their identities. The prolonged legal wrangling over the San Juan Teotihuacan cacicazgo was in some sense an exemplary process whose intensity corresponds to the historical moment in which all the privileges afforded to elite native families were disappearing. The stakes were absolute for a family facing the loss of a generations-long social standing. One could thus argue that the status and privileges Alva Ixtlilxochitl enjoyed during his lifetime allowed a mestizo intellectual like himself to work as part of the República de indios, but as the República de indios declined, the network that afforded elite Indians and mestizos a special place in society also weakened. It is not incidental, then, that Alva Ixtlilxochitl represents one of the last mestizo or Indian chroniclers in New Spain. In the seventeenth century, as the dual republic system was coming to an end, so was the kind of linkage it afforded between historical knowledge from the Indian communities and European historiography. The passing of Alva Ixtlilxochitl's archive to Sigüenza mediated between the two communities and marked these wider changes in colonial society.

Alva Ixtlilxochitl, the Cacica, and the Legacy of Nobility

There is an intimate connection between don Fernando de Alva Ixtlilxo-chitl's historiographical project and his family's struggles over land. In the closing paragraphs of his *Sumaria relación de las cosas de la Nueva España*, Alva Ixtlilxochitl laments how his family had continually lost status and possessions since the arrival of the Spaniards: "They have taken all our towns and lands and authority that we used to have" [se nos han quitado todos los pueblos y tierras y mando que teníamos]. He goes on to explain that not only are he and his family the natural lords of the lands they claim, but that they are of the "best Indians in New Spain" [los mejores indios en la Nueva España], because those Indians had quickly converted to Christianity during the conquest and recognized Hernando Cortés's authority (1975–1977, 1:392). In a tone of dismay and disbelief, Alva Ixtlilxochitl protests that even though his forebears had been such loyal Christian vassals from the very beginning, their descendants "are very poor and in need of income" [vivimos muy pobres y necesitados sin ninguna renta] (1:393). The greatest injustice, he says, is that the people who in pre-Hispanic times were *macehualtin* and their underlings are now accustomed to being addressed as gentlemen, while the "sons and daughters, granddaughters and relatives of Nezahualcoyotl and Nezahualpilli go about plowing and digging just to have enough to eat" [los hijos y hijas, nietas y parientes de Nezahualcoyotzin y Nezahualpiltzintli, andan arando y cabando para tener qué comer] (1:392–93).

In these passages, Alva Ixtlilxochitl condenses the concerns that motivate his legal and historical writings into three common threads: (1) he and his family were descendants of esteemed pre-Hispanic leaders who ruled the lands to which his family laid claim; (2) his ancestors had been loyal vassals and good Christians since the arrival of the Spaniards; and yet, (3) despite their noble lineage and their loyalty, his family members were treated like nonelite Indians. To emphasize this last point, Alva Ixtlilxochitl bemoans the fact that he and his family were forced to pay taxes just like the *macehualli*, even though they were "descendants of royal stock" [descendientes de la real cepa] (1:393). Alva Ixtlilxochitl's legal and historical writings were produced in this context of lost recognition and failing privilege.

The colonial Andean chronicler Felipe Guaman Poma de Ayala spent many years immersed in legal struggles to reclaim what he saw as patrimonial lands. In one of her illuminating studies of Guaman Poma's extensive legal and literary activities, Rolena Adorno observed that "when his decade-long efforts failed, Guaman Poma took the extraordinary step of devoting at least as many years to writing a twelve-hundred-page chronicle of ancient Andean history and a treatise on colonial reform" (2012, 63). Though Alva Ixtlilxochitl's historical works and legal petitions were written simultaneously rather than consecutively, his experience followed numerous aspects of Guaman Poma's. For instance, as Adorno has remarked, Guaman Poma de Ayala invoked the European motif of the "world upside down," where, as she says, "the objects of his ire are low-born Andeans living as kings" and "he intimates that this social chaos drove him to write his chronicle of Andean history and treatise against injustice" (70). Alva Ixtlilxochitl's frustrations parallel those of Guaman Poma: both authors were litigants in a context of social change that was in part a result of demographic shifts in which the Indian population continued to decline, thus causing further instability in social positions, customs, and specifically claims to native lands.

Alva Ixtlilxochitl's life spanned a period of continued and marked population decline among the native communities. In 1568, just a decade before his birth, the native population in central Mexico is estimated to have been 2.65 million, while the numbers dropped to half a million by 1646, just four years before his death (Cook and Borah 1979, 3:97; Borah 1983, 26). Even closer to home, the native population of Teotihuacan in 1568 had been 4,689, and by 1646 it was a mere 510 (Cook and Borah 1979, 3:20).[20] Alva Ixtlilxochitl himself was living in Mexico City in 1646, though he was still closely tied to the concerns of the cacicazgo of San Juan Teotihuacan. The population demise accompanied by the geographical mobility of the native population created a situation in which the cacicazgos were vulnerable to incursion. With fewer and fewer native inhabitants, the value of a cacicazgo came to rest more and more on the land itself rather than the labor of its inhabitants, which made the cacicazgo a tempting target for nonnative interlopers. A royal decree from 1602 indicates that, for instance, Spaniards had been attempting to occupy land within Tetzcoco, and then orders these Spaniards to vacate.[21] Conflicts in 1611 and 1643—and the legal paperwork they generated—demonstrate that as the native population of the cacicazgo lands declined, the incursions by Spaniards became much more frequent and their tactics for making legitimate claims to the lands became much more aggressive.

In 1611 Alva Ixtlilxochitl mobilized a defense of his mother's position and his family's claims to the cacicazgo, as "some people who maliciously and with sinister intent are attempting to petition lands within her dominion and inherited estate" [algunas personas maliciosamente y con siniestra relación pretenden pedir tierras en las de su patrimonio y señorío natural] (Alva Ixtlilxochitl 1975–1977, 2:294). On July 20, 1611, on behalf of his father, Juan de Peraleda, and his mother, doña Ana Cortés Ixtlilxochitl, Alva Ixtlilxochitl petitioned the viceroy to provide an *amparo* (order of protection) assuring the authorities that the San Juan Teotihuacan lands belonged to doña Ana, thus prohibiting others from staking a claim. The petition was accompanied by testimony from fourteen witnesses who attested to the extent of the lands included in the cacicazgo of San Juan Teotihuacan and the tenure of those lands, tracing back to pre-Hispanic times (Alva Ixtlilxochitl 1975–1977, 2:294–333). On August 23, 1611, the viceroy don Luis de Velasco, Marqués de Salinas, granted this petition.

The documentation concerning this event provides insight into Alva Ixtlilxochitl's position within the native community. He was able to rally the support of fourteen Indians, many of whom held titles that indicated noble status and positions of authority within the government of the República de indios. Their experience and age allowed these witnesses to serve as legitimate sources of knowledge that could convincingly tell the story about his mother's family. The thesis of Alva Ixtlilxochitl's petition, with support from the witness statements, was that his mother had right-fully inherited the cacicazgo from her mother and that their family had been recognized as having seigneurial rights to that land for many generations. As he reminded the viceroy in his petition, his mother had indeed received the title of cacica from her mother, doña Francisca, as she was the eldest child and there were no male offspring. He went on to affirm that "the viceroy Gaspar de Zúñiga Acevedo y Fonseca, Count of Monterrey, confirmed that the town [of Teotihuacan] granted the recognition of her title and service, which her ancestors had always enjoyed" [el virrey conde de Monterrey verificó en ella el reconocimiento y servicio que el dicho pueblo daba . . . que siempre sus padres y abuelos tuvieron] (1975–1977, 294).

The fourteen witnesses included Indians who resided in the town, as well as Indians who were governors, caciques, or other nobles from towns nearby. They were all asked, under oath and with the assistance of an interpreter, to respond to fifteen questions drafted by Alva Ixtlilxo-chitl that were intended to prove that his mother's native ancestors had been rulers in Teotihuacan and Tetzcoco for many generations. The wit-nesses confirmed doña Ana Cortés Ixtlilxochitl's position as cacica of San Juan Teotihuacan because she was the descendant of the first cacique, don Francisco Verdugo Quetzalmamalitzin Huetzin, and his wife, doña Ana Cortés Ixtlilxochitl, who was the granddaughter of Nezahualpilli and the great-granddaughter of Nezahualcoyotl, ruler of Tetzcoco. The knowledge of these witnesses about the genealogy of Alva Ixtlilxochitl's family provides the substance of their testimony. As elders in their com-munities, these men were able to speak with authority to the history of the leadership of the cacicazgo of San Juan Teotihuacan and pre-Hispanic leadership in the region.

One of the witnesses was Gabriel de Segovia, an eighty-seven-year-old Indian noble from Tetzcoco. Asked about doña Ana, Segovia confirmed the genealogy that connected her to the pre-Hispanic *tlatoque* of Tetzcoco—Nezahualcoyotl, Nezahualpilli, and don Hernando Cortés Ixtlilxochitl—as well as the leaders of Teotihuacan, the conquest-era governor Xiuhtototzin and don Francisco Verdugo Quetzalmamalitzin. Segovia attested that he knew doña Ana Cortés Ixtlilxochitl's grandparents, don Francisco Verdugo Quetzalmamalitzin and doña Ana Cortés Ixtlilxochitl. He also testified that he had heard stories about don Francisco's parents, Xiuhtototzin and doña Magdalena Tecucihuatzin, just as he also knew of don Hernando Cortés Ixtlilxochitl and Nezahualpilli (Alva Ixtlilxochitl 1975–1977, 2:326). This octogenarian witness, as with many of the other elders Alva Ixtlilxochitl consulted, would have been born just a few short years after the arrival of the Spaniards. His life spanned the period of conquest and colonization, and their impact on native society and culture, and he would have been a source for local history and also for greater knowledge about the region of Alva Ixtlilxochitl's ancestors. Segovia represents the kind of oral authority Alva Ixtlilxochitl sought out in his efforts to defend the family's titles and in his own historical writings. By incorporating those sources into his own writings as well as into his legal petitions, Alva Ixtlilxochitl marks the passage of this oral tradition into a modern European textual medium and demonstrates directly the linkages between the various aspects of his intellectual and textual life.

It is significant and noteworthy that Gabriel de Segovia also served as a source for Alva Ixtlilxochitl's historical writings. In *Sumaria relación de las cosas de la Nueva España*, he is described as "Gabriel de Segovia Acapipiotzin, noble Indian from Tetzcoco, grandson of the famous prince Acapipiotzin, nephew of the king of Tetzcoco, eighty-eight years old, who also was able to see the royal archives of Tetzcoco and he spoke often with historians and the sons of the king of Tetzcoco, his cousins" [Gabriel de Segovia Acapipiotzin, indio principal de Tezcuco, nieto del famoso infante Acapipiotzin, y sobrino del rey de Tezcuco, de edad de ochenta y ocho años, que también alcanzó vido los archivos reales de Tezcuco, y comunicó mucha veces con los historiadores y los hijos del rey de

Tezcuco, sus primos] (Alva Ixtlilxochitl 1975–1977, 1:286). Since Segovia's age in the legal document is just one year younger than what is given
in the historical text, it would appear that the texts were written within
a year of each other.[22] This coincidence offers a specific example of the
ways in which Alva Ixtlilxochitl drew from various sources, including oral
testimony provided by elders, in order to pursue legal matters related to
the cacicazgo and at the same time in order to build his historical studies
of the region. Alva Ixtlilxochitl's legal and historical work was a crucial
moment of transition between native oral traditions and the literate world
of colonial Mexico and western historiography.

On the heels of the resolution of the 1611 dispute, Alva Ixtlilxochitl
embarked on his career as a colonial administrator within the República
de indios. Just as Alva Ixtlilxochitl demonstrated his mother's rightful
possession of the cacicazgo by reminding the authorities of her illustrious
heritage and service to the Crown, he capitalized on this same lineage and
history to procure positions as governor within the República de indios.
In 1612, he was designated by the viceroy as *juez gobernador* (governor)
of Tetzcoco; in 1616 he was named *juez gobernador* of Tlalmanalco; and,
in 1618 he was named to the same post in Chalco. Later he served as an
interpreter in the General Indian Court in New Spain. In 1620, Alva Ixtlilxochitl made a petition to the Royal Crown for an appointment based
on the deeds of his ancestors and received in return a royal decree favoring
him for employment by the viceroy.[23] This type of request was not un-
common during the colonial period. Many residents of the Indies sought
recognition and recompense for their contributions and those of their
family members to the Spanish colonial project through petitions known
as *relaciones de méritos y servicios*.[24] Just as the personal and the family
concerns overlapped in the arena of law and government, the public and
private research interests were closely connected in Alva Ixtlilxochitl's
writings and he was able to translate (quite literally, as an interpreter) his
legal and historical work into effective administrative authority.

New Spain had changed in the three decades between the first and
second major legal disputes over the cacicazgo. The native population had
continued to decline and there was a growing movement toward natives
residing in Mexico City rather than on ancestral lands. Alva Ixtlilxochitl's
family had maintained houses in Mexico City for several generations and

it seems that their daily lives were as much tied to the urban center as to the ancestral homelands. Though more and more Spaniards moved onto cacicazgo lands, not all were rapacious land thieves; many are simply described as workers and residents in San Juan Teotihuacan. Some were even married to doña Ana's children. This trend, of the native elite marrying Spaniards, is at the crux of the legal dispute from 1643.

Alva Ixtlilxochitl was the bearer of the family archive, even when he no longer served as his mother's legal representative. In 1643, the family was forced to defend its claim to the cacicazgo of San Juan Teotihuacan yet again. Unlike in 1611, Alva Ixtlilxochitl did not play an active role in the proceedings. By 1643 he was living in Mexico City, interpreting in the General Indian Court. Perhaps because Alva Ixtlilxochitl's professional obligations kept him in Mexico City, his brother-in-law Diego de Yebra Turrillo, a Spaniard, organized doña Ana's defense. Alva Ixtlilxochitl, however, held in his possession the collection of documents that were requested to prove his family's legitimate claims to the cacicazgo. Doña Ana and then in turn Yebra Turrillo were pressed to submit for examination their "titles and records" [títulos and recaudos], and the documents indicate that "Fernando de Alva, who resides in Mexico City, is in possession of them and he will send for them and present them" [los tiene remitidos a don Fernando de Alva, su cuñado, vecino de la ciudad de México a donde enviará por ellos y los exhibirá] (Alva Ixtlilxochitl 1975–1977, 2:357).

Whereas the legal actions from 1611 were centered around the question of to whom the lands belonged, which was established by proving a history of ownership, in 1643 there was a new series of legal petitions filed that aimed to cast doubt on the rights of Alva Ixtlilxochitl's mother to occupy the position of cacica. In a 1643 petition asking that she demonstrate she had proper title to the cacicazgo, she and her children are described as Spaniards: "They are all Spaniards, Ana Cortés, daughter of said Juan Grande, who was married to Juan Pérez de Peraleda, Spaniards, deceased, from which marriage were left children . . . all Spaniards" [son todos españoles, como lo son doña Ana Cortés, hija del dicho Juan Grande que fue casada con Juan Pérez de Peraleda, español, difunto, de cuyo matrimonio quedaron hijos . . . todos españoles] (Alva Ixtlilxochitl 1975–1977, 2:358). The 1643 dispute was conflictive. In 1611, Alva

Ixtlilxochitl's family had responded to the incursion of "some people" [algunas personas] onto their lands. By 1643, the conflict is more clearly framed. The problems arose when a group of five Spaniards who were residing in San Juan Teotihuacan petitioned for a study of doña Ana Cortés's lands, including an analysis of the documents that supported her title.[25] Additionally, these five men informed the viceroy that they were willing to offer their service in the newly formed Windward Fleet along with five hundred *pesos de oro* (gold pesos) in exchange for any lands within San Juan Teotihuacan that were determined to not belong to doña Ana Cortés. This offer gives us some idea of how valuable the cacicazgo in question was thought to be. The petition by the Spaniards was facilitated by the government officials who were involved in the case. Both Andrés de Urbina Eguilus, the judge appointed by the viceroy to survey lands and waters, and Juan de Cárdenas Eguirao, the judicial investigator (*agente fiscal*), clearly favored the position of the Spaniards and repeatedly asserted that doña Ana Cortés did not carry a legitimate title to the cacicazgo.

Just as witnesses were called to give testimony in 1611, in 1643 four residents of San Juan Teotihuacan provided their perspective on the question of whether the heirs to Juan Grande were Spaniards or Indians. Even though they resided in an Indian town, all four witnesses were Spaniards. In turn, each witness detailed the backgrounds of the family members, and two of the four concluded that all the family members were recognized as Spaniards, while one declared they were *castizos* (Alva Ixtlilxochitl 1975–1977, 2:357–58). The fourth witness, Diego de Yebra Turrillo, demurred, and instead of addressing the issue of whether or not Juan Grande's heirs were Spaniards he simply named the descendants and their spouses. Yebra Turrillo, himself a Spaniard, was married to don Fernando de Alva Ixtlilxochitl's sister doña Juana de Navas Ixtlilxochitl, and as the son-in-law of doña Ana Cortés he served as her legal representative in the 1643 dispute.

The crux of the 1643 dispute was whether doña Ana had a legitimate claim to the cacicazgo as the daughter of a Spaniard. In response to the argument that doña Ana Cortés Ixtlilxochitl and her children should be denied rights to the cacicazgo, Yebra Turrillo and Alva Ixtlilxochitl's son don Juan de Alva explained that it was erroneous and misleading to argue that doña Ana's claims were illegitimate because she was a descendant of Juan

Grande, since the line of inheritance did not pass through the paternal line but rather through the maternal line, which, as they said, was thoroughly supported in the documentation that had been provided (Alva Ixtlilxochitl 1975–1977, 2:364). Some of the language used to contest the legitimacy of her claims speaks to an underlying tension between the Indian and Spanish communities that was not present in the 1611 dispute. For instance, in 1643 Eguirao states that the fourteen witnesses called in 1611 were "all Indians of little capacity or talents and as such their statements should not be given credence" [todos son indios de poca capacidad y talento y tales que no se les puede dar fe ni crédito a sus dichos] (Alva Ixtlilxochitl 1975–1977, 2:366). With the increasingly precarious demographic position of the natives, it was apparently easier to denigrate their value as legal subjects. Ultimately, there is no evidence in the surviving documents that the Spaniards succeeded in taking any parts of the cacicazgo. The disputes of 1643, however, were not the end of conflicts over the cacicazgo. Yet, unlike the disputes from 1611 and 1643, the later struggles were strictly intrafamilial and drew in collaborators entirely outside the Ixtlilxochitl family and San Juan Teotihuacan—collaborators like Sigüenza. While we are used to thinking of Sigüenza as an essentially urban figure who was disassociated from the problems of the countryside, such as those facing the Ixtlilxochitl family, the legal work Sigüenza carried out on behalf of the Alva Ixtlilxochitl family went far beyond the paper-dominated procedures of New Spain's bureaucratic system.

Sigüenza, the Cacique, and the Capellanía

In April 1682, Sigüenza walked the perimeters of San Juan Teotihuacan in order to confirm the rights of possession to the lands held by his friend don Juan de Alva Cortés, to be inherited by don Juan's brother, don Diego de Alva Cortés. Establishing the boundaries of the land was a critical step for defending it against intrusions. Sigüenza documented the hills, valleys, and other property markers, and noted that the lands had belonged to the family since before the arrival of the Spaniards:

> I request that your majesty honor the possession of all the lands,
> hills, springs, rivers, trees, nopals, magueys, rocks and houses

that belong to said cacicazgo and that since pre-Columbian times their ancestors possessed. Carlos de Sigüenza y Góngora

[Suplico a Vuestra Merced se sirva de dada posesion de todas las tierras, montes, ojos de agua, rios, arboles, nopales, magueyes, piedras y casas que por el dicho cacicazgo le pertenecen y que desde la gentilidad poseyeron sus antepasados. Carlos de Sigüenza y Góngora] (AGN-V volume 232, folio 151)

The image of Sigüenza meticulously working his way around the lands of Teotihuacan on behalf of his friend's family offers a fascinating contrast to his historical reputation as a bookish intellectual. Mentioned alternately in the archival documents as "Licenciado Carlos de Sigüenza y Góngora," "procurador Sigüenza," and "Licenciado Carlos de Sigüenza y Góngora presbítero y cathedratico de mathematicas en la Real Universidad" (Bachelor Carlos de Sigüenza y Góngora, legal advocate, priest, and professor of mathematics at the Royal University), Sigüenza worked tirelessly to defend don Diego's position as cacique after his brother's death.

After the death of Alva Ixtlilxochitl's mother, doña Ana Cortés Ixtlilxochitl, the cacicazgo passed to her eldest son, don Francisco de Navas. But when he died childless, it was apparent that there would be various contenders for the title of cacique. Upon his death in about 1660, one of don Francisco's younger brothers, don Luis de Alva, ended up taking control of the cacicazgo, but this was against the inheritance practice that gave precedence to siblings and their offspring in order of birth. Don Juan de Alva Cortés thus argued that doña Ana's second son—his father, don Fernando de Alva Ixtlilxochitl—would have been don Francisco's heir had he lived, and the elder son of don Fernando (don Juan himself) subsequently the next in line to inherit the estate (Alva Ixtlilxochitl 1975–1977, 2:373–78). In 1666, don Juan filed multiple petitions asking for his right to the cacicazgo to be recognized. Don Francisco had signed a document indicating that don Luis should in fact inherit the cacicazgo after his death, but don Juan stated that it was the product of a manipulation by don Luis, who had taken advantage of don Francisco's advanced age and feeble mind (2:381). In July 1666, the Real Audiencia issued a decree granting the cacicazgo to don Juan (2:388–89). Don Juan then served as cacique until his own death in 1682, but before he died he wanted to ensure that his younger brother, don Diego, would be able to inherit the title, and he called on his friend Sigüenza to aid in that process.

Among the forty paragraphs of don Juan's will, he explicitly stated that the cacicazgo of San Juan Teotihuacan should be inherited by his brother, Diego de Alva Cortés (O'Gorman 1975–1977, 392). He went on to say that his brother was in need of a representative because he was disabled [de poca capacidad] and unscrupulous relatives might try to take advantage of him (392). From what we know, it seems that don Diego was blind and never active in legal matters on his own behalf (Munch 1976, 56). From 1682 until 1685, Sigüenza helped don Diego rebut multiple attempts by his cousin, don Felipe, the youngest son of don Luis, to assume the position of cacique. In his defense of don Diego, Sigüenza emphasized the right of inheritance based on the genealogy of the Alva Ixtlilxochitl family, as we see in a precisely executed genealogical tree penned by the creole scholar himself (Figure 5).

The genealogy begins with "Don Francisco Verdugo Indio," Alva Ixtlilxochitl's great-grandfather, and it ends with don Diego de Alva's son, Antonio. Sigüenza organized the genealogy in such a way that it explicitly supports the argument that Fernando de Alva Ixtlilxochitl's sons are the legitimate heirs to the cacicazgo. He emphasized this point in a statement found beneath the family tree:

> Since the hereditary line of don Francisco ended, [the line
> of inheritance] followed that of don Fernando. Now, if that
> line were to end and don Luis's line were to enter, who would
> not see that it was his son Lorenzo and his children and
> grandchildren [who should follow] and that all of them are
> missing. Geronimo and his descendants, and then Ana and
> her line, and afterward Magdalena and then lastly Felipe,
> who unjustly brought suit against don Diego . . . For Felipe
> to be [cacique] more than forty people would have to die.

> [Por haver faltado la linea de D Francisco se siguio la de D
> Fernando, luego si faltara la de D Fernando y entrara la de D Luis
> quien no ve que primero era Lorenzo y sus hijos y nietos y la falta

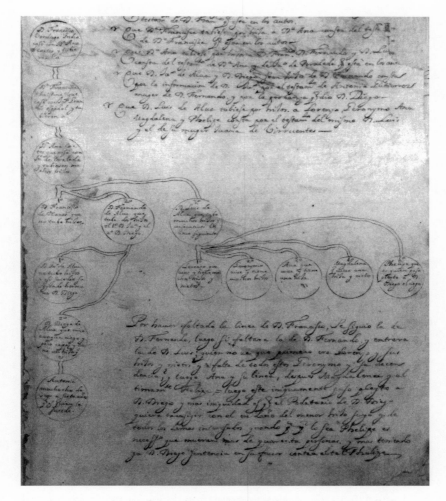

Figure 5. Genealogy of the Alva Ixtlilxochitl family in the hand of don Carlos de Sigüenza y Góngora. AGN-V volume 232, folio 328. Courtesy of the Archivo General de la Nación, Mexico City.

de todos estos. Geronimo y su decendencia, y luego Ana y su linea,
despues Magdalena y ultimamente Felipe, luego este iniquamente
puso pleyto a D Diego . . . para que lo sea Phelipe es necesario que
mueran mas de quarenta personas.] (AGN-V volume 232, folio 328)

The family tree and the text that accompanies it established that the line of
inheritance led to Fernando de Alva Ixtlilxochitl's sons, don Juan and don
Diego, as it would have first gone to the children of doña Ana's eldest son,
and since he did not have children, the cacicazgo should thus have passed
to the sons of the second oldest, don Fernando. As the youngest son of
doña Ana's youngest son, don Felipe would have been the last in line, and
thus his many attempts to usurp don Diego's position were ungrounded—
egregiously so, according to Sigüenza, who argued with more than a bit
of hyperbole that a full forty lives or more separated the litigant from his
claim. The intricacies of the line of inheritance and the family genealogy
surrounding that line become the grist for the story told and retold in the
legal documents concerning the cacicazgo of San Juan Teotihuacan.

Sigüenza did secure don Diego's position as cacique, but other family
members made attempts to discredit his involvement in the legal matters, and ultimately the creole scholar was dismissed as don Diego's *podatario*. Expressing his extreme frustration at these developments, in
1685 Sigüenza noted for the court that don Diego had a new *podatario*,
Sebastián de Alva, whom he described disparagingly as a "mestizo shoe-
maker" [mestizo zapatero] (Munch 1976, 56). Yet, Sigüenza's involvement
in legal matters related to San Juan Teotihuacan did not end when he
was relieved of his advocate's position. Don Juan de Alva Cortés had also
bequeathed to his friend lands separate from the cacicazgo. The will stated
that Sigüenza, who as its executor wrote this stipulation in the first person,
"shall serve as the *capellán* and after my death I shall decide who should
succeed me" [y que yo la sirva y después quien yo quisiere] (O'Gorman
1975–1977, 2:394). According to John Frederick Schwaller, the *capellanía*
(chantry) "provides for masses for the spiritual benefit of the founder and
others, usually family members, designated in the foundation documents"
(2011, 82). There was an intricate financial system created to support the
capellanías and the *capellanes*. This system relied on mortgages, rents, or
liens on lands for financial support (von Wobeser 1998, 120; Schwaller

2011, 82). Often the *capellán* (priest) designated to say the masses was a family member. In fact, Alva Ixtlilxochitl's great-grandmother, doña Francisca Cristina Verdugo, requested in her will of 1596 that a *capellanía* be founded using certain rents from lands in San Juan Teotihuacan (Alva Ixtlilxochitl 1975–1977, 2:291). Although that wish was not granted, in March 1683 the *capellanía* was finally founded in honor of don Juan de Alva Cortés, with Sigüenza, a nonrelative and a creole, as the first *capellán*. His position as an outsider eventually caused tensions with the native inhabitants of San Juan Teotihuacan, including the man he was intended to protect, don Diego de Alva Cortés.

In Sigüenza's will and testament from August 9, 1700, he stated that he was the executor for don Juan de Alva Cortés and that he had been appointed the "patrón y capellán" at the *capellanía* in San Juan Teotihuacan.[26] This *capellanía*, he clarifies, had been established on lands that belonged to don Juan personally and not to the estate (Pérez Salazar 1928, 176). Don Juan had designated those lands to be used as collateral in the process of establishing the *capellanía*, and thus he had essentially transferred that asset to Sigüenza upon his death. However, beginning in 1685, there were a series of legal struggles between Sigüenza and other interested parties—including local officials and don Diego de Alva Cortés—over the legitimacy of his claims to the lands associated with the *capellanía*. The struggle over the *capellanía* lands explains Sigüenza's falling out with don Diego and his being relieved of his position as don Diego's *podatario*. Ultimately the court awarded Sigüenza a much smaller plot, which was declared to have been the personal property of don Juan and not entailed to the *cacicazgo*.[27] By the time of his death, Sigüenza's connections to the lands of San Juan Teotihuacan were strictly through this small share of the *capellanía*, despite his long and complex relationship with the area's leading native family.

In his will, Sigüenza named his twelve-year-old nephew Raphael de Sigüenza to succeed him as *capellán*. Since Raphael was so young, Sigüenza appointed his elder nephew and the executor of his will, don Gabriel López de Sigüenza, as the administrator of the *capellanía* until the younger boy became of age (Pérez Salazar 1928, 178). The ownership of the lands associated with the *capellanía* continued to be a point of contention between Sigüenza's heirs and other interested parties. Between

1703 and 1709, local residents and officials of San Juan Teotihuacan, including its governor, don Theodoro Ambrosio, sought to have the claims
of Sigüenza's nephews to the *capellanía* lands dismissed (AGN-T volume 1779, file 3, folio 38). Don Gabriel López de Sigüenza responded
to their petition by arguing that the lands were part of a *capellanía* to
which Sigüenza had been named and so they had come to him by family
inheritance (folios 30–31). The nephew included in his response a petition drafted by don Carlos in 1690. Asking that the lands be officially
recognized as belonging to him, don Carlos stated: "I submit that it was
declared that the chantry that don Juan de Alva, deceased, ordered to be
founded belonged to me and that I am *capellán* and owner of its lands"
[demuestro se declaró pertenecer a la capellanía de misas que mando fun-
dar D. Juan de Alva Difunto y de que yo soy capellan propietario las
tierras que en el se expresan] (folio 33). In 1709, the complainants were
ordered to return the lands to López de Sigüenza.

The legal documents related to the cacicazgo and the *capellanía* provide fresh insights into Sigüenza's involvement with the Alva Ixtlilxochitl
family, just as they allow us an important perspective on the position of the
native elite in seventeenth-century Mexico and the relationship between a
prominent creole and a prominent Indian family. Sigüenza's positions—as
executor of don Juan de Alva Cortés's will, *podatario* for don Diego de Alva
Cortés, and *capellán* in San Juan Teotihuacan—shaped the last two decades
of his life and formed a significant part of his legacy. His work advocating
for don Diego allowed him access to a wealth of native documents and
manuscripts that would inform his own writings, and the *capellanía* provided him with financial assets that he was able to leave for his nephews.
Fernando de Alva Ixtlilxochitl and Carlos de Sigüenza y Góngora were
keen to collect and study materials related to the Indian past, and though
their individual motivations for accumulating that knowledge traveled
along different trajectories, they did share at least one goal: to aid in the
family's preservation of the cacicazgo of San Juan Teotihuacan.

Contrasting Historiographies and *Parayso occidental*

As described at the beginning of this chapter, don Juan de Alva Cortés
asked don Carlos de Sigüenza y Góngora to produce a *vida* of Marina de

la Cruz, bequeathing a sum of money to his friend to do so (Alva Ixtlilxochitl 1975–1977, 2:393). Sigüenza published his study of don Juan's aunt
as book 2 of his *Parayso occidental* (1684). As Sigüenza's lengthiest surviving text, the three-book *Parayso occidental* has been astutely studied as an
example of colonial religious writing (Lavrin 2008; Córdova 2009; Díaz
2010) and as an example of creole intellectual production in seventeenth-
century Mexico (Brading 1991; Ross 1993; More 2013). However, the
connection with the Alva Ixtlilxochitl family that underlies the project has
not been a focus of scholarly attention. In fact, a careful reading of *Parayso
occidental* reveals the degree to which Sigüenza's connections with an elite
native family informed the writing of the text and, just as importantly,
the ways in which that family imprinted their own agenda on the creole
scholar's work. All these connections make this text a vivid, if less than
obvious, example of how knowledge moved between intellectual spheres
via a complex web of power and agency.

The epigraph to this chapter, detailing the box Sigüenza fashioned to
house the skull of Mother Marina, is found near the end of book 2. The
strained syntax of the description and the excessive ornamentation of the
box itself, not to mention the skull that is the centerpiece of the passage,
could be considered hallmarks of Sigüenza's baroque style, and have provided numerous scholars with illuminating insights into his work (Ross
1993; Merrim 2010; More 2013). My focus, however, is the symbolic
function this box and the skull have within the personal ties between
Sigüenza and the Alva Ixtlilxochitl family. The box continued to hold
sway over Sigüenza's thoughts until his death, as in his own will he strove
to secure funding for a replacement:

> I declare that don Alonso Gallegos, who leases the ranch in San Juan
> Teotihuacan, owes me rent from November of last year forward. . . .
> And whatever remains should be spent to make a box, the finest
> possible, which could hold the head of the pious woman Marina
> de la Cruz, nun at the Royal Convent of Jesús María in this city.

> [Declaro que Dn. Alonso Gallegos quien tiene en arrendamiento
> el Rancho de San Juan Teotiguacan me está deviendo la Renta
> desde Noviembre del año pasado, y lo que va corriendo. . . . Y

lo que restare se gaste en hazer una Caxa lo mas decente que
se pudiere para que se guarde en ella la Cabeza de la Beata
marina de la Cruz Religiosa que fue del Convento Rl. de
Jesús María de esta Ciud.] (Pérez Salazar 1928, 188–89)

With his friendship with don Juan de Alva Cortés at its center, Sigüenza's
web of connections with various members of the Alva Ixtlilxochitl family
extended out to both the living and the dead. He demonstrates this not
only in his custody of Fernando de Alva Ixtlilxochitl's manuscript collection, but also in the legal documents through which he accumulated a
detailed knowledge of the family's genealogy, in his chronicle of the Royal
Convent of Jesús María, and perhaps most poignantly in his enduring
concern for a relic of the family that presented no gain to his interests,
material or intellectual.

Book 2 of *Parayso occidental* concludes with a genealogical narrative
that echoes those found in the legal documents related to the cacicazgo
conflicts. In addition to his detailed descriptions of Mother Marina's parents and immediate family members, Sigüenza offers one of her nephew
Juan Pérez de Peraleda, who came to New Spain to be with his aunt
and eventually married doña Ana Cortés Ixtlilxochitl. Doña Ana was, as
Sigüenza explains,

> daughter of Juan Grande and doña Francisca Cristina,
> who in turn was the daughter of don Francisco Verdugo
> Quetzalmamalitzin, cacique of San Juan Teotihuacan, and of
> doña Ana Cortés, daughter of don Fernando Cortés Ixtlilxochitl
> and granddaughter of Nezahualpilli, king of Tetzcoco.
>
> [hija de Iuan Grande, y Doña Francisca Christina [*sic*],
> siendo esta hija de D. Francisco Verdugo Quetzalmamalitzin
> Cacique del Pueblo de S. Juan Teotihuacan, y de Doña Ana
> Cortes hija de D. Fernando Cortes Ixtlilxochitl, y nieta de
> Nezahualpiltzintli Rey de Tetzcoco.] (1995 [1684], 128r–128v).

The paragraph continues to trace out the family line, and it ends with the
man deemed by Sigüenza to be the rightful inheritor of the cacicazgo:

Don Juan de Alva Cortés, interpreter in the Royal High Court
and the Indian Court, cacique of San Juan Teotihuacan, a very
upright man in his personal dealings and also a very religious
man, by whose death without offspring entered don Diego de
Alva, his younger brother, in the cacicazgo of said town.

[*D. Iuan de Alva Cortes*, Interprete que fue de la Real Audiencia,
y Jusgado de Indios, Caciques del Pueblo de S. Juan Teotihuacan,
hombre muy ajustado en sus procederes, y devotissimo de los
Santos, por cuya muerte sin sucession entró D. Diego de Alva su
segundo hermano en el Cacicazgo de dicho Pueblo.] (128v).

Beyond reiterating the details of the Alva Ixtlilxochitl family tree, these
lines hint at a personal intimacy that bound Sigüenza to don Juan de Alva
and prompted his involvement in legal and biographical matters related
to don Juan's family. *Parayso occidental* is thus understood, in light of the
extensive relationship to the Alva Ixtlilxochitl family, as one of Sigüenza's
most personal works, even as it continues with some of his well-worn
tropes for connecting the Mexican past to European antiquity.

For instance, book 1 of *Parayso occidental* opens, somewhat incon-
gruously, with a detailed treatment of the pre-Hispanic Mexican vestal
virgins, whom Sigüenza represents as counterparts to the ancient Romans: "The barbarous Mexica were like the ancient Romans in sending
virgins to care for the perpetual flame" [Concordaron los barbaros Mexicanos, con los Romanos antiguos en destinar Virgenes puras, para que
cuydasen de la perpetuidad del fuego] (1995 [1684], 1v). According to
Sigüenza, the fourth Mexica leader, Itzcoatzin, initiated the tradition of
bringing together these virgins (*cihuatlamacazque* in Nahuatl) to live in
single dwellings the author calls "Indian convents" [Indianos Conventos]
(2r).[28] Sigüenza not only proposes a similarity between the Mexica virgins
and their Roman counterparts but also suggests that these pre-Columbian
women shared two important features with the colonial Catholic nuns:
both are examples of communities of virginal women brought together for
religious worship. Sigüenza cites as his source for this knowledge a series
of Nahuatl songs that, he says, don Fernando de Alva Ixtlilxochitl had
transcribed directly from his Nahua elders and then translated. Praising

the linguistic and rhetorical skill of the Tetzcoca chronicler, Sigüenza introduces passages purportedly drawn from Alva Ixtlilxochitl:

> The following sentence, which is found among those that were
> taken from the mouths of the ancients, was conserved in the
> manuscripts of the Cicero of the Mexican language, don Fernando
> de Alva; I'll use the same words chosen by Alva, who translated
> it directly from the originals and with extraordinary precision.

> [La oración siguiente, que se halla entre las que de boca de
> los Antiguos conservó en sus Manuscritos el Ciceron de
> la lengua Mexicana, D. Fernando de Alva, la qual referiré
> con las mismas palabras, que la tradujo por corresponder
> a las originales con propiedad muy precissa.] (2v)

The creole author then cites four lengthy paragraphs from Alva Ixtlilxochitl's text that offer a prayer for the young woman about to enter the pre-
Hispanic and pre-Christian convent. Beginning with the phrase "Lord
and God Unseen" [Señor, y Dios invisible] (2v), this address is reminiscent of the phrase frequently used by Alva Ixtlilxochitl, "The Lord of the
Near and the Far" [In Tloque, In Nahuaque], but the language appears
more closely tied to biblical phrasing than Nahuatl speech.[29]

In fact, except for the occasional Nahuatl name or term, the texts
Sigüenza cites are roundly Christian and European in tone and content.
For instance, Sigüenza introduces a passage allegedly from Alva Ixtlilxochitl's translation that addresses the *cihuatlamacazque*, whom the author
calls *vírgenes sacerdotisas* (virginal priestesses). According to Sigüenza,
these young women were asked to remove their fancy clothing and cut
their hair in order to enter the living space for religious women. Reminding us of the advice offered to a young novice in a Catholic convent, the
text exhorts the young woman in this manner: "Enter, then, my child,
with all your will to serve the omnipotent God and you will be and you
will live with the chaste and penitent young women; but see that I charge
you to be pure of body and soul, because the virgins of heart and body
are in always closest to God" [Entra pues, Hija, con toda tu voluntad a
servir al Omnipotente Dios y estarás, y vivirás con las Doncellas castas, y

penitentes; pero mira, que te encomiendo, que seas puríssima en cuerpo, y alma, porque las Vírgenes de coraçon, y cuerpo, son en todos tiempos las mas llegadas a Dios] (3v). Though Sigüenza claims that his discussion of the vestal virgins is heavily indebted to the texts from don Fernando de Alva Ixtlilxochitl that he had in his possession, there is no evidence of these passages in any extant text produced by Alva Ixtlilxochitl. This fact should give us pause as we consider and weigh the impact of native knowledge on the emerging creole discourse.

Alva Ixtlilxochitl's *Sumaria relación de las cosas de la Nueva España* provides a compilation of historical knowledge of pre-Hispanic Anahuac that relied heavily on oral traditions maintained by elders in the community, many of whom had had access to the archives in Tetzcoco.[30] This text would fit Sigüenza's description of the work he claimed to have consulted and in which he found the explanation of the *cihuatlamacazque*. Yet, we find no passage in the *Sumaria relación* that is remotely similar to what Sigüenza cites. In fact, when Alva Ixtlilxochitl does address pre-Hispanic female sacred practices in the text, it is with a note of critique, as we see in this passage: "The women went to the temples and they lay with the priests and committed other grave and abominable sins" [Las señoras iban a los templos . . . y se revolvían con los sacerdotes y hacían otros pecados graves y abominables]. He then provides details of a specific woman who became involved with a specific priest and though they had both made a vow of chastity, they broke the vow and she went on to bear his child (1975–1977, 1:277). Quite unlike the passages cited by Sigüenza, Alva Ixtlilxochitl's text does not offer the reader a model of pre-Hispanic sacred practices that served as a foundation for colonial-era Catholic traditions. There are no *cihuatlamacazque* or vestal virgins by any other name in Alva Ixtlilxochitl's works.

In fact, it is more likely that Sigüenza took inspiration from Spanish authors in his construction of pre-Hispanic female religious practice. In *Historia natural y moral de las Indias* (1590), José de Acosta includes a chapter titled "Regarding the monasteries for young women that the devil invented for his own service" [De los monasterios de doncellas que inventó el demonio para su servicio] (Acosta 1985 [1590], 240–44). Sigüenza's aim was to establish a clear link between those pre-Hispanic practices and the Hispano-Catholic colonial context of the Royal Convent of Jesús

María. Acosta's focus was squarely on the nefarious spiritual traditions that existed in the Indies before the arrival of the Spaniards. Yet, there are clear parallels between the two descriptions of religious women. For example, according to Acosta, in Mexico, upon entering the house for religious women, girls of twelve to thirteen years of age cut their hair and don simple white shifts (241). Just as Sigüenza would assert roughly one hundred years later, Acosta says that these young women from Mexico and also Peru are similar to the "vestal virgins from Rome" [las vírgenes vestales de Roma]. For Acosta the religious practice of the ancients was performed "in service to Satan" [en servicio a Satanás] (242; 244), but for Sigüenza the *cihuatlamacazque* signal a positive precursor to the convent life of colonial Mexico. One can suspect that in addition to pursuing his own historiographical interests in connecting pre-Columbian Mexico with ancient Greece and Rome, Sigüenza is also creating a sanitized version of indigenous tradition in order to place a revered member of a family dear to him in a more positive light. Again, *Parayso occidental* was among the most personal of Sigüenza's surviving works and one whose peculiarities are perhaps best understood within the more constrained limits of service and obligation that characterized the colonial economy of letters I have been tracing.

In her careful and extended reading of *Parayso occidental*, Kathleen Ross focused on the Spanish American baroque as the prism through which to study the text, and she views the language and style of the *barroco de Indias* as intimately tied to the creole historiography. She identified Sigüenza's narrative strategies in *Parayso occidental* as an "operation of textual domination" carried out over the voices of the female religious and their *vidas*, which were the true object of the text's exposition (1993, 10). For Ross, the Indian vestal virgins embody the "syncretic idea of pre-Conquest Mexico as a land with direct parallels to Western historiography," and the heart of the opening chapter of the text is "Sigüenza's transcription of a selection from early manuscripts of Fernando de Alva Ixtlilxochitl" (67; 69). What happens to this analysis when we pose the possibility that the presumed writings from Alva Ixtlilxochitl were not in fact from him, but rather originated from Sigüenza's pen? I suggest that we pursue this scenario as a way of rethinking the relationship between the creole and mestizo scholars. The Alva Ixtlilxochitl family, well after the death of Alva Ixtlilxochitl, sought to inscribe their family further into Catholic traditions related to sainthood, and Sigüenza's sanitizing of the vestal virgins tradition can be understood in that light less as an appropriation or even transcription from a native tradition and more as an alteration in the indigenous historical record corresponding to pressures from within the native elites, who themselves wanted to pursue a pattern of integration with the dominant society. Further, Sigüenza's relationship with the Alva Ixtlilxochitl family was real and enduring, and to truly approach an understanding of his debt to Alva Ixtlilxochitl, we need to take into account the extent to which Sigüenza was immersed in the family's land dealings, legal struggles, and genealogical history, including the notably physical efforts of documenting the Alva Ixtlilxochitl cacicazgo.

Conclusion

In his influential study of creole patriotism, David Brading described Sigüenza's role in the following way: "Sigüenza's greatest contribution lay in his zealous care of Ixtlilxochitl's collection, possibly augmenting it with other manuscripts and codices, all of which he bequeathed to the Jesuit college of St Peter and St Paul" (1991, 367).[31] For Brading, Sigüenza—and really Alva Ixtlilxochitl as well—was simply a conduit that brought the trove of native materials into the hands of eighteenth-century historians. This analysis underestimates the interpretive value of the subjective circumstances that explain why and how Sigüenza came to possess Alva Ixtlilxochitl's collection. As we look at the movement of the material collection from Alva Ixtlilxochitl's family to Sigüenza, there is a rich and understudied context to take in. Sigüenza was a close personal friend of don Juan de Alva Cortés and he took on the mantle of advocate for don Juan's younger brother, don Diego de Alva Cortés. In this capacity he fought to protect the claims of an Alva Ixtlilxochitl son to the family's cacicazgo at San Juan Teotihuacan. During that same period, Sigüenza wrote a number of historical texts, including *Parayso occidental*, which don Juan had effectively commissioned through his will.

The relationship between Alva Ixtlilxochitl's sons and Sigüenza underlines the ways in which the divisions between the República de indios and the República de españoles were transgressed, and yet not fully dissolved. Frederick Cooper has called on scholars to undertake a more rigorous historical practice in colonial and postcolonial studies. Specifically, "historical practice suggests that however varied the impetus and context for the actions of men and women, interactions unfold over time; contexts are reconfigured and shape future possibilities and closures" (2005, 13). By digging deep into the impetus for the gift to Sigüenza, we gain a more subtle understanding of the movement of native knowledge from an elite native landholding family to a creole scholar. Yet as the manuscripts shifted ownership, they were recontextualized and reinterpreted.

The legal struggles over the cacicazgo provide a context and specific circumstance for the collection and circulation of knowledge of local history and genealogy. Alva Ixtlilxochitl sought to collect local knowledge from the native elders in order to support his mother's claims to the title of cacica. A generation later, Sigüenza inherited a diverse collection of materials from Alva Ixtlilxochitl's older son so that he could provide strong legal support for Diego de Alva Cortés's rights to the cacicazgo. In this sense, there is a parallel between Alva Ixtlilxochitl and Sigüenza, as both men were advocates for the Alva Ixtlilxochitl family and both helped preserve the family's landholdings, founding the legitimacy of their claims on the family's genealogy. Yet their individual historiographical projects followed different paths. That will be the subject of the following two chapters.

CHAPTER 3

Configuring Native Knowledge

SEVENTEENTH-CENTURY MESTIZO HISTORIOGRAPHY

Every historical book worthy of the name ought to include . . .
"How can I know what I am about to say?"
　　　　　　　　　　　　—Marc Bloch, *The Historian's Craft*

I<small>N HIS UNFINISHED STUDY ON THE</small> work of the historian, Marc Bloch says
that writing history is heavily contingent on the moment in which it is
produced and thus it is ever shifting.[1] "The past," he said, "is, by definition, a datum which nothing in the future will change. But the knowledge
of the past is something progressive which is constantly transforming and
perfecting itself" (1954, 58). To study the writings of don Fernando de
Alva Ixtlilxochitl in the twenty-first century requires facing underlying
questions and concerns related to his knowledge and discussion of the
native past. Do we look on his five historical studies as a more or less
transparent window into the native past—a source of material for gaining
a greater understanding of pre-Hispanic and conquest-era Mexico? Or do
we view his writings as a product of the linguistic and cultural impositions
of the colonizers and thus, perhaps, of dubious value as a representation of
native history and experience? This chapter works with the premise that
for us to advance our understanding of Alva Ixtlilxochitl's historical writings we must first look carefully at his historiographical methods. To be
clear, I am concerned with Alva Ixtlilxochitl's process and methodology

as a historian and for this we must take careful stock of his project and
the context in which he undertook it. In other words, referencing the epigraph from Bloch: How can Alva Ixtlilxochitl have known what he said?

Edmundo O'Gorman's 1975–1977 edition of Alva Ixtlilxochitl's historical works includes five texts: *Sumaria relación de todas las cosas que han
sucedido en la Nueva España, Relación sucinta en forma de memorial, Compendio histórico del reino de Texcoco, Sumaria relación de esta Nueva España*, and
Historia de la nación chichimeca.[2] The material Alva Ixtlilxochitl drew from
for his five historical works was wide-ranging and diverse.[3] At various points
in his texts he mentions alphabetic manuscripts and pictorial texts produced
by native authors, as well as the names of native elders with whom he consulted and traditional songs he heard.[4] He also cites European sources, including Francisco López de Gómara's *Historia general de las Indias* (General
history of the Indies), Juan de Torquemada's *Monarquía Indiana* (Monarchy
of the Indies), and ancient authors like Plato and Xenophon. In addition
to the materials Alva Ixtlilxochitl cites, we have several manuscript copies
that appear to be in his hand, including Juan Bautista Pomar's *Relación de
Tetzcoco*, originally written in 1582 for the king (Figure 6).[5] This volume is
one of the few we have that clearly belonged to Alva Ixtlilxochitl's collection
and which he cites explicitly in his own writings. In a passage in the *Historia
de la nación chichimeca*, Alva Ixtlilxochitl states that, among other materials,
he has drawn from the historical relations written by various figures from
Tetzcoco, including "Juan de Pomar" (1975–1977, 2:137).

Just as Alva Ixtlilxochitl would lament in his own histories, Pomar
notes at the beginning of his *Relación* that he had struggled to gather
knowledge of Tetzcoco's past, since many of the *altepetl*'s documents had
been destroyed when the royal archives were burned during the reign of
the first archbishop of Mexico, Fray Juan de Zumárraga. Pomar attributes the
actual destruction of the materials to the people of Tetzcoco, who feared
that their pictorials would be misinterpreted as part of idol worship.[6]
Alva Ixtlilxochitl, however, lays the blame alternately on Zumárraga and
Hernando Cortés. For example, citing unnamed historians as he narrates
the conquest of Mexico in the "Thirteenth Relation" of the *Compendio
histórico del reino de Texcoco*, Alva Ixtlilxochitl directly criticizes Cortés and
his men for sacking and plundering the royal palaces: "They were the first
destroyers of the histories of this land" [Fueron los primeros destruidores

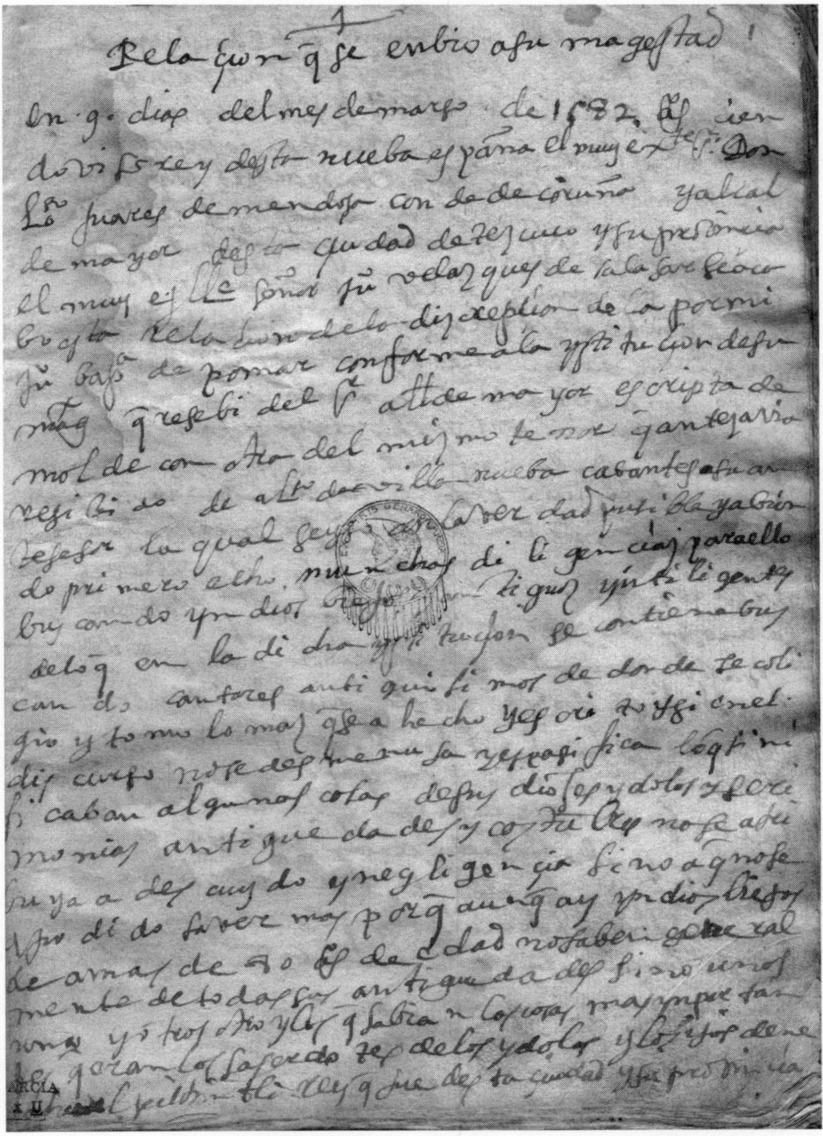

Figure 6. Alva Ixtlilxochitl's copy of Juan Bautista Pomar's *Relación de Tetzcoco*. Ms. G57–G59, folio 1r. Courtesy of the Nettie Lee Benson Latin American Collection, University of Texas Libraries, The University of Texas at Austin.

de las historias de esta tierra] (1975–1977, 1:468). However, in the *Historia de la nación chichimeca*—Alva Ixtlilxochitl's lengthiest and most developed work—he makes a sweeping criticism of the first archbishop when he blames Zumárraga not only for the destruction of documents, but also myriad other cultural artifacts that the priest "ordered destroyed, believing they were some form of idols" [mandó hacer pedazos, entendiendo ser algunos ídolos] (1975–1977, 2:115). In each text, Alva Ixtlilxochitl offers a slightly different interpretation of the account he read in Pomar and perhaps secured from other sources as well. This example helps to remind us that Alva Ixtlilxochitl's use and interpretation of sources was not static and, in fact, to gauge how he knew what he said we must look to the broader social context in which he wrote.

Scholars have tended to describe Alva Ixtlilxochitl as a "mestizo historian." As an identity marker or a discursive descriptor, "mestizo" contains multiple contradictions. Understood as a category, it presumes a set of common features among a group of individuals, yet at the same time the suggestion of mixing that the term communicates connotes non-belonging. Mestizos are neither fully Spanish nor fully Indian. In the concluding lines to their persuasive article "Beyond 'Identity,'" Rogers Brubaker and Frederick Cooper assert that "to criticize the use of 'identity' in social analysis is not to blind ourselves to particularity. It is rather to conceive of the claims and possibilities that arise from particular affinities and affiliations, from particular commonalities and connections, from particular stories and self-understandings, from particular problems and predicaments in a more differentiated manner" (2000, 36). Recognizing the importance of the particular over the categorical, my analysis of Alva Ixtlilxochitl as a mestizo historian draws from specific circumstances that defined his work and writing in order to underline his access to two cultural traditions as the defining feature of his mestizo histories. Alva Ixtlilxochitl used his bicultural vantage point to make the stories derived from native sources relevant to the Hispano-Catholic context in which he lived and worked.

Collecting and Configuring Native Knowledge

In *The Writing of History*, Michel de Certeau emphasized that a historical study is the "product of a place" because, he says, it is "bound to the complex of a specific and collective fabrication more than it is the effect merely of a personal philosophy or the resurgence of a past 'reality'" (1988, 64). In this sense, a historical study tells us as much about the moment in which it was written as it does about the past it presumes to describe. Alva Ixtlilxochitl saw himself as part of a time in which native knowledge was disappearing, as troves of material history had been destroyed and the elders were dying and taking their memories of pre-Columbian times with them. In this context of loss, Alva Ixtlilxochitl took on the role of local historian. Nowhere does he more eloquently address this project than in the prologue to the *Historia de la nación chichimeca*, where he explains in the opening sentence that unlike other historians, he roots his narrative in native sources:

> Given the variety and contradictory opinions of the
> authors who have addressed the history of this New
> Spain, I have not wanted to follow any of them. Instead,
> I have relied on the paintings and glyphs with which the
> native histories are written and memorized since they
> were painted at the time when the events happened.
>
> [Considerando la variedad y contrarios pareceres de los
> autores que han tratado las historias de esta Nueva España,
> no he querido seguir a ninguno de ellos; y así me aproveché
> de las pinturas y caracteres que son con que están escritas y
> memorizadas sus historias, por haberse pintado al tiempo y
> cuando sucedieron las cosas acaecidas.] (1975–1977, 1:527)

Positioning himself as the intermediary between this native knowledge and a readership that reaches beyond the native communities, Alva Ixtlilxochitl claims access to original sources and the interpretative skills to make sense of those materials.

In this prologue, he goes on to describe the various genres in which the ancients wrote: annals that described events in each year, month, day, and hour; genealogies of kings and people of great standing; pictures and maps describing the physical limits of cities, provinces, and towns; books on laws, rites, and ceremonies; and paintings and songs documenting the knowledge of philosophers and intellectuals(1975–1977, 1:527). Following this passage, Alva Ixtlilxochitl plaintively states that the arrival of the Spaniards marked a new time in which the social and political order that had buttressed the writing of history changed dramatically. Alva Ixtlilxochitl notes that the kings were no longer kings; after the demise of the reigning leaders, their descendants had endured great trials and their vassals had suffered a dire and calamitous demographic collapse.[7]

Alva Ixtlilxochitl's texts were imagined and produced in a colonial context that, for him, was defined by loss, and he proposes himself as the guardian of the remaining local knowledge of Tetzcoco in the conclusion to the prologue of the *Historia de la nación chichimeca*, where he movingly describes the challenges faced by the inhabitants of Tetzcoco and the native intellectuals:

> Not only did [the Tetzcoca] not continue with what was good
> and not at all contrary to our Catholic faith, but the majority
> of their histories were inadvertently and inconsiderately burned
> by order of the first friars. This was one of the greatest injuries
> suffered in this New Spain. All the aforementioned books,
> texts, and materials were kept in the royal archives in the city
> of Tetzcoco, since it was the metropolis of all knowledge,
> traditions, and good customs since its kings were proud of this
> and they were the lawmakers in this new world. The materials
> that escaped from the fires and calamities were guarded by
> my ancestors, from whom I obtained them, and from them I
> have taken and translated the history that I promise here.

> [No tan solamente no se prosiguió lo que era bueno y no contrario
> a nuestra santa fe católica, sino que lo más de ellos se quemó
> inadvertida e inconsideradamente por orden de los primeros
> religiosos, que fue uno de los mayores daños que tuvo esta Nueva
> España; porque en la ciudad de Tetzcuco estaban los archivos
> reales de todas las cosas referidas, por haber sido la metrópoli de
> todas las ciencias, usos y buenas costumbres, porque los reyes que
> fueron de ella se preciaron de eso y fueron los legisladores de este
> nuevo mundo; y de lo que escapó de los incendios y calamidades

referidas que guardaron mis mayores, vino a mis manos, de donde
he sacado y traducido la historia que prometo.] (1975–1977, 1:527)

This passage condenses critical elements of Alva Ixtlilxochitl's writings:
he wrote in an explicitly Hispano-Catholic context; for him, Tetzcoco
was the intellectual center of pre-Hispanic New Spain; upon their arrival, the Spaniards sought to destroy diverse material forms of native
knowledge; and, Alva Ixtlilxochitl salvaged from the remains of those texts
and memories the histories of his people. Aligning himself with both the
Catholic faith and his native ancestors, Alva Ixtlilxochitl's vantage point
is tied explicitly to the moment in time he inhabited. The two verbs that
drive the last line of this passage underline the way he imagined his own
historiographical project: "to take out" (*sacar*) and "to translate" (*traducir*).
A century after conquest and colonization, Alva Ixtlilxochitl drew from
the surviving material and human sources and he deciphered those stories
for a seventeenth-century audience whose worldview was informed by,
though not necessarily limited to, Hispanic tradition and Catholic faith.

In his 1611 dictionary, Sebastián de Covarrubias defines the verb *traducir* in this way: "From the Latin verb *traduco*, meaning to carry something
from one place to another or to set it on its path. . . . In Latin it can have
other analogous meanings, but in Spanish it means to turn the sentence
from one language into another" [Del verbo latino *traduco*, is, por llevar de
un lugar a otro alguna cosa o encaminarla. . . . En lengua latina tiene otras
sinificaciones analógicas, pero en la española sinifica el bolver la sentencia
de una lengua en otra] (1943 [1611], 972). Following—as he says—the
advice of Horace, Covarrubias goes on to caution that one should not
attempt to translate literally or word for word.[8] This question of how to
best and most effectively translate from one language to another is the
object of philosophical discussion as well as serious methodological consideration by practitioners of translation.[9] In an influential essay, "The Task
of the Translator" (1923), Walter Benjamin provides insight into the act of
translation that, we might observe, heeds the ancient advice of Horace
and the cautionary words of Covarrubias: "The task of the translator consists in finding the particular intention toward the target language which
produces in that language the echo of the original" (1996[1923], 258).
As much art as science, translation relies on the translator's ability to find

words, phrases, and concepts that give meaning to the original text, yet in a new linguistic and perhaps cultural context. Lawrence Venuti, a practicing translator and a theorist of the art of translation, recently commented that "translating is readily seen as investing the source text with a significance that is specific to the translating language and culture" (2012, 11). This emphasis on making a text intelligible in a second language and for a secondary audience is at the heart of Alva Ixtlilxochitl's historiographical project, and as he was active as an interpreter for the Indian court system, these are issues with which he would have had a lived investment.

As we saw in Chapter 1, Alva Ixtlilxochitl mentions at various points his reliance on the *original historia*. Throughout Alva Ixtlilxochitl's historical works, he positions himself as a medium through which this original, native history can be accessed and interpreted. According to Alva Ixtlilxochitl, Spanish historians are at a distinct disadvantage trying to gather and record native history, while he has a privileged perspective that should lend more credence to his work, "having the histories in my possession, knowing the language of the same natives, since I was raised among them, and knowing all of the elders and notables from this land . . . always seeking the truth of each of these things about which I have written and will write in the history of the Chichimecs" [tener las historias en mi poder, y saber la lengua como los mismos naturales, porque me crié con ellos, y conocer a todos los viejos y principales de esta tierra . . . procurando siempre la verdad de cada cosa de estas que tengo escrito y escribiré en la historia de los chichimecos] (1975–1977, 1:288). Alva Ixtlilxochitl knows the people, he knows their stories, and he knows the language in which they are told and retold. However, finding a definitive version of history, Alva Ixtlilxochitl makes clear, is difficult in his sources as well.

Alva Ixtlilxochitl concludes the *Sumaria relación de las cosas de la Nueva España* with two illuminating anecdotes. After enumerating important sources for his histories, Alva Ixtlilxochtil addresses the challenge of locating the truth in the stories he has been told by native elders. By way of example, he presents a personal story of an occasion when he went to visit a gentleman friend, don Lope Zerón, and searching—as Alva Ixtlilxochitl always was—for more informants, he asked don Lope about "the notable people in the town and some of the elders" [la gente principal del pueblo y de algunos viejos]. Don Lope directed him to a certain elderly man who had been appointed governor thirty or forty years prior, since he was "very well spoken in Spanish, though belonging to the native community" [muy ladino, aunque villano de nación]. Notwithstanding the informant's bona fides, Alva Ixtlilxochitl complained that the elderly man told him "so many outlandish things, just like those our Spaniards have written" [tantos disparates, como los que nuestros españoles han escrito] (1975–1977, 1:287).

To further emphasize his point, Alva Ixtlilxochitl offers another example of an experience that demonstrates the challenges and pitfalls of finding sources for his histories. Though the story is secondhand, it illustrates clearly the historian's oft-times frustrated journey to the truth:

A certain gentleman who was descended from the house of Tetzcoco when upon asking an elderly nobleman from Tepetlaoztoc who were the parents and grandparents of Ixtlilxochitl, the father of Nezahualcoyotl, he responded to him by telling him that Ixtlilxochitl had no father or mother. Rather, a very large eagle came and made a nest in a big tree that was in the city and he put a big egg in it. After some time, the egg hatched and out came a little boy. The eagle brought him down from the nest and placed him in the middle of the plaza in the city. Seeing all this, the Acolhuas raised him and since they did not have a king, they made him their king and they gave him the name Ixtlilxochitl.

[Cierto caballero descendiente de la casa de Tezcuco que preguntando de una historia a un viejo de Tepetlaóztoc, principal, que quién fueron los padres y abuelos de Ixtlilxóchitl, padre del rey Nezahualcóyotl, le respondió diciéndole que Ixtlilxóchitl no tuvo padre ni madre, sino que vino una águila muy grande y hizo un nido en un árbol grande que estaba en la ciudad, y puso un huevo muy grande, y de allí a cierto tiempo quebró y sacó un niño, y lo bajó del nido poniéndolo en medio de la plaza de la ciudad; y viendo esto los aculhuas lo criaron, y como no tenían rey le alzaron por rey, y le pusieron el nombre llamándole Ixtlilxúchitl.] (1:288)

Upon hearing this tall tale, Alva Ixtlilxochitl's acquaintance let out a big laugh and told the man that what he had said was pure nonsense. The elderly man explained that he would respond to anyone who asked him that question the same way, especially to the Spaniards. It certainly is possible that the interaction Alva Ixtlilxochitl reports actually occurred. But even if the story had been embellished or entirely fabricated, Alva Ixtlilxochitl's point would be the same: in gathering oral sources, the informant may or may not reveal the truth.

Though still influential, Aristotle's foundational distinction (established in *Poetics*) between history and poetry, where the historian describes what has been and the poet describes what might be, may not provide the most productive barometer for analyzing the historical writings of seventeenth-century New Spain. In fact, David Boruchoff has suggested that the lines between poetry and history are particularly blurry in the early modern Hispanic world: "Early modern authors continually stretched the traditional concept of history as a documentary medium by employing fictional devices to attain higher truths that exist not in the facts of history as for Hegel, but beyond these facts in philosophy and religion" (2004, 276). Boruchoff points out that fictional speeches are chief among the devices employed by sixteenth- and seventeenth-century historians to bring to the fore one of the higher truths intended by the author.

Another way to think of the importance of the passage that addresses the fantastical birth of the pre-Hispanic leader is that Alva Ixtlilxochitl is signaling to the reader that informants can withhold stories. Michel-Rolph Trouillot discusses the function of silence in the production of history (1995).[10] In the passage about the elderly man from Tepetlaoztoc, the author recognizes that his oral source actively chooses to silence aspects of native history and that choice signals an exertion of power. According to Trouillot it is important to recognize that there is agency behind these silences:

> Thus the presences and absences embodied in sources
> (artifacts and bodies that turn an event into fact) or archives
> (facts collected, thematized, and processed as documents and
> monuments) are neither neutral or natural. They are created. As
> such, they are not mere presences and absences, but mentions
> or silences of various kinds and degrees. By silence, I mean
> an active or transitive process: one "silences" a fact or an

individual as a silencer silences a gun. One engages in a practice of silencing. Mentions and silences are thus active, dialectical counterparts of which history is the synthesis. (1995, 48)

In Alva Ixtlilxochitl's anecdote about sources, the elderly storyteller openly communicates that he has fabricated an untrue story, just as he has silenced a true one. Alva Ixtlilxochitl himself, we should hasten to add, makes those same choices about silencing or voicing the past as he understood it throughout his writing process. Alva Ixtlilxochitl's personal connections to the native communities aided him in his process of unearthing native stories. Yet, to discern the nature of Alva Ixtlilxochitl's sources is merely a first step in accounting for the production of his historical narratives. We must also look at the ways in which he voices and silences, reveals and conceals the native stories as he understood them.

Frank Salomon's classic essay on colonial Andean chronicles, which he calls "literature of the impossible," reminds us of the inherent difficulties in producing indigenous histories in alphabetic form (1982). Salomon notes that whereas Andean history was recounted in a cyclical fashion, European history was represented as uni-directional. Recognizing such fundamentally different perspectives, he suggests that "the project of reclaiming such knowledge for the purposes of postconquest historicizing involved compromises so drastic as to take it from the category of transposition to that of resynthesis or reconceptualization" (11). He goes on to say that "when one considers the indigenous chronicles as unified works, rather than as quarries from which to extract pieces of pristine Andean lore, there is no escaping the problem of cultural doubleness" (12). There are certainly particularities to Andean writing and recording systems that make the disjuncture between alphabetic writing and native forms of record-keeping, such as the *khipu*, more pronounced in the Andes than what we find in Mesoamerica. Nonetheless, Salomon's emphasis on the mediations that occur as pre-Hispanic narratives are recontextualized in the Hispano-Catholic colonial context is germane to central Mexico and to Alva Ixtlilxochitl's position as a mestizo writer working within two traditions. In fact, historian James Lockhart has addressed the question of cross-cultural writing through the phrase "double-mistaken identity," in which "each side of the cultural exchange presumes that a given form or concept is functioning in the way familiar within its own tradition and is unaware or unimpressed by the other side's interpretation" (1999, 99). Though there may have been convergences, he cautions, between European and central Mexican societies, those convergences should not be misconstrued as pointing to the same identity. Both Salomon's "literature of the impossible" and Lockhart's "double-mistaken identity" encourage us to recognize the gaps between European and native social practices and narrative traditions.

Alva Ixtlilxochitl had access to native knowledge through various means and media. His historiographical project was to make that knowledge intelligible within the Hispano-Catholic context in which he lived. In these dual influences we find the key to understanding his historical oeuvre. That body of work does not represent a transparent window onto the native past, nor should it be construed as a Europeanized and thus inauthentic version of native history. Rather, Alva Ixtlilxochitl's five historical texts are each a product of the colonial context in which he lived and worked, and in this sense, in the words of Salomon, they are imbued with a "cultural doubleness." The vantage point that informs his methods as a historian is defined by the sources and knowledge derived from native communities and the mores and discourses of the Hispano-Catholic society in which he lived.

Alva Ixtlilxochitl, Mestizo Historian

In his foundational study of Nahuatl letters, *Historia de la literatura náhuatl* (1954), Ángel María Garibay attempted to locate the writings of a range of authors who shared a similar project of writing historical texts about pre-Hispanic Mexico based on Nahuatl documents. He called these writers "mestizo historians" [historiadores mestizos] Garibay hastened to clarify that his use of the term "mestizo" was not intended to signal racial mixing; in fact, he said, a Spanish writer like Fray Diego Durán could also be considered under his use of the term, since his focus was pointedly literary or even documentary *mestizaje*.[11] He further emphasized that his use of "*mestizaje*" could also be expressed by the term "interculturation," which, he admitted, was less than elegant (1971 [1954], 2:291). Garibay focused his interest in these mestizo historians on the texts, which they

wrote and also from which they drew source material and historiographical models. For him, Alva Ixtlilxochitl is highly esteemed because of his
ability to both interpret native documents and draft a history in the European style (293).

Though it is undoubtedly true, as Jongsoo Lee (2014) has pointed
out, that Garibay's use of the term "mestizo" is, in part, indicative of his
intellectual affinity with the mid-twentieth-century nationalist impulse
to incorporate indigenous culture into a burgeoning sense of the Mexican nation as a mestizo nation, we should be wary to dismiss Garibay's
development of this term as simply a symptom of his era. "Mestizo" has
remained a key term in descriptions and studies of Alva Ixtlilxochitl and
other bicultural authors throughout the decades following *Historia de la
literatura náhuatl*, and Garibay's analysis of "mestizo historians" allows us
an early glimpse at the promise and challenge of the concept. "Mestizo" has
been used at times to highlight, as Garibay did, the "intercultural" nature
of writings that drew from native and European sources and historiographical models (Lienhard 1991; Velazco 2003; Voigt 2006). Other scholars
have used the term to emphasize his mixed ancestry and in this way locate
Alva Ixtlilxochitl in the social context from which he wrote (Florescano
1994 [1987]; Pagden 1987). In both cases, the use of the term "mestizo"
potentially connotes an author and text that simultaneously borrow from
and belong to the European and Indian social and cultural contexts.

Rolena Adorno has eloquently addressed this bicultural position of
Alva Ixtlilxochitl, noting that "Alva Ixtlilxochitl occupied a subject position that is not that of the pure indigenous pre-Hispanic past, but rather
that of a colonial subject whose conscious attempts to accommodate
himself to new doctrinal and literary historiographic norms bespeak an
ethnic ambition and an effort to remake cultural identity" (2007, 145).[12]
She urges scholars to acknowledge that Alva Ixtlilxochitl's efforts to engage with both Spanish and native values should not invite us to "deny
the legitimacy of the position of the colonial subject" (146). Then she
poignantly notes that "this complex and compromised subject position
does not fit the neat model of binary opposition; the acknowledgement
of a third or intermediate position is closer to historical reality than is any
abstract, binary model that in itself is a feature of the reductive outlook
imposed by the colonizing culture" (146). Locating and understanding

this intermediate position, as she calls it, is a challenge faced by many scholars who have engaged with Alva Ixtlilxochitl's works, most of whom have opted to communicate this in-betweenness by describing Alva Ix-tlilxochitl as mestizo.

"Mestizo" is the most common reference that scholars have utilized when referring to him and to his works. Martin Lienhard and Salvador Velazco have emphasized the ways in which Alva Ixtlilxochitl embodies a specifically mestizo tradition, by combining native narratives and European literary and historical discourses. Lienhard's study draws attention to the heterogeneous nature of the text (rather than the author). Indian-Hispanic writing, he argues, reflects a potentially new perspective on the world that is articulated through European and indigenous voices and traditions (1991, 52). In this sense, mestizo writing is a framework that can apply equally to Indian writers (such as the Andean author Felipe Guaman Poma de Ayala) and biologically mestizo writers (such as Alva Ixtlilxochitl).[13] Velazco also focuses on the text, rather than the individual. However, he prefers a slightly different approach to that of Lienhard and he suggests that instead of a "mestizo" chronicle, we should speak of trans-cultural discourse (2003, 22).

Unlike Lienhard and Velazco, Enrique Florescano (1994 [1987]) underlines the importance of Alva Ixtlilxochitl's mixed ancestry, which for him signals an impurity in his social identity and associated general untrustworthiness. He goes so far as to say that Alva Ixtlilxochitl and two other mestizo chroniclers, Juan Bautista Pomar and Diego Muñoz Camargo, falsely represented themselves as Indians.[14] Though to different ends, Anthony Pagden (1994) also focused on the social context as the most salient aspect of Alva Ixtlilxochitl's mixed identity. Pagden said of Alva Ixtlilxochitl, Diego Muñoz Camargo, and Garcilaso de la Vega, "El Inca," that "for all of them the true American society was to be a mestizo one, a hybrid culture mixing Spanish laws and the Christian religion with Indian customs" (1987, 70). Unlike El Inca, however, Alva Ixtlilxochitl does not describe himself as "mestizo."[15] In fact, self-identification is rarely a focus in his work. Whether that mixed identity is construed as a positive harbinger of mixing that would come to define New World society, following Pagden, or a negative trend toward biological and cultural mixing, associated with treachery and deceit, following Florescano, the emphasis on mixed ethnic identity per se offers a limited model for understanding Alva Ixtlilxochitl's work as a historian since it tends to foreclose important questions related to the historiographical process.

Ethnographic work on history and *mestizaje* provides alternative models for how to rethink the complex category of "mestizo" beyond a strictly biologically based identity category. In her efforts to "rescue mestizos from *mestizaje*—and thus challenge the conceptual politics (and political activism) that all too simplistically, following a transitional teleology, purify mestizos *away* from indigeneity," Marisol de la Cadena has suggested that we consider that "mestizo and *mestizaje* house several hybridities" (2005, 262–63). Her discussion of multiple hybridities attempts to destabilize the empirical version we are used to, which is, as she says, "the scientific observation of 'mixture' in mestizo's bodies, cultures, races and so forth" (263). De la Cadena turns her attention to the "hybridity inscribed in the discursive formation of *mestizaje*" (263). In a way, de la Cadena's work takes us full circle, back to the early influences of Garibay, where the emphasis was also on the text as the locus of cultural mixing.

Joanne Rappaport's recent study of the "disappearing mestizo" also approaches the topic through close and sustained analysis of the particular context in which the term was utilized, and she concludes that the term "mestizo" cannot embody a singular referent (2014). Rappaport cautions against constructing "mestizo" as a facile socioracial category; instead, she emphasizes that "there is no single mestizo narrative in the early colonial period, nor did mestizos automatically merge into a single social group because they were of mixed descent" (93). Astutely, she notes that "mestizos had no specific obligations to a collectivity, as was the case with Indians and Spaniards" (11). In her exploration of the range and usage of this slippery term, Rappaport offers a series of carefully developed case studies that demonstrate the ways in which colonial individuals adopted, rejected, and fell into or out of the category of "mestizo." That her focus is New Granada, today's Colombia, does not detract from the relevance of her insights for other regions of colonial Spanish America, including New Spain.

In a chapter that focuses on mestizo caciques, Rappaport describes how the case studies she has looked at demonstrate that her subjects "consistently imagined themselves to be superior candidates for chiefly status precisely because they were mestizos" (134). Each of the sixteenth-century northern

Andean figures Rappaport studies projected his status and lineage "as a very privileged kind of mestizo, one who could best serve his native community because he was lettered and cosmopolitan, at once versed in the intricacies of the colonial legal system, fluent in both Spanish and Muisca, a legitimate successor to the caciques who came before him, and a pious Catholic" (134). But for the language and the fact that he did not achieve the position of cacique himself, we can find parallels in Alva Ixtlilxochitl for each of these descriptors offered by Rappaport: Alva was lettered, cosmopolitan, adept at the colonial legal system, fluent in Spanish and Nahuatl, a legitimate successor to the caciques of Teotihuacan who came before him, and a thoroughly pious Catholic. Rappaport emphasizes that for the individuals she studies, their bilingualism and biculturalism were viewed as assets rather than markers of illegitimacy. Though Alva Ixtlilxochitl did not himself assume the label "mestizo," he certainly represented his dual cultural inheritance as an asset that allowed him to effectively translate native knowledge and history for a seventeenth-century Hispano-Catholic audience. He is mestizo in the sense of his doubleness—the double cultural nature of his work (in Salomon's sense) and the double-mistaken identity it has provoked (in Lockhart's sense).

I thus follow the line of thinking—found from Garibay to Lienhard, Velazco, de la Cadena, and Rappaport—that locates *mestizaje* in the text and the context rather than the bloodline, just as I recognize Adorno's foundational analysis, which situates Alva Ixtlilxochitl firmly in a colonial context rather than attempting to align him with a specifically and singularly Indian or Spanish identity.[16] As a Christian and Spanish-speaking mestizo historian who was active in colonial government and family legal matters in seventeenth-century Mexico, Alva Ixtlilxochitl strongly identified with his Indian ancestors and community. Yet, we should add the cautionary words from Brubaker and Cooper about the pitfalls inherent in the study of identity, where they emphasize that discussions of identity should be rooted in particular circumstances and experiences. In this sense, Alva Ixtlilxochitl is a mestizo historian within the particular social context and textual corpus that influenced his reconstruction of the pre-Hispanic and conquest-era history of central Mexico. Alva Ixtlilxochitl, as he himself emphasizes throughout his writings, resided in a time of disappearing native cultural traditions, and his stated project was to salvage the remains of those pre-Hispanic stories and songs for posterity. Yet, to make that history relevant for the Hispano-Catholic context in which he lived and worked, Alva Ixtlilxochitl drew from European textual and discursive traditions.

Humanism provided Alva Ixtlilxochitl with the conceptual framework in which to incorporate pre-Hispanic native knowledge into that Hispano-Catholic context. In a prefatory piece to his *Historia de la nación chichimeca*, he places himself squarely at the crossroads of European historiography and native history:

> Since adolescence I have always had a great desire to know
> about the historical events in this new world, which were no
> less important than those of the Romans, Greeks, Medes, and
> other great pagan republics that were universally known.

> [Desde mi adolescencia tuve siempre gran deseo de saber las cosas
> acaecidas en este nuevo mundo, que no fueron menos que las de los
> romanos, griegos, medos y otras repúblicas gentílicas que tuvieron
> fama en el universo.] (1975–1977, 1:526; CC, volume 1, folio 1r.)[17]

This explicit reference to European antiquity has led many to connect Alva Ixtlilxochitl to the humanist educational project developed at the Colegio de Santa Cruz de Santiago Tlatelolco. In *Historia de la literatura náhuatl* (1954), Ángel María Garibay asserted numerous times that Alva Ixtlilxochitl was a student at the Franciscan school in Santiago Tlatelolco. After citing this same passage from the dedication to the *Historia de la nación chichimeca*, Garibay states that "Alva Ixtlilxochitl's affection for history stems from the humanistic studies of his adolescence. The years he spent at Tlatelolco served to familiarize him with the changing fates of empires" [La afición a los estudios históricos tiene su raigambre en los estudios humanísticos de su adolescencia. Los años de su estancia en Tlatelolco sirvieron a Ixtlilxóchitl para conocer las mudanzas de los imperios] (2:310).

It is unlikely that Alva Ixtlilxochitl was ever a formal student pursuing advanced studies at Tlatelolco.[18] By the time of his birth in the last quarter of the sixteenth century, the school was no longer a center of higher learning. Founded in 1536, it was originally intended as a seminary for native elite to train for service in the clergy. This plan was dismissed after a few years, but the Colegio continued to develop as a center of higher learning and as a research institute where the friars and native scholars studied religion, classical European texts, and pre-Hispanic culture. Though Alva Ixtlilxochitl was not part of the earlier generation of native intellectuals affiliated with Tlatelolco, such as Pablo de Nazareo and Antonio de Valeriano, there are traces of humanistic education in his writings that reflect his acquaintance with books that may have formed part of the Franciscan library and also, perhaps, with older scholars who were connected to the Colegio.

Numerous scholars have suggested that Alva Ixtlilxochitl collaborated with the Franciscan friar Juan de Torquemada (ca. 1562–1624), who was the guardian of the priory at Tlatelolco from 1603 to 1612 (Brading 1991, 277; Townsend 2014, 6–9). Others, however, have urged caution in imagining a working relationship between Alva Ixtlilxochitl and Torquemada since neither makes specific reference to such an arrangement (O'Gorman 1975–1977, 1:84). It is clear, however, that Alva Ixtlilxochitl was familiar with Torquemada's magnum opus, *Monarquía indiana* (1615), which is cited three times in the *Historia de la nación chichimeca* (Alva Ixtlilxochitl 1975–1977, 2:137; 184; 235). Further, as O'Gorman notes, Alva Ixtlilxochitl mentions Torquemada among a list of sources he has consulted, and he refers admiringly to Torquemada as "the most diligent and first discoverer of the meaning of the pictorials and songs" [el diligentísimo y primer descubridor de la declaración de las pinturas y cantos] (2:137). A sprawling work, spread out over three tomes, the *Monarquía indiana* drew from well over one hundred sources, including Spanish chroniclers, such as López de Gómara and Antonio de Herrera; native or mestizo historians, such as Diego Muñoz Camargo and Juan Bautista Pomar; and dozens of ancient writers, among them Virgil, Plutarch, and (as we shall see) the most relevant to this analysis, Xenophon.[19] This dispersed and diverse set of authorities and sources has prompted Brading to remark that Torquemada's substantial history "lacked intellectual coherence" because of the "variegated, often conflicting group of sources" (1991, 278). What is certain is that Torquemada had at his fingertips reference to a rich selection of printed and manuscript sources, and it is possible to imagine that beyond reading the *Monarquía indiana* itself, Alva Ixtlilxochitl may have had access to portions of the Franciscan's library. Through some method, the mestizo historian gained a reading knowledge far beyond what he would have been exposed to in San Juan Teotihuacan, his neighborhood of Santa Catalina in Mexico City, or the various postings he had as an official in Tetzcoco, Chalco, and Tlalmanalco.

Alva Ixtlilxochitl certainly lived and worked in the long shadow of the Franciscan school at Tlatelolco and its humanist project, even if his education was most likely self-guided. In this sense he reminds us of the great Andean mestizo humanist Inca Garcilaso, who was also an autodidact. Observing the impact of Renaissance humanism on Alva Ixtlilxochitl, we are left with a key question: How do we qualify the impact of classical texts on native or mestizo histories? In *The Darker Side of the Renaissance* (1995), Walter Mignolo traces how "the rebirth of the classical tradition [served] as a justification of colonial expansion," specifically in the Spanish New World territories (1995, vii). The centerpiece of his argument is that beyond their military and religious endeavors, the Spaniards undertook a cultural and intellectual colonization of the Indians by imposing their own forms of literacy on the new subjects. For scholars such as Mignolo, once a figure like Alva Ixtlilxochitl became conversant in European traditions and knowledge, he ceased in some important ways to be Indian. However, the line between European knowledge and Indian knowledge was not always so impermeable. Though European intellectual currents circumscribed the educational process, other scholars have convincingly argued that the humanistic tradition allowed for more nuanced ways of addressing native forms of knowledge within the bounds of the colonial infrastructure.

In her study *On the Wings of Time: Rome, the Incas, Spain, and Peru* (2007), Sabine MacCormack looks at the influence of texts from European antiquity on colonial Peru. MacCormack emphasizes the broad impact of the classical heritage on New World history written by Spaniards as well as native authors. For MacCormack, "the legacy of Greece and Rome was part and parcel of the cultural identity of the Spanish and creole elite." But, she goes on, "classical texts, images, myths, and histories reached Andean people" as well, and Andeans created their own interpretations of these traditions. Thus, according to MacCormack, "paradoxically, classical traditions and ideas arising from them at times became instruments of Andean autonomy" (21). Alva Ixtlilxochitl's mestizo project is indebted to traditions founded in European antiquity just as it is rooted in the knowledge held by the native community. Nowhere is this more clear than in Alva Ixtlilxochitl's construction of the figure of Nezahualcoyotl, whom he represents as a pre-Hispanic leader in the model of a Renaissance ideal prince.

Nezahualcoyotl and Mestizo Historiography

As Alva Ixtlilxochitl makes clear in the dedication to the *Historia de la nación chichimeca*, he wished to insert the deeds of his pre-Hispanic ancestors among the feats of the ancient Romans and Greeks, and Medes and Persians. Alva Ixtlilxochitl's principal object of study in this regard was the fifteenth-century *tlatoani* (ruler) from Tetzcoco, Nezahualcoyotl (ca. 1400–1472). Alva Ixtlilxochitl depicts Nezahualcoyotl as a great and stalwart leader whose qualities were deserving of emulation. Renaissance scholars redefined their own cultures by studying ancient Greece, Rome, and the Near East; Alva Ixtlilxochitl was conscious of the significance of the ancients, yet he turned to the deeds of his Indian ancestors for models of New World societies in a way similar to that of Europeans turning to the ancient Mediterranean civilizations.

Alva Ixtlilxochitl explicitly mentions the ancient Greek historian Xenophon (430 BCE–354 BCE). The work of Xenophon was resurrected during the Renaissance and his biography of King Cyrus of Persia (r. 559 BCE–530 BCE), *Cyropaedia* (*The Education of Cyrus*) was influential in the emergence of the *speculum principis* (mirror of princes) tradition.[20] Through his portrait of Cyrus, Xenophon models how to create and maintain an empire (Tatum 1989). Alva Ixtlilxochitl drew from Xenophon's biography of Cyrus in his representation of Nezahualcoyotl as an illustrious pre-Hispanic leader.

Alva Ixtlilxochitl begins the eleventh of his thirteen relations in the *Compendio histórico del reino de Texcoco* by highlighting Nezahualcoyotl as an exemplary model of leadership. He is represented as an ideal prince in the same fashion as Xenophon's Cyrus:

> As they say about Xenophon, which is something everyone says
> of him, in the biography he wrote about Cyrus, the King of the

Persians, his intent was not so much to write a biography of a specific man as to paint the portrait of a good king with all the aspects that he should have; and so, whoever should want to paint such a portrait and make such a description of a good monarch, albeit a barbarous one, among all those that existed in this new world, would need only look at the life of Nezahualcoyotzin.

[Lo que se cuenta de Xenofonte, que todos dicen de él, que en la vida que escribió de Ciro, rey de los persas, no fue tanto su intento escribir vida de un hombre en particular, cuanto pintar un buen rey en las partes que conviene que tenga, y así parece que quien quisiera pintar y hacer relación de un buen monarca, aunque bárbaro, de cuantos hubo en este nuevo mundo, no tenía que hacer más de poner delante la vida de Nezahualcoyotzin.] (1975–1977, 1:439)

Nezahualcoyotl provided Alva Ixtlilxochitl with material similar to what Cyrus offered Xenophon as a means for discussing the nature of an excellent and effective leader. Xenophon's biography of Cyrus, as Alva Ixtlilxochitl notes, was not meant to be understood in literal terms, but rather as an allegorical representation of the necessary qualities of a prince. Both Xenophon's Cyrus and Alva Ixtlilxochitl's Nezahualcoyotl were meant to embody the estimable qualities and deeds of an ideal prince in the pre-Christian Old World and the New.

It should also be noted that this passage offers a trace of the humanist education that we see in Alva Ixtlilxochitl's work. He points to a context in which he learns of Xenophon's history: "everyone says of him." Of course we cannot know what Alva Ixtlilxochitl had in mind by "everyone," but it is apparent that either through reading or conversation (or both), he had engaged in an ongoing dialogue about ancient historiography and what it had to offer a seventeenth-century historian. There is a breadth to the influences on Alva Ixtlilxochitl's work that forces us to recall that he was always responding to discourses tied both to the local, native community with which he identified and discursive threads that dominated early modern European historiography.

For example, despite his wide reading, it is doubtful that Alva Ixtlilxochitl would have had access to Niccolò Machiavelli's seminal discussion of early modern political leadership. It is likely, however, that he would have been familiar with the contours of Machiavelli's arguments through the polemics surrounding his essay, especially through the Spanish counter-Machiavellian authors. In 1513, Machiavelli composed *The Prince* as a gift for a Medici prince in hope of gaining an office as a reward.[21] *The Prince*, however, was placed on the *Index librorum prohibitorum* (Index of prohibited books) in 1559 by Pope Paul IV, a sanction that essentially put an end to the publication and circulation of the text. The book continued, however, to be a touchstone for political thinkers, many of whom constructed their arguments in reference to and more specifically against Machiavelli's 1513 treatise. While Machiavelli's infamous political treatise was not published in Spanish translation until the nineteenth century, there is clear evidence of its currency in debates around government affairs from the sixteenth century onward. Antonio Maravall, for example, has noted that after 1559, the year of the Vatican censure, anti-Machiavellian treatises became much more the norm than the exception (1984). A central tenet of texts by Spanish anti-Machiavellian writers, such as Pedro de Rivadeneira and Diego de Saavedra Fajardo, was to convert religion into a means of governance—an *instrumentum regni* (Maravall 1984, 66). Rivadeneira's *Tratado del príncipe cristiano* (Treatise on the Christian prince) (1595) was addressed to the future Philip III of Spain and aimed to offer him a guidebook for effective Christian political virtues. Rivadeneira's text provides a *speculum principis* by offering the young ruler-to-be a series of historical examples of virtuous regal behavior that he should try to emulate. Rivadeneira blamed the growing ills in Europe on those—such as Machiavelli and Jean Bodin—who found that the successful government of state was not possible without departing from God's law. Rivadeneira affirms that effective government can only be wrought in conjunction with Christianity. The argument that Christian ethics are central to effective government is echoed in the seventeenth-century treatise by Diego Saavedra Fajardo, *Idea de un príncipe político-cristiano representada en cien empresas* (Idea of a Christian political prince represented in one hundred emblems) (1640). Saavedra Fajardo relied on the emblematic tradition to communicate advice for good governance to princes and kings.[22] Thus, Spanish authors of political treatises constructed their advice to the Crown in the tradition of the mirror of princes and thereby maintained a presence for this genre via their anti-Machiavellian polemics.

Significantly, Rivadeneira and Saavedra Fajardo both cite Xenophon and his illustrative stories of Cyrus. Among extensive and lengthy quotations from Aristotle, Plutarch, and Tacitus, Saavedra Fajardo incorporates lessons from *Cyropaedia* on how to best raise and instruct a prince (1927–1930 [1640]). Describing Xenophon as a "very serious philosopher and historian," Rivadeneira enthusiastically puts forth the ancient author's biography of Cyrus as a model of how to make a prince: "Xenophon wrote eight books about the *Education of King Cyrus*, whom he paints and puts forth as an example and model of all the great kings and prudent governors, in peace and war" [(Jenofonte) escribió ocho libros de la *Institucion del rey Ciro*, á quien pinta y pone por dechado y modelo de todos los grandes reyes y prudentes gobernadores, en paz y en guerra] (1868, 460). Rivadeneira highlights the way in which Xenophon's Cyrus was defined by his religious faith, which although false was earnest and devout: "Thus it appears that the beginning, middle, and end of all the endeavors of this great king was the religion, albeit false, dedicated to his imaginary gods" [De manera que parece que el principio, medio y fin de todas las empresas de este gran rey era la religion, aunque falsa, de sus vanos dioses] (461). The Cyrus captured by Rivadeneira is a model for how Alva Ixtlilxochitl incorporated this ancient king into his own rendering of pre-Hispanic Mexico.

In much the same vein, Alva Ixtlilxochitl portrays an ideal New World ruler in the figure of Nezahualcoyotl. In the *Relación sucinta en forma de memorial*, Alva Ixtlilxochitl explains the three names that were associated with Nezahualcoyotl in writings and in songs: "Nezahualcoyotl Acolmiztli Yoyontzin had these three names, each one signifying his great valor" [Nezahualcoyotl Acolmiztli Yoyontzin tuvo estos tres nombres, cada uno a significación de su gran valor] (1975–1977, 1:404). Alva Ixtlilxochitl also describes Nezahualcoyotl not only as valorous but wise—more wise than Plato, in fact. The ancient Tetzcoca leader, unlike the ancient Greek philosopher, intuited the presence of a single god, which he knew as *in tloque in nahuaque*:

[Nezahualcoyotl] was a wise man, and from his great knowledge he declared these words that follow, which even the divine Plato and other great philosophers did not declare, which was to say: *Ypan yn Chahcohnauhtla manpan meztica intloque nahuaque ypal nenohuani teyocoyani ic el teotl oquiyocox ynixquex quexquix mita ynamota,* which when interpreted well means "after the nine levels there is the creator of the heaven and the earth, through whom live all creatures, and a single god who created all things visible and invisible."[23]

[[Nezahualcoyotl] fue hombre sabio, y por su mucho saber declaró estas palabras que se siguen que el divino Platón y otros grandes filósofos no declararon más, que fue decir: *Ypan yn Chahcohnauhtla manpan meztica intloque nahuaque ypal nenohuani teyocoyani ic el téotl oquiyócox yníxquex quéxquix mita ynamota,* que bien interpretado quiere decir: "después de nueve andanas está el criador del cielo y de la tierra, por quien viven las criaturas, y un solo dios que crió las cosas visibles e invisibles."] (Alva Ixtlilxochitl 1975–1977, 2:404)

Alva Ixtlilxochitl's emphasis on the monotheism of Nezahualcoyotl, to the exclusion of other Tetzcoca and Nahua leaders or peoples, is distinctive and characteristic of his writings. His interpretation of the singularity of the Nahuatl *in tloque in nahuaque,* which in the precontact period would have referred to multiple deities, underlines how Alva Ixtlilxochtil sought to maintain favor in the colonial community of Spaniards by demonstrating his and his family's devotion to Christianity, which he implied had existed even before the arrival of the first friars.

The Franciscan friar Alonso de Molina, in his authoritative sixteenth-century Nahuatl-Spanish dictionary, defines the omnipresent *in tloque in nahuaque* in a similar fashion as Alva Ixtlilxochitl: "Tloque Nahuaque. Encompasses he who is the being of all things, maintaining them, and sustaining them" [Tloque nauaque. Cabe quien esta el ser de todas las cosas, conservandolas y sustentandola] (1992 [1571], 148r).[24] Miguel León-Portilla and his mentor Ángel María Garibay both published numerous studies of this Nahua religious concept. In his study of Nahua belief systems, for example (translated by Jack Emory Davis), León-Portilla endorsed Molina's interpretation of this term as an omnipresent god: "The deity's ubiquitous presence is not a static quality, but an active principle which gives foundation to the universe" (1963, 93).[25] A distinctive feature of Alva Ixtlilxochitl's use of the term *in tloque in nahuaque*, however, is that he limits its application to his Tetzcoca ancestors and even more specifically to Nezahualcoyotl.

Alva Ixtlilxochitl presumably drew from the same native texts and songs consulted by Garibay and León-Portilla. As mentioned earlier, he had copied out by hand both Pomar's *Relación de Tetzcoco* and the Nahuatl *Romances de los señores de la Nueva España*. However, Alva Ixtlilxochitl's narrative about a latent pre-Columbian monotheism varies significantly. Pomar, for example, writes that some of the elites from the city began to have misgivings about the practice of sacrifice to the idols and gods and, he notes, among the Tetzcoca, Nezahualcoyotl was the one who was most doubting and searching for "the true God and Creator of all things" [verdadero Dios y Creador de todas las cosas] (1986, 69). Yet, Pomar does not focus on Nezahualcoyotl as the sole monotheist. Rather, always using the third-person plural, he describes the monotheistic impulse of the Tetzcoco community as a whole:

> And never—although they did have many idols that represented different gods—never when communications were directed to them did they name all of them in general or individually, but rather **they said** in their language *IN TLOQUE IN NAHUAQUE*, which means "the lord of the heavens and the earth": a very clear signal that they certainly did not have more than one (emphasis mine).

> [Y jamás, aunq[ue] tenían muchos ídolos q[ue] representaban [a] diferentes dioses, nunca, cuando se ofrecía tratarlos, nombraban a todos en general, ni en particular a cada uno, sino decían en su lengua IN TLOQ[UE] IN [N]AHUAQUE, q[ue] quiere decir "el s[eñ]or del [ci]elo y de la tierra": señal evidentísima de que tuvieron por cierto no haber más de uno.] (70).

Pomar goes on to confirm that in Tetzcoco "not only the most prudent and discreet, but even the common people spoke in this way" [no sólo los más prudentes y discretos, pero aun la genta común lo decía así]. This practice was documented, he clarifies, in the songs that were generated by the nobles, which reflected their past "in the form of chronicle and history" [en forma de crónica e historia] (70).

Alva Ixtlilxochitl, however, writes in the *Historia de la nación chichimeca* that Nezahualcoyotl was unique in his belief in one god: "He held as false those gods that the people of this land worshipped, saying that they were nothing more than statues of demons, enemies of the human race" [Tuvo por falsos a los dioses que adoraban los de esta tierra, diciendo que no eran sino estatuas de demonios enemigos del género humano] (1975–1977, 2:136). Alva Ixtlilxochitl says that Nezahualcoyotl named this god "in tloque, yn nahuaque," which, as he explains in the opening of the *Historia*, means "the universal god of all things, creator of them and according to whose will live all creatures, father of heaven and of the earth, etc." [el dios universal de todas las cosas, creador de ellas y a cuya voluntad viven todas las criaturas, señor del cielo y de la tierra, etcétera] (2:7). Conforming closely to the language in the Pomar passage cited above, Alva Ixtlilxochitl makes a single yet revealing change to emphasize that Nezahualcoyotl, and not the community in Tetzcoco as a whole, embraced monotheism fully fifty years before the arrival of the Spaniards:

> Never ever (although there were many idols that represented
> different gods) when communications were directed to the deity,
> neither did he name them in general or in particular, but rather
> **he said** *Intloque yn Nahuaque, y palnemo alani*, which means
> that which has been previously explained (emphasis mine).

> Nunca jamás (aunque había muchos ídolos que representaban
> diferentes dioses) cuando se ofrecía tratar de deidad, los nombraba
> ni en general ni en particular, sino que decía Intloque yn Nahuaque,
> y palnemo alani, que significa lo que está atrás declarado (2:137).

Alva Ixtlilxochitl then explains that Nezahualcoyotl attempted to dissuade the Mexica from the practice of human sacrifice, though he was not completely successful:

> Although he was unable to end human sacrifice in accordance
> with the rites of the Mexica, he still managed to convince

them to sacrifice only prisoners of war, slaves, and captives, and not their children as had been their custom.

[No pudo de todo punto quitar el sacrificio de los hombres conforme a los ritos mexicanos todavía alcanzó con ellos que tan solamente sacrificasen a los habidos en guerra, esclavos y cautivos, y no a sus hijos y naturales como solían tener de costumbre.] (2:137).

This pre-Columbian believer in a single and most powerful god further admonished his own children and heirs to not worship the idol gods of the Mexica, as they were the devil in disguise (2:137). In this passage, and throughout his writings, Alva Ixtlilxochitl emphasizes the exceptionality of Nezahualcoyotl, who is consistently described as "the most powerful, brave, wise, and fortunate prince and captain that there ever was in this New World" [el más poderoso, valeroso, sabio, venturoso príncipe y capitán que ha habido en este nuevo mundo] (2:136). Alva Ixtlilxochitl suggests that just as Xenophon's Cyrus was emblematic of Old World pre-Christian leadership, Nezahualcoyotl was emblematic of New World pre-Christian leadership. Drawing from the classical example and the Renaissance reinterpretation of it, Alva Ixtlilxochitl represents his ancestor as a model leader within the humanist-inflected Hispano-Catholic political discourse of the seventeenth century.

The textual image of Nezahualcoyotl as a pre-Hispanic model of the ideal prince has its visual equivalent in the full-length portrait of him that is part of the *Codex Ixtlilxochitl* (Figure 7), which among its three parts contains a section with illustrations of four Tetzcoca lords, the god Tlaloc, and a pyramid. In a still-influential analysis, John Eric S. Thompson (1941) argued that this portion of the text first belonged to Pomar's *Relación de Tetzcoco*. Excised from their original context, the illustrations eventually became incorporated into the bound volume with two other unrelated components, all of which passed through the hands of Alva Ixtlilxochitl, Sigüenza, and later historians.[26] This portrait of Nezahualcoyotl and another in the same group of Nezahualpilli influenced later depictions of native rulers, particularly the stunning painting of Motecuzoma by Antonio Rodríguez now housed in the Museo degli Argenti in Florence (Escalante Gonzalbo 2004, 171–77). The impact of the

Figure 7. Nezahualcoyotl, *Codex Ixtlilxochitl* [*Códice Ixtlilxochitl*], folio 106. Courtesy of the Bibliothèque Nationale de France, Paris.

figurative—rather than stylized—visual interpretations of these leaders is analogous to the textual rendering of Nezahualcoyotl in Alva Ixtlilxochitl's historical writings, where he is described in terms and traditions that are accessible to a nonnative audience.

Alva Ixtlilxochitl's project on ancient Mexico mimics the emphasis on exegesis and interpretation of ancient languages that was a hallmark of Renaissance humanism. Within such a historical endeavor he adapts that linguistic model to a colonial context and uses it as a means to question and supplant the dominant European narratives. In that way Alva Ixtlilxochitl appropriated the norms of humanist historiography into his writings in order to make his narratives of ancient Mexico comprehensible to European readers, but he also created a counternarrative to contest other versions of New World history, some of which were themselves informed by Renaissance discourses, including humanism.

Catholic humanism offered a platform for dissent in Spain in figures like Alfonso de Valdés (1490–1532), Juan de Valdés (1509–1541), and Miguel de Cervantes (1547–1616), but humanism's incorporation into the colonial project is more ambiguous. Pagden has shown how humanism formed part of the early conceptions of empire in the court of the Spanish king Charles V (Pagden 1995). Significantly, it was a humanist scholar, Juan Ginés de Sepúlveda (1494–1573), who argued in favor of the enslavement of Indians, in a debate against the reformist Dominican cleric Bartolomé de las Casas (1484–1566). At the same time, however, peripheral intellectuals such as Alva Ixtlilxochitl used humanism against the grain of the empire to create a discourse of critique. While humanism has long been viewed as signaling progress in the rebirth of classical knowledge and the beginning of European modernity, a counternarrative articulated by Mignolo projects humanism as a mechanism for the European will to power and global domination. The double-discourse of mestizo figures like Alva Ixtlilxochitl suggests, in line with scholars like MacCormack, that humanism became a tool of resistance in the hands of some native communities. Alva Ixtlilxochitl, we could say, fashioned himself as a native humanist, familiar with the genres and discourses of Renaissance humanism. A figure like Fernando de Alva Ixtlilxochitl suggests that the line between European knowledge and Indian knowledge was not always simple to draw or impermeable to subtle negotiations. Alva

Ixtlilxochitl put into dialogue the historical narrative forms from Europe and those from the Americas in an attempt to communicate the history of Anahuac and its people effectively. Using his knowledge of Nahuatl and Nahua generic traditions such as genealogies and pictorials, he questioned the legitimacy of the court-sponsored histories against which he wrote.

Conclusion

In her foreword to Gabriela Ramos and Yanna Yannakakis's *Indigenous Intellectuals: Knowledge, Power, and Colonial Culture in Mexico and the Andes* (2014), Elizabeth Hill Boone remarks instructively that colonial indigenous intellectuals should be distinguished from the pre-Hispanic *tlamatinime*, which is often taken to mean "wise people":

> They were taught to speak Latin and Spanish, to write these
> languages as well as indigenous ones alphabetically, and to read
> the newly introduced European art of pictorial illusionism. They
> learned the literature of the European classical authors, to the
> extent that some became great rhetoricians, considered by the friars
> to be as accomplished as the great classical rhetoricians Cicero
> and Quintilian. Moreover, they were forged in a pragmatism
> necessitated by the conquest, the demographic collapse, and
> the domination by European systems and expectations. (xi)

Don Fernando de Alva Ixtlilxochitl's historical writings are indebted to the legacy of these early colonial Mexican *tlamatinime* at the Colegio de Santa Cruz de Tlatelolco, who pursued studies of ancient Europe while at the same time documenting their own cultural traditions. Alva Ixtlilxochitl likewise drew from native sources and European historiographical models and traditions in order to craft his history of pre-Hispanic and conquest-era New Spain.

If we are to return to the question borrowed from Bloch and posed at the beginning of this chapter—how can Alva Ixtlilxochitl have known what he said?—we can recognize his access to and use of native oral, pictorial, and alphabetic sources. These materials were central not only to the context of his historical writings, but also to the authority he established for himself as a historian during his lifetime and to this day. We must also recognize, however, that Alva Ixtlilxochitl was a colonial subject whose intellectual formation and discursive production were influenced heavily by the Hispano-Catholic context in which he was raised and in which he wrote. In this sense, Alva Ixtlilxochitl's historiographical methods were founded on his access to native knowledge as well as his social, intellectual, and political formation in seventeenth-century New Spain. He was a *tlamatini*, "one who knows something," in the time period in which he lived and wrote, and what he knew was drawn from multiple sources and cultural contexts.

CHAPTER 4

Circulating Native Knowledge

SEVENTEENTH-CENTURY CREOLE HISTORIOGRAPHY

From all the many communications I have had with the Indians in order to learn of their things, I can speak with great certainty about their idolatry, superstitions, and vain practices, all of which they hold today; I would be delighted if I were asked to write about how to remedy this.

[DE LO MUCHO que he comunicado a los indios para saber sus cosas puedo decir el que me hallo con cierta ciencia de las idolatrías, supersticiones y vanas observaciones en que hoy entienden, y de que me alegrara me mandasen escribir para su remedio.]
                           —Carlos de Sigüenza y Góngora, *Parayso occidental*

DON CARLOS DE SIGÜENZA Y GÓNGORA sought earnestly to share his wealth of knowledge about the native people and their traditions, yet he was never commissioned to write a text dedicated to this topic about which he was so passionate. In the prologue to his *Parayso occidental* (1684), Sigüenza bemoans the fact that he was unable to bring to light books he had written on a range of topics connected to the native inhabitants of New Spain, and he informs his readers that these texts "will probably die with me" [probablemente morirán conmigo] (1995 [1684], c2). Though he was unable to publish these studies he longed to share, Sigüenza did manage to incorporate his knowledge of native culture in many of the texts that were printed in his lifetime. Sigüenza's interest in and concern for native traditions and practices was not an isolated phenomenon. Other creole scholars and religious figures of the seventeenth century also studied Indian communities, producing works that ranged from histories of pre-Hispanic central Mexico to treatises seeking to root out holdover native practices that imperiled the adoption of the Christian faith.

In 1699, Sigüenza came close to achieving some of the institutional authority he strove to wield when he was named a *corrector de libros*, or post-publication censor (AGN-I, volume 710, file 54; personal communication with Kenneth Ward, September 4, 2013).[1] In a memorandum written to the Santo Oficio (Inquisition authorities) on November 24, 1699, Sigüenza accepts with relish his new assignment, as he confirms that even his own library holds books that need to be expurgated. Some of these works, he says, could be found to be heretical, while others simply suffer from errors. Sigüenza makes it clear that if he possesses books worthy of censorship, then there must certainly be a great deal of such material on bookshelves all over New Spain. Concluding the short document, Sigüenza emphasizes that "I have desired greatly and do desire to serve this Inquisition and that I can achieve this in service as a censor to which I shall apply all of my attention and ravage" [lo mucho que e deseado y deseo servir a este santo oficio y que lo puedo lograr en el ministerio de su corrector de libros a que aplicare toda mi atencion y desuelo] (AGN-I, volume 710, file 54). For most of Sigüenza's varied career, however, he was removed from any position that would have allowed him the authority to intervene on matters directly related to governance. He was, nevertheless, an important and early figure to articulate a point of view that would later be more firmly tied to creole discourse, and his involvement with the native community was key to this process.

The seventeenth century has been looked upon as the period in which the creole sector emerged as a differentiated and distinct group; they articulated a unique relationship to the history and land of the Indies that served to distance them from the peninsular counterparts (Brading 1991; Mazzotti 2000; Bauer and Mazzotti 2009; Vitulli and Solodkow 2009; More 2013). The role of the incorporation of native traditions and history into this emergent creole discourse is key and has, most often, been viewed as a simple process of appropriation. This chapter deals with the role of native culture in the written works of Sigüenza. As the most emblematic example of seventeenth-century creole discourse in New Spain, I explore the early—creole—writings about the Virgin of Guadalupe. Though scholars who have studied the Guadalupe cult concur about the central role of these creole clerics in the construction and consolidation of the Guadalupe story, there are varying opinions about the relationship between the creole authors and the native community, specifically around the question of who influenced whom, and who responded to whom (Maza 1981; Lafaye 1987 [1974]; Brading 2001; Poole 1995, 2006; Burkhart 1993, 2001). Was this a cult manufactured by the creole community and then introduced to the natives? (As Poole and Burkhart argue.) Or, were the creole writers responding to incipient worship among the native community and then documenting and propagating those stories? (As Lafaye and Maza argue.) My interest is in looking at the emergence of the Guadalupe textual corpus as a moment in which the native archive—specifically Alva Ixtlilxochitl's native archive that Sigüenza had inherited—becomes the creole archive.

Sigüenza, Creole Historian

Carlos de Sigüenza y Góngora is considered to be the quintessential Mexican creole author and intellectual. Born in Mexico City to Spanish parents, he clearly identified with native people and considered their history his own, and in this sense he distanced himself from peninsular cultural models. The Indian is key to Sigüenza's works, particularly in his *Teatro de virtudes políticas* (1680), with its adulatory praise of Mexica leaders, and in his *Alboroto y motín* (1692), with its vitriolic anger at the Indians and *castas* for their perceived betrayals to the *patria*. These two texts are often put forth as examples of how Sigüenza, as a paradigmatic New World creole, adored the dead Indians but could not abide the living ones (Cogdell 1994; Moraña 2000).

One of the most influential discussions of creole consciousness and protonationalism in Mexico is found in Jacques Lafaye. Early in his analysis, Lafaye points to Sigüenza as the embodiment of a Mexican national consciousness: "Within this society," Lafaye states, "there gradually took form a Mexican national consciousness whose components, it seems, Sigüenza y Góngora first brought together in his writings" (1987 [1974], 60). For Lafaye, the unifying feature in all of Sigüenza's works is the exaltation of the Indian, yet the French critic hastens to clarify that the Indian who forms such a central part of Sigüenza's studies and writings is "a dead Indian" (65). This position is central to how Sigüenza is taken as both a key agent and a symbol of an emergent creole patriotism that legitimizes itself through the Indian past.

Exactly how to define and demarcate "creole patriotism" is an ongoing focus of scholarly activity. Usually it is associated with early nationalism, the baroque, and the appropriation of native history and traditions. Sigüenza has been evoked in each of these contexts from sometimes widely disparate perspectives. José Lezama Lima, for example, declared him to be the "señor barroco," a symbol for all the exuberant excesses, tensions, and contradictions that the Cuban poet and essayist saw as characteristic of the baroque. The baroque for Lezama was the "art of counter-conquest," in the sense that it created an American identity rather than destroying one in the way the Spanish invasion had (1993, 80). For Lezama, Sigüenza was emblematic of the intellectual and artistic tendencies inherent to the innovative aesthetics that Lezama called "American expression." The American baroque famously provided Lezama a moment of cultural synthesis for this proposition, in which the Amerindian, African, and European elements were brought together in the same discursive space.

From a very different frame of reference, Irving Leonard also viewed Sigüenza as an intellectual whose work and ideas ran counter to those that predominated in the seventeenth century. Against Lezama, however, Leonard offers a disparaging representation of the baroque, which for Leonard represented the repressive orthodoxy of the Counter-Reformation, during which "reason fell under the sway of rigid authority and conclusions reached through rational processes were predetermined" (1959, 24). In Leonard's analysis, Sigüenza was an exception whose "spirit clearly foreshadowed the end of the Age of the Baroque and the beginning of the Age of Reason in Hispanic America" (214).[2] If the contradictions inherent in these two analyses point to anything, it may be the diverse nature of the style, themes, and genres deployed throughout Sigüenza's oeuvre. Against that dispersion, scholars trying to understand

Sigüenza's works as a whole seem tempted to synthesize the great variety of the texts into a singular character, theme, or style marker.

Kathleen Ross's pioneering study of Sigüenza's historical texts, *The Baroque Narrative of Carlos de Sigüenza y Góngora* (1993), attempts such a synthetic analysis of his work, using some of the same terms employed by both Lezama and Leonard. For her, Sigüenza's writings—specifically *Parayso occidental*—are representative of what she terms a "criollo Baroque historiography." This is a style she describes as the confluence of sometimes contradictory discourses present in Sigüenza's works and it demonstrates "a fundamental shift of perspective [that] puts the center in America and makes the New World better than the Old, indicating the growing consciousness of a separate, less dependent colonial subjectivity" (45). Ross follows Lezama in seeing baroque literature as the medium for opposing an Old World expression to that of the New World, such that Sigüenza can rewrite the story of the conquest. For Ross, the role of the baroque in the Indies develops in conjunction with the creole perspective, which became increasingly dis-identified with Spanish cultural identity and eventually with Spanish political identity as well. Though she is careful to point out that creole baroque historiography is not motivated by the nationalist impulse associated with the independence activities of a later century, Ross argues that a combination of baroque style and creole social status allowed for the development of a new colonial subjectivity that can summarize the work of a figure like Sigüenza.

A key element in the way that Sigüenza's work has been studied is the problem of how to address the great diversity of his textual production. Sigüenza's texts subscribe to a variety of discursive genres, ranging from narratives (such as the chronicle, the history, and the *vida*) to scientific treatises, as well as epistolary, poetry and even cartography, each imbued with its own set of concerns. This generic dispersion is often cited as a reason why he is considered emblematic of the baroque, an aesthetic or intellectual period often associated with proliferation and excess. For instance, Ross has attempted to synthesize the diversity in Sigüenza's works by arguing that the criollo historiography of the *barroco de Indias* "is a way of retelling the past through a discourse of shifting power relationships, represented by a complicated, self-contradicting language" (1993, 47). The question of how Sigüenza can typify an emergent creole subjectivity rarely extends far beyond such formulations, which often fall into a kind of tautological reasoning: if the baroque is dispersion, display, contradiction, paradox, and variety, the eclectic forms pursued by Sigüenza become (when taken as a whole) emblems of the baroque. Comparatively less attention is paid to the complex relationships between form, content, and context that mark each of his texts in its own right. The fact that Sigüenza seems to say many things in diverse ways, or the way that he seems to say the same kinds of things in a variety of forms, seems sufficient evidence that his work is typical of a period, a social class, or the spirit of an age.

One exceptional element that seems to transcend the dead end of baroque forms in the search for a unifying theme in Sigüenza's work is his consistent interest in pre-Columbian history. Not surprisingly, this element has predominated in critical assessments of Sigüenza's role in the formation of what has been called a nascent creole discourse and protonationalism (Lafaye 1987 [1974]; Brading 1991; Ross 1993; More 2013). Lafaye articulates an enduring analysis related to creoles and the native population, where creole intellectual production is viewed as intimately connected to the demise of the Indian communities and the appropriation of their history: "The process of rooting colonial society in the American soil, landscape, and historico-mythical background accelerated from the moment the Indian ceased to appear as a vital threat to creole society" (1987 [1974], 67). For Ross, Sigüenza's identification with native people is similarly taken as a major component of his creole social identity, yet she reaches a slightly different conclusion from that presented by Lafaye. On this point she asserts that "if Sigüenza became an ethnographer and collector of books on indigenous culture, it was not so much due to feelings of nascent nationalism in the modern sense, as to a desire for justification of his own New World existence" (1993, 34).

The lines of analysis represented by Leonard, Lafaye, Brading, and Ross have been eloquently reiterated in Anna More's study of Sigüenza and the creole archive, where baroque patriotism prevails as the critical model. For More, the crisis of the Spanish monarchy in the second half of the seventeenth century led to a need for local and regional history to support governance, and the keepers of this local history were the creoles. Creole scholars, and specifically Sigüenza, built their own archives based on materials they had gathered from previous collectors like don

Fernando de Alva Ixtlilxochitl. More argues there is a specific rhetoric through which creoles authorized themselves, and this rhetoric turned on creating an image of the local history as a mystery to be interpreted by people with specific forms of knowledge. In this way, she responds to a common critical stance with a novel approach to the material: "What has often been interpreted as a paradoxical Creole appropriation of pre-Columbian indigenous artifacts and history even as they emphasized their own European roots, therefore, was in fact a bid to establish an authority based on knowledge available only to those who understood both traditions" (2013, 13). For More this process of creole interpretation and recontextualization of native knowledge was removed from direct dealings with native peoples and was fundamentally allegorical (14).

My interest in Sigüenza as a creole historian is more closely tied to the ways in which he pursued and represented relationships with members and segments of the Indian community, where the defining feature was variability. The surviving examples of Sigüenza's writings suggest an unusually varied talent. However, the principal reason for the lack of generic coherence in his published texts may have less to do with the inherent complexity of baroque intellectual life than with the specific exigencies that surrounded his work as a *letrado*. For the most part Sigüenza was only able to publish texts that he wrote on commission, a fact that he laments at different moments in his writings and one that should not be quickly dismissed from analyses of his work. As discussed in Chapter 1, Sigüenza often bemoans the fact that he was unable to publish many of his own texts in part because he lacked the economic resources to do so.

During Sigüenza's lifetime, a fascination with pre-Columbian Anahuac was evidently not always the basis for a shared sense of *patria* by a majority of fellow creoles. The prologue to *Parayso occidental* makes evident the tensions between the depth of Sigüenza's intellectual interests and his limited ability to publish the kinds of studies he wanted to circulate in seventeenth-century New Spain. Sigüenza's fascination with pre-Columbian Nahua culture and history was clearly central to his investigations, and his knowledge of the topic appears wherever he can work it into the texts he wrote on commission. In that effort to make his most heartfelt investigations relevant, Sigüenza struggled to insert aspects of pre-Columbian history into the prevailing discursive structures in which he was forced to work in order to find a public space for his writings. Two of his most studied texts can serve as examples: the letter on a riot in Mexico City from 1692 and the explanation of the triumphal arch he constructed for the arrival of a new viceroy in 1680.

Native Knowledge in the Public Space: 1692 and 1680

For many, works such as Sigüenza's letter to Admiral Pez regarding the 1692 corn riot in Mexico City (known in Spanish as *Alboroto y motín*) and his earlier *Teatro de virtudes políticas* (1680), which extolled the virtues of historic Mexica leaders, point to the fundamental paradox in Sigüenza's identification with the native population: he praises long-dead native figures while condemning the living inhabitants of New Spain. Irving Leonard brought to light *Alboroto y motín* and published it for the first time as an English translation titled "Letter to Admiral Pez."[3] In this missive Sigüenza narrates for his friend Andrés de Pez the events leading up to and including the 1692 urban uprising in Mexico City. Though there is disagreement on the precise origins of the rebellion, critics generally concur that the participants consisted of lower-class citizens of varied racial and ethnic backgrounds.[4] Sigüenza emphasizes the class status of the mob in his letter and he clearly adopts a disparaging and derogatory tone in his description of the rioters, as the following oft-cited passage demonstrates:

> Your Grace is probably asking me how the populace behaved at this time. I'll answer briefly, well and less well, because they are such an extremely rabble-like mob that they can only be termed the most infamous *canaille*. This is because it is composed of Indians, Creoles, *bozales* from various nations, *chinos*, mulattoes, *moriscos*, mestizos, *zambaigos* (Indian and chinos half-breeds), *lobos* (half-breeds), and Spaniards as well who, in declaring themselves "saramullos" (which is the same as knaves, rascals, and cape-snatchers) and in falling away from their allegiance, are the worst of them all in such a vile rabble. (Leonard 1929, 240)

> [Preguntaráme vuestra merced cómo se portó la plebe en este tiempo y respondo brevemente que bien y mal; bien, porque siendo plebe

tan en extremo plebe, que sólo ella lo puede ser de la que se reputare
la más infame, y lo es de todas las plebes por componerse de indios,
de negros, criollos y bozales de diferentes naciones, de chinos, de
mulatos, de moriscos, de mestizos, de zambaigos, de lobos y también
de españoles que, en declarándose zaramullos (que es lo mismo que
pícaros, chulos y arrebtacapas) y degenerando de sus obligaciones,
son los peores entre tan ruin canalla.] (Sigüenza 1984b, 113)

This famous sentence can be taken to mark a change in Sigüenza's work
from the earlier heroic studies of Indians to this later disenchantment
with the native population.[5] Yet, we must acknowledge that this angry
description is directed not simply at the *indios* but rather at the behavior
of a variety of subjects who are incorporated into a single class: the plebes.
Sigüenza perceives the demonstrators as a plebeian mob of mulattoes,
mestizos, *indios*, and Spaniards alike, all of whom are united in his mind
by their class identification in struggle against the viceregal government.

To understand Sigüenza's assessment of the 1692 riot, it may be useful
to recall other evocations of the urban environment in his works. For
example, his *Piedad heroyca de don Fernando Cortés* is a text meant to be a
tribute to Cortés by way of the hospital the conquistador founded amid
the ruins of the Aztec capital he had himself destroyed. Now known as the
Hospital de Jesús, the Hospital de la Inmaculada Concepción still serves
patients in the historic center of Mexico City. Sigüenza served as the chaplain at this hospital and thus knew its workings intimately. His text on the
institution's history underlines the virtue and piety of Cortés, but he also
takes advantage of the opportunity to recount the historical emergence
of Mexico City itself. Sigüenza constructs Motecuzoma as a formidable,
though misguided, leader of a city that was equally grand and misguided.
The "fortissimo and dichossissimo" (most strong and lucky) Cortés inter-
venes to bring Christian leadership to the noble unfaithful. A spatial allegory then takes over. Just as Motecuzoma's Tenochtitlan underlay Mexico
City, a discourse of Indian memory and knowledge seems to run beneath
an otherwise Eurocentric paean to the conqueror. Sigüenza relates how
the foundation for the hospital buildings was built in three months by the
Indian cacique don Antonio Cortés Chimalpopoca, and Sigüenza turns
to a text by the Nahua historian Hernando Alvarado Tezozomoc as his

source for the history of the ground beneath those buildings. The original of this text, Sigüenza tells us, is in Sigüenza's own library. This manuscript also once formed part of the collection that Alva Ixtlilxochitl's older son bequeathed to Sigüenza, underlining once again the many moments in which authority was constructed by means of this native archive. But at a remove of 150 years from the events of the conquest, Sigüenza inscribes Cortés into the foundation not of a homogenous Spanish or even creole colony, but of a multilingual, multicultural Mexico where civic unity, inclusive of both Spaniards and Indians, defines the hospital and thereby the colonial enterprise.

We find a less idealized version of Mexico City in *Alboroto y motín*, where the Indians are a threat, and their menace is tied to the conquest. Throughout his writing life, Sigüenza was passionate in his admiration and dedication to his *patria*, Mexico City, but the environmental, political, and social crises that climaxed in the June riots of 1692 draw into focus his conflicted sentiments about the origins of the capital of New Spain. The unrest was precipitated by floods and crop damage that led to food shortages in the city. Mexico City was also directly impacted by the heavy rains, and Sigüenza, working as a civil engineer, took part in work on the *desagüe* (drainage system) in the months leading up to the summer riots. In this context of his discussion of the repairs to the city's infrastructure, Sigüenza informs the reader that at an earlier moment in the city's history, workers cleaned out the irrigation ditches:

> An infinite number of tiny objects of superstition were taken
> out from beneath the Alvarado bridge. A great number of little
> pitchers and pots which smelled of pulque, and a still greater
> number of manikins or tiny figures of clay, were found. All of the
> latter represented Spaniards and all were either pierced by knives
> and lances formed of the same clay or had signs of blood on their
> throats as if they had been gashed. (1929 [ca. 1692], 246)

> [Se sacó debajo de la puente de Alvarado infinidad de cosillas
> supersticiosas. Halláronse muchísimos cantarillos y ollitas que
> olían a pulque, y mayor número de muñecos o figurillas de
> barro y de españoles y todas travesadas con cuchillos y lanzas

que formaron del mismo barro o con señales de sangre en
los cuellos, como degollados.] (Sigüenza 1984b, 116–17)

These clay figurines, in Sigüenza's estimation, represent an attempt to
harm the Spaniards through "ancient superstitions" [supersticiones an-
tiguas] (117). They were found, significantly, on the exact spot where
Cortés fled Tenochtitlan during the Noche Triste, the infamous night in
the summer of 1520 when the Mexica pushed the Spaniards and their
Indian allies out of Tenochtitlan. We can infer from Sigüenza's remarks
that there is a popular historical memory tied to this location—a memory
of the triumph this midsummer defeat of the invaders represented for
the Indians. According to Sigüenza, the native histories attribute that triumph to Huitzilopochtli, "their most important deity (which is the God
of War)" [su mayor dios (que es el de las guerras)] (117). Sigüenza emphasizes that he knows the stories of the natives very well, both through
his studies of their written histories and through conversations he has
had. For this reason he is capable of explaining to the Spanish authorities
what the threatening clay figurines mean. Sigüenza positions himself as a
cultural mediator in a way we can fruitfully contrast to the perspective of
his contemporary Diego Villavicencio.

As David Tavárez has said in his study of native spiritual practices, "Diego
Jaimes Ricardo Villavicencio was one of the most zealous secular ministers
who engaged in idolatry eradication in the late seventeenth century" (2011,
179).[6] In 1692, the same year as the corn riots, Villavicencio published a
treatise on native superstition and idolatry titled *Luz, y methodo, de confesar
idolatras*. A useful counterpoint to Sigüenza's assessment of the urban un-
derclasses, *Luz, y methodo* is an anti-idolatry treatise-cum-confessional guide
that pretends to offer the means to root out holdover unorthodox religious
practices among the native population. *Luz, y methodo* founds its discussion
of the Indian problem in the moment of the conquest, but Villavicencio
is not informed by any native versions of events. He relies on Bernal Díaz
del Castillo's history of the conquest, though Villavicencio draws his own
horrific images of native priests, or "papas," as he calls them:

Stained with human blood, their long hair knotted with clots of
blood, they had their ears slashed and their faces bandaged because

this is how they indicated when they were going to sacrifice to the gods of their idols. . . . These devilish priests, who were the bloody butchers, were so covered in blood and disgusting that they smelled of burnt and rotten flesh; and, with the horrible appearance of their faces and clothing they seemed to be the very demons they served and to whom they sacrificed as their ministers.

[Manchados de sangre humana los cabellos largos y muy enredados con costras de sangre las orejas las tenian rasgadas y fajadas las caras porque assi se señalavan quando se sacrificavan a los dioses de sus Idolos. . . . Estos malditos Papas eran los sangrientos carniceros estavan tan ensangrentados y asquerosos que hedian a carne quemada y podrida y con la horrible figura de sus caras y trages se parecian a los demonios a quien servian y sacrificavan como ministros suyos.] (1692, 41–42)

Luz, y methodo represents a condemnation of Indian culture that contrasts with Sigüenza's interpretive works. Even in the heat of his anger and frustration with the Indians in *Alboroto*, Sigüenza reveals his intellectual fascination with native life and his dedication to learning their stories and histories. His annoyance is directed at the class insurrection rather than the survival of native culture, and this is the one trait he in fact shares with Villavicencio.

Both Sigüenza and Villavicencio underline the *calidad* (social quality or class) of the Indians—the "indios plebeyos" whom they describe as depraved, barbaric, and, as Sigüenza emphasizes throughout *Alboroto*, seditious. In the final pages of the *Alboroto*, Sigüenza decries the riots in the city of Tlaxcala, which followed those in Mexico City. The natives of Tlaxcala were the greatest of the Spaniards' Indian allies during the conquest, but by the end of the seventeenth century Sigüenza saw them undertaking the same unfounded route of public revolt. Sigüenza's sense of disappointment and betrayal inspires his portrayal of the 1692 riots, but his criticisms are clearly aimed at the "indios plebeyos," whom we should not confuse with the indigenous elites with whom he maintained the kinds of friendship that, as we have seen, made him an important point in the custody of Alva Ixtlilxochitl's native archive.

Since its rediscovery by Leonard, *Alboroto y motín* has become a canonical text, often used to illustrate the racial and class-based hierarchies of colonial Mexico. It is frequently assigned in classes and has been a common object of scholarly work, all because it tells us something about colonial society in an engaging way. With a focus on urban violence, this text offers action and drama, in which Sigüenza casts himself as a protagonist pitted against a series of foes. Given the usual image of Sigüenza as a learned, deeply bookish man, it is more than a little amusing to think of him as a man of action in the midst of an urban uprising, abandoning his studies and being drawn into the violence on the streets. We can imagine him, Clark Kent–style, doffing his glasses and donning a cape as he pushes his way through the raging mob to save what he considered to be the most innocent victim of the entire event: the archive at the viceregal palace.[7] As he tells it,

> with a bar and with an axe I cut beams and pried open
> doors by my own efforts and not only some apartments of
> the Palace but whole halls and the best archive of the city
> were rescued from the fire. (1929 [ca. 1692], 268)

> [cuando yo con una barreta, ya con una hacha cortando vigas,
> apalancando puertas por mi industria se le quitaron al fuego de
> entre las manos no sólo algunos cuartos del Palacio sino tribunales
> enteros y de la ciudad su mejor archivo.] (1984b, 130)

With this depiction of Sigüenza's bravery, *Alboroto y motín* may be read less as a document of racial or class hatred than as a desperate plea for the preservation of knowledge, which Sigüenza clearly understood as a bulwark against disorder. This question of how to maintain order most effectively in colonial Mexico was a topic which Sigüenza himself had addressed previously in two closely related ways: in designing a triumphal arch to celebrate the arrival of a new viceroy in 1680 and in the textual commentary he wrote in order to explain the allegorical contents of his arch.

In November 1680, the twenty-sixth viceroy of New Spain, known by name and titles as Tomás Antonio de la Cerda, Conde de Paredes, Marqués de la Laguna, arrived in Mexico City, where he was greeted by two enormous triumphal arches. Sigüenza designed the principal arch in the Plaza of Santo Domingo, and Sor Juana Inés de la Cruz contributed a second arch outside the cathedral. The former was funded by the municipality and the latter by the cathedral chapter. Triumphal arches were ephemeral architectural structures erected in honor of kings and viceroys. In ancient Rome, they served to recognize a successful return from battle but in the Renaissance they had become associated with a transition in power. The arrival of viceroys to New Spain was celebrated in ritualistic fashion, marking the path of the conquistador Hernando Cortés, from the disembarkation in Veracruz to the grand entrance into Mexico City, where the incoming viceroy would be greeted by the multitudes.[8] Mimicking the symbolic power of festive architecture dedicated to the kings and queens of Europe, the triumphal arch in New Spain and Peru concentrated the public's attention on the incoming ruler and the authority he embodied. These impressive urban structures were decorated with images from Greek and Roman antiquity to represent the virtues of an ideal leader. Francisco de Solano catalogs the various Greek and Roman heroes and gods who were called up to represent various virtues embodied by New Spanish viceroys: Mars (Duke of Albuquerque), Apollo (Marquess of Mancera), Perseus (Duke of Veragua), Neptune (Count of Paredes), and Cadmus (Count of Galve) (1984, 252).

   Both of the triumphal arches erected in Mexico City in 1680 followed the classical model: they were immense monuments that provided an arch through which the incoming viceroy would parade. Like so many others, Sor Juana's arch, titled "Neptuno alegórico," displayed a series of mythological figures from ancient Greece and Rome. Sigüenza, however, drew his inspiration from the Indian past. The images Sigüenza chose for his arch and the explanation he offered of the Mexica figures in his accompanying handbook offered a challenge to the established conventions surrounding the triumphal arch and the associated tradition of the *speculum principis*.

   The triumphal arch itself would have demonstrated the very specific scope of Sigüenza's subject in *Teatro de virtudes*. He had engraved in the façade of the arch a lengthy inscription welcoming the viceroy and advising him to take heed of the images on the arch and the wisdom they held. Significantly, Sigüenza dates the arch to "the 30th of December of the year

353 after the foundation of Mexico" [el día treinta de diciembre del año 353 de la fundación de México] (1984b, 189). The Marqués de la Laguna, the twenty-sixth viceroy, arrived in 1680. Sigüenza's reference is thus to 1327, the year of the arrival of the Mexica to what would become Mexico Tenochtitlan, the *altepetl* that would rise to dominate most of central Mexico and would be conquered by Hernando Cortés in 1521. Sigüenza skips over the history of colonial New Spain and correlates the founding of the viceroyalty to the Mexica's founding of Tenochtitlan. The author then turns to the twelve Mexica leaders to demonstrate the exemplary qualities necessary to govern New Spain. Though the virtues described are conventional—clemency, prudence, piety, and so on—the figures Sigüenza deploys to embody these virtues could be viewed as con-troversial. He includes in his pantheon of emblematic leaders Huitzilo-pochtli, the infamous Mexica Tenochca god of war who, in the enduring representations of Bernal Díaz del Castillo, inspired the multitude of human sacrifices performed before the arrival of the Spaniards. Sigüenza also points to the exemplary qualities possessed by Cuauhtemoc, the last of the Mexica leaders who resisted Cortés's conquest of Mexico-Tenochtitlan and was tortured and executed by the conquistador in 1521.

In *Teatro de virtudes políticas* Sigüenza follows Alva Ixtlilxochitl in adapting the contemporary genre of the mirror of princes. Also like Alva Ixtlilxochitl, Sigüenza simultaneously affirms and contests that tradition via the use of indigenous figures as emblems of lordly virtue. This deploy-ment of the pre-Columbian past is an American gesture directed at the newly arrived Spanish authority, the Marqués de la Laguna. Sigüenza uses vivid terms to ascribe to them the native legacy on which he will base his advice on governing New Spain: "It was their fortune's destiny that on some occasion the Mexican monarchs should be reborn from among the ashes in which they are held in oblivion, so that the phoenixes of the West might immortalize their fame" [Era destino de la fortuna el que en alguna ocasión renaciesen los mexicanos monarcas de entre las cenizas en que los tiene el olvido, para que como fénixes del Occidente los inmortalizase la fama] (167). In heroic terms, Sigüenza announces that he will pull the Mexica leaders from the ashes and return them to their proper glory.[9]

The influence of the traditions around the mirror of princes is evident throughout the opening sections of the text, while at the same time it is clear that Sigüenza is making departures from the scope of the genre. Sigüenza directly states that, just as other triumphal arches, *Teatro de virtudes* should serve as a "mirror where they pay attention to the virtues with which the triumphal arches are adorned" [espejo donde atiendan a las virtudes con que han de adornarse los arcos triunfales] (171). Sigüenza forcefully asserts that local heroes are required to communicate to the incoming viceroy the nature of the *patria*:

> And it is clear that if the intent was to propose examples to imitate, it was an insult to the *patria* to beg foreign heroes from whom the Romans learned to exercise their virtues, and moreover when there is a surplus of instructive models, even among the people who are reputed to be barbarous, that establish the civilized customs.

> [Y claro está que si era el intento proponer para la imitación ejemplares, era agraviar a su patria mendigar extranjeros héroes de quienes aprendiesen los romanos a ejercitar las virtudes, y más cuando sobran preceptos para asentar la política aun entre las gentes que se reputan por bárbaras.] (174)

The *patria* for Sigüenza is directly tied to its pre-Hispanic peoples and traditions, and he ties his authority to the native materials he has in his possession. When describing those materials in *Teatro de virtudes*, Sigüenza emphasizes that the pictorial and alphabetic texts he consults require an expert knowledge that most readers do not have. For instance, he states that he has chosen not to go into a detailed explanation of "the original ancient histories" [las historias antiquísimas originales] that he possesses or the "characters or Mexican hieroglyphs, since some would think it a contemptible triviality and, thus, an unworthy object of his sublime studies" [los caracteres o jeroglíficos mexicanos, que algunos tendrán por trivialidad despreciable y, por el consiguiente, indigo objeto de sus estudios sublimes] (181–82).

In *Teatro de virtudes*, Sigüenza writes for an audience that is not connected to his specialized interest in and knowledge of the native past.[10] As he does not imagine an interlocutor who shares his passion and understanding of native culture, Sigüenza makes that knowledge appear even more esoteric. We see a very different process at work in Sigüenza's writings about the Virgin of Guadalupe, where he interjects himself into an ongoing and developing textual narrative of the cult dedicated to her worship.

The Virgin of Guadalupe and Creole Historiography

There is probably no clearer point at which the native archive intersects with what has been called a creole or national consciousness in Mexico than the Virgin of Guadalupe. The Virgin of Guadalupe is considered the spiritual patroness of Mexico and has been a focal point in articulating what are specifically Mexican religious and cultural traditions. Nationalist armies from the period of Mexico's independence in the early nineteenth century through the Mexican Revolution in the early twentieth century have marched under her banner, and her figure remains one of the few things likely to generate a sense of shared identity in a diverse and often internally divided country. In large measure the Virgin of Guadalupe derives this national status because of her association with popular, indigenous culture dating back to the early colonial period.

The canonical story is that on December 12, 1531, the Virgin of Guadalupe appeared to a *macehual* (lower-class indigenous man) named Juan Diego on a hill called Tepeyac, and left an imprint of her image on his *tilma* (cloak).[11] At the time, Tepeyac was on the outskirts of Mexico City, and it has long been believed that the site had pre-Columbian religious associations with a deity known as Tonantzin. However, this is probably a later attribution because, as Louise Burkhart has noted, the name *Tonantzin* taken literally means "honored mother" in Nahuatl and was used by the early Catholic missionaries and Indian converts in Mexico simply to refer to the Virgin Mary (2001, 209).[12] What is most significant about the appearance of the Virgin to Juan Diego is that it included a miracle—that is, the manifestation of an image of a dark-skinned woman, a *virgen morena*, as Guadalupe is often called—on his cloak. This iconic image has long been at the center of the Guadalupe cult, and its status as a prodigious gift to a poor indigenous man has lent the veneration of Guadalupe the possibility of a distinctly populist sensibility.[13] The social articulation of that populism is complex and variable, but the official church has supported the cult of Guadalupe, going so far as to canonize the name of Juan Diego in 2002. That validation notwithstanding, almost every aspect of the Guadalupe story has been examined, contested, defended, reasserted, and reconsidered by historians, detractors, believers, and a multitude of interested parties, almost since the stories of the apparition first circulated. However, even anti-apparitionist scholars such as Stafford Poole agree on the centrality of her deep and abiding connection to Mexican culture and religious experience.[14]

The origin and genealogy of the written narratives associated with Guadalupe have themselves been the source of controversy and confusion almost from the beginning. The scholarly consensus today is that the apparition stories were first written and published in the seventeenth century and that the authors of these texts were all creole clerics.[15] The principal authors and their texts were Miguel Sánchez (1606–1674), *Imagen de la Virgen María Madre de Dios de Guadalupe* (1648); Luis Laso de la Vega (ca. 1600–ca. 1660), *Huei tlamahuiçoltica* (1649); Luis Becerra Tanco (1603–1672), *Felicidad de México* (1675); and Francisco de Florencia (1620–1695), *La estrella del norte de México* (1688). In an influential study from 1953, Francisco de la Maza referred to these authors as the "four evangelists," and the epithet has stuck. Significantly, these texts all date from within Sigüenza's lifetime, and in that sense his own foray into discussions of Guadalupe joined a debate that was very much a part of his times and of concern to his own social class.

Among Guadalupana literature, Sigüenza's *Piedad heroyca de Don Fernando Cortés* (ca. 1689) has become important in its own right. As the title implies, the text is primarily about Hernando Cortés. However, it also includes a significant and oft-cited anecdote about materials related to the apparition:

> I say, and swear, that I found this Relation among don Fernando de Alva's papers, of which I have all, and that it is the same one Luis Becerra [Tanco] claims in his book [*Felicidad de México*] (page 30 in the Seville edition of 1685) to have had. The original in Nahuatl is in the hand of don Antonio Valeriano, Indian, who is its true author, and at the end are added some miracles in the hand of don Fernando, also in Nahuatl. The text I loaned to the Reverend

Father Francisco de Florencia was a periphrastic translation
of both texts done by don Fernando, and also in his hand.

[Digo, y juro, que esta Relación hallé entre los papeles de
D. *Fernando de Alva*, que tengo todos, y que es la misma que
afirma que el Licenciado *Luis de Bezerra* en su libro (pag. 30 de
la impresion de Sevilla) haver visto en su poder. El original en
Mexicano está de letra de *Don Antonio Valeriano* Indio, que es su
verdadero autor, y al fin añadidos algunos milagros de letra de *Don
Fernando*, también en Mexicano. Lo que presté al R. P. Francisco
de Florencia, fué una tradución parafrastica, que de uno y otro hizo
Don Fernando, y también está de su letra.] (1960 [ca. 1689], 65)

Sigüenza's references in this passage encapsulate the contentious ground
on which the narrative tradition of the apparition is founded. Sigüenza
ties the written story of the Virgin of Guadalupe's apparition to two
Nahua intellectuals: Alva Ixtlilxochitl himself and don Antonio Valeriano
(ca. 1520–1605). Valeriano, a native *letrado*, was an active scholar and
colonial administrator from a generation before Alva Ixtlilxochitl. Unlike
Alva Ixtlilxochitl, Valeriano was also an early pupil and then an instructor
of Latin and other subjects at the Colegio de Santa Cruz de Tlatelolco.
Later in life he was governor of the Indian portion of Mexico City. As the
apparition of Guadalupe was a distinctly Mexican phenomenon and one
tied in some ways to indigenous culture, it is not surprising that Sigüenza
returns again here to the native archive of Alva Ixtlilxochitl to authorize
his own knowledge on the topic. In fact, Sigüenza tells us that among
Alva Ixtlilxochitl's library he found the documents pointing to Valeriano
and Alva Ixtlilxochitl as the authors of the original written narrative of
the apparition of the Virgin of Guadalupe and the miracles associated
with her. This assertion would come to be a salient detail in the overall
authorization of the Guadalupe cult's roots in Mexican culture.

Founding the apparition story in the native community and specifically in the hands of native intellectuals is a central tenet of much popular
understanding of the Guadalupe legend and is still a common approach
to Guadalupe scholarship in academic circles.[16] Some historians, however,
have come to cast doubt on the native authorship of the apparition story

and subsequent miracle tales (Poole 1995 and 2006; Sousa, Poole, and Lockhart 1999; and Brading 2001). My interest here is to explore the genealogy and significance of Alva Ixtlilxochitl's association with the Guadalupe legend as an example of the colonial economy of letters—that is, as a case in which we can follow the close and even personal relationships that developed between creole historiography and the works and renown of native intellectuals. By highlighting Alva Ixtlilxochitl and Valeriano, Sigüenza is moving the origins of the apparition story back as much as two generations from the work of the four Guadalupe evangelists, all of whom were contemporaries or near contemporaries of Sigüenza. In the process he is implying a historical continuity for both the story itself and for the people involved in its creation and preservation. Becerra Tanco, for example, wrote of knowing Alva Ixtlilxochitl personally, and it is thought that Sigüenza shared some of Alva Ixtlilxochitl's archive with Florencia. This larger context of friendship, collective inquiry, and intellectual exchange provides the background for all of the earliest known writing related to the story of Guadalupe.

Miguel Sánchez is indisputably the first author of an extant scripted narrative of Guadalupe's apparition. As the title of his text might lead us to imagine, the *tilma* image is the focal point of his text.[17] *Imagen de la Virgen María Madre de Dios de Guadalupe* (Image of the Virgin Mary Mother of God of Guadalupe) (1648) presents a commentary on the significance of the Guadalupe image in the context of Western intellectual tradition and Catholic practices within New Spain. The miraculous appearance of the Virgin of Guadalupe's likeness on the *tilma* both provides a climax to the tale of the multiple apparitions of the Virgin to Juan Diego and allows the creole writer to underline a preeminently Nahua theme in the story. The Virgin, as Sánchez and later authors emphasize, appeared to Juan Diego, a *macehual* and Nahua neophyte, rather than to a Spaniard or a native person of higher social standing. Her blessing of Juan Diego was intended as a blessing for the Indians of the New World who had recently arrived to the faith and as a blessing for the new Catholic realm in Mexico more broadly.

Sánchez wrote for an educated audience in what is often described as baroque prose that is heavily laden with theological digressions, including abundant Latin passages. This was not a text aimed at the general populace.

In fact, Mateo de la Cruz published an extracted and simpler version of Sánchez's text, intended for wider reading, under the title *Relación de la milagrosa aparición de la Santa Virgen de Guadalupe* (1660). Though the most notable difference between Sánchez's and later Guadalupe texts is that it is more encumbered by erudition, another important distinction is that *Imagen de la Virgen* is fundamentally about the image of the Virgin, and the author, though not for want of trying, does not engage with a written record of the apparition story. Sánchez looked through archives and fruitlessly sought documentary evidence related to the apparition: "Determined, eager, and diligent, I searched for papers and writings that dealt with the sacred image and its miracle; I did not find them, even though I searched through all the archives that could have held them" [Determinado, gustoso y diligente busqué papeles y escritos tocantes a la santa imagen y su milagro, no los hallé, aunque recorrí los archivos donde podían guardarse] (1982 [1648], 158). Without textual sources to cite as authorities, his narrative became an exegesis of the image. Decades later, Becerra Tanco, Florencia, and Sigüenza foregrounded the ways in which they engaged with a written tradition of the Guadalupe legend that emerged out of the native community and was authored by Antonio Valeriano and Fernando de Alva Ixtlilxochitl. Though these three creole authors do not specifically suggest that Valeriano and Alva Ixtlilxochitl wrote the *Huei tlamahuiçoltica*, their seventeenth-century works serve as the foundation of just such a connection.[18]

Published in Nahuatl in 1649, *Huei tlamahuiçoltica omonexiti in ilhuicac tlatocacihuapilli Santa Maria totlaçonantzin Guadalupe in nican Huei altepenahuac Mexico itocyocan Tepeyacac* (By the great miracle the Heavenly Queen, Saint Mary, Our Precious Mother of Guadalupe, appeared here near the Great Altepetl of Mexico, in a place called Tepeyacac) contains a text known as the *Nican mopohua* (Here is recounted), the story of the apparition of the Virgin, and another known as the *Nican motecpana* (Here is an ordered account), which recounts miracle stories associated with her.[19] The stated author of the text was Luis Laso de la Vega, a secular cleric and vicar at the Guadalupe chapel at Tepeyacac. The main text is preceded by a preface written in Nahuatl and signed by Laso de la Vega. There is a note from a Jesuit priest, Baltasar González, that supports the publication of the text and again attributes authorship to Laso de la Vega.

There is also a notarized decree from Pedro de Barrientos Lomelín, vicar general of the archdiocese, that gives Laso de la Vega permission to publish the text. When looking at the text itself, it thus seems that everything indicates Luis Laso de la Vega is the author. Lisa Sousa, Stafford Poole, and James Lockhart, the editors of the 1998 translation and edition of the text, state as much in their introduction.[20]

And yet, as with many aspects of the Guadalupe cult, all these clear signs about authorship have not kept the *Huei tlamahuiçoltica* from being caught up in a confusing series of attributions that have led many scholarly and popular authorities alike to claim that this Nahuatl version of the Guadalupe story was written by Valeriano and Alva Ixtlilxochitl. Stafford Poole, in his meticulous account of the Guadalupe tradition, writes that Lorenzo Boturini Benaduci was the first to identify Valeriano as the author of the *Nican mopohua* and that the nineteenth-century Jesuit historian Mariano Cuevas is responsible for popularizing the attribution (Poole 1995, 167–69). Poole separates the *Huei tlamahuiçoltica* from the Nahuatl sources mentioned by Becerra Tanco, Florencia, and Sigüenza, affirming that "the 'Relación' is not the same as the *Nican mopohua* and in fact is substantially different from it" (169). The question of authorship of the *Huei tlamahuiçoltica*, as well as the issue of sources for that text and the other seventeenth-century narratives, is complicated and polemical. The most thorough treatments of the topic are found in Poole (1995) and David Brading (2001), though even these two eminent historians at times differ in their opinions. Brading, for example, offers a more cursory reading than Poole's of Sigüenza's *Piedad heroyca* and suggests simply that the creole author named "Antonio Valeriano as the author of the *Nican mopohua*" (117) when, in fact, that is not quite what Sigüenza states, as Poole explains (167). The issue of concern here is what role, if any, did Alva Ixtlilxochitl have in the emergence of the Guadalupe narratives.

Becerra Tanco was the first to present Alva Ixtlilxochitl as an active player in recording the apparition and early miracles associated with the Virgin. Unlike Sánchez, who claims early on that his efforts to make a full written account of the apparition were frustrated by his fruitless search for related documents, Becerra Tanco dedicates lengthy portions of his text to enumerating crucial oral and written sources from the native community. Becerra Tanco announces in the prologue of *Felicidad de México* that since he was a native Nahuatl speaker, having grown up in a Nahuatl-speaking community near Taxco, he found himself obliged to write down everything he knew and had learned during his adolescence from Nahua pictorial records [las pinturas y caracteres de los indios mexicanos] (1982 [1675], 310). Becerra Tanco's original account was included in the 1666 capitular inquiry that relied on the testimony of twenty witnesses to seek a grant of a special feast, mass, and office in honor of the Virgin of Guadalupe (Poole 1995, 138). Though Rome did not grant the request, the stories accumulated for the inquiry served as yet another milestone in the development of the apparition narrative and the miracles tales wrought around Guadalupe. Becerra Tanco reworked his written testimony from 1666 and this second version was published posthumously as *Felicidad de México en el principio, y milagroso origen que tubo el Santuario d ela Virgen Maria N. Señora de Guadalupe* (The felicity of Mexico in the beginning and the miraculous origin of the Sanctuary of Our Lady of Guadalupe) (1675).[21]

Felicidad de México provides the foundation for a narrative of the apparition that is rooted in the native community, and Becerra Tanco sees himself as singularly suited to bear witness to that story. But many of the men on his list of oral sources who confirm the apparition turn out to have been creole men—often religious—who were enmeshed in the Indian community. Their skills and proficiency in Nahuatl—or *mexicano*—are described as akin to those of classical orators, like Cicero in Latin or Demosthenes in Greek. These learned and intercultural creoles are then supposed to have communicated to Becerra Tanco the stories they had gathered from learned and intercultural Indians. For example, the maternal uncle of Becerra Tanco, Gaspar de Prabez, is described as a grandson of one of the first conquistadors and a "Nahuatl Cicero" [Cicerón de la lengua mexicana]. He is said to have related to his nephew what he had heard of the tradition directly from Antonio Valeriano (Becerra Tanco 1982 [1675], 329). The line of evidence is thus rather extended.

Nevertheless, Becerra Tanco himself maintained close ties to the native lettered community. Most significantly, if not surprisingly, he highlights the materials he read and studied that were in the possession of "Don Fernando de Alva, interpreter in the Indian Court of this viceregal government, capable and elderly man who understood and spoke Nahuatl with eminence, and who understood the pictorial records of the natives"

[D. Fernando de Alva, intérprete que fue del juzgado de indios, de los señores virreyes en este gobierno, hombre muy capaz, y anciano, y que entendía y hablaba con eminencia la lengua mexicana, y tenía noticia de los caracteres y pinturas antiguas de los naturales] (325). Becerra Tanco claims to have held while among Alva Ixtlilxochitl's papers "a notebook written in our alphabet and in Nahuatl, in the hand of one of the most esteemed Indians from the College of Santa Cruz [de Tlatelolco]" [un cuaderno escrito con letras de nuestro alfabeto en la lengua mexicana, de mano de un indio de los más provectos del Colegio de Santa Cruz] (326). Presumably this is a reference to Valeriano. The central innovation Becerra Tanco provides here for the apparition story is its connection to these two men—Valeriano and Fernando de Alva Ixtlilxochitl—who in later decades would be further implicated in the emergence of the narrative of Guadalupe and who in later centuries would be put forth as the true authors of the *Huei tlamahuiçoltica*. Though Becerra Tanco was forty years older than Sigüenza, the two men enjoyed a friendship that was based on not only a shared passion for Indian history but also a common interest in mathematics. Becerra Tanco was named the first chair of the mathematics department at the Royal University in 1672, just a few months before he died. Sigüenza then succeeded him in the same position (Leonard 1929, 10). Sigüenza and Francisco de Florencia were also friends, and Sigüenza shared some of the materials he had inherited from Alva Ixtlilxochitl with the Jesuit historian. For all three of these creole clerics, Alva Ixtlilxochitl served as a source of information and authority for their studies of the apparition. The interactions of the creole clerics extend in important ways the reach of the colonial economy of letters as it was tied across generations to the native archive that accrued around Alva Ixtlilxochitl. A seemingly marginal reference by Sigüenza to a manuscript from Alva Ixtlilxochitl's collection demonstrates the foundational importance of the native archive to the written tradition around Guadalupe.

As we have seen, Sigüenza's *Piedad heroyca de don Fernando Cortés* (ca. 1689) offers a history of the hospital Cortés founded in Mexico City. Intended as a tribute to Hernando Cortés, the text places this hospital amid the ruins of the Aztec capital and it constructs Motecuzoma as a formidable though misguided leader of a grand though misguided city. The "extraordinarily pious" [piadosissimo] Cortés then appears in order to bring Christian leadership to the noble pagans (1960 [ca. 1689], 4). Early in the *Piedad heroyca* Sigüenza takes a not atypical opportunity to insert his knowledge and interest in indigenous history. Despite the fact that a text ostensibly about an institution founded after the conquest should have little or nothing to do with the pre-Columbian past, Sigüenza uses the location of the Hospital Amor de Dios as a pretext to demonstrate his knowledge of the layout of the city from before the arrival of the Spanish. Later he announces a coming digression in the title of chapter 10, "The University was not founded in a structure belonging to this hospital. Incidentally, it is explained where the image of most holy Mary of Guadalupe appeared" [No se fundó la universidad en casa perteneciente a este hospital. Dicese incidentemente donde se aparacio la imagen de Maria Santissima de Guadalupe] (53).

This curious and tangential chapter opens with a detailed refutation of the suggestion that the Royal University had been founded in a building belonging to the Hospital Amor de Dios. Sigüenza goes on to explain that the university was first installed in a building adjacent to the archbishop's residence. The mention of that building allows one more metonymic digression through which Sigüenza arrives at the miraculous apparition of the Virgin of Guadalupe. After appearing to Juan Diego, he says, the Virgin instructed him to gather roses in his *tilma* and take them to the house of the bishop, Juan de Zumárraga (Zumárraga was named the first archbishop of New Spain in 1548, though he died before receiving the news). While standing before Zumárraga, Juan Diego opened his *tilma* and they both beheld a miraculous image of the Virgin imprinted on it. Though there is no connection between the Hospital Amor de Dios and the apparition of the Virgin of Guadalupe, it is important for Sigüenza to clarify where Zumárraga's dwelling was located because Francisco de Florencia, a Jesuit priest, published an account of the Virgin of Guadalupe in 1688 titled *La estrella del norte de México* (The north star of Mexico City). In this text Florencia asserts that the bishop resided in a different building that, by the seventeenth century, belonged to the Count of Santiago. In his obsession with details, Sigüenza takes offense at this perceived error and states adamantly that his version of the story is confirmed by numerous accounts, including an ancient and trusted manuscript in his possession [una antiquíssima, que aun tengo M.S. y estimo en mucho] (63). Though

Sigüenza had loaned the manuscript to Florencia, the Jesuit author apparently did not completely follow its story. The ghost of the native archive again haunts this moment in which Sigüenza constructs his own, highly local authority.

In the final paragraphs of this same chapter, Sigüenza reminds the reader of his close personal ties to Luis Becerra Tanco and Francisco de Florencia, even as he expresses dismay at the latter's conclusions about the author of a manuscript Sigüenza had lent him. Florencia declared the author of the manuscript to be Gerónimo de Mendieta, a Franciscan friar who had died well before many of the miracles recounted in the text had occurred. Sigüenza then goes on to explain that the relation was found among Fernando de Alva's papers and that the original is in the handwriting of don Antonio Valeriano. According to Sigüenza, Alva Ixtlilxochitl had then added some miracle stories (65). Exactly which relation Sigüenza is referring to continues to be the source of confusion. For example, in his translation and edition of the *Nican mopohua*, Miguel León-Portilla, perhaps the most eminent Nahuatl scholar alive in Mexico, cites precisely this passage from the *Piedad heroyca* to support his own assertion that Antonio Valeriano is the true author of the Nahuatl text.[22] León-Portilla reads Sigüenza's reference to a relation as a reference to the *Nican mopohua*, whereas Poole understands the relation to be a separate document.[23] Doubts like Poole's and the obvious confusions found in the texts themselves have not prevented many scholars and popular writers alike from following León-Portilla in relying on this one note from Sigüenza in order to tie Valeriano and Alva Ixtlilxochitl to the *Nican mopohua* and the *Nican motecpana*.

What emerges from this occasionally dense and often confusing web of references, cross-references, recriminations, and citations is a thin line of allusion that ties the Guadalupe legend to indigenous sources by means of a tangential comment in one of Sigüenza's lesser texts. Underlying that tangential remark is Sigüenza's relationship to the Alva Ixtlilxochitl family and, crucially, his custody over the native archive amassed by Fernando de Alva. Portrayed as both the guardian of Antonio Valeriano's account of the apparition and as the author of miracles attributed to the Virgin, Alva Ixtlilxochitl served as the point of exchange between the Indian and Hispanic cultural and intellectual spheres with regard to the Guadalupe cult. The details of Alva Ixtlilxochitl's involvement in the development of the Guadalupe narrative are riddled with contradictions and confusions, yet he continues to have a significant presence in popular and academic versions of the story.[24] Alva Ixtlilxochitl's own texts do not bear out any proof either of devotion to Guadalupe or of participation in the documentation of the narrative of her apparition.[25]

Since the authors of the foundational Guadalupan texts were creole clerics, scholars have focused on these authors as participants in an emerging creole discourse that aimed to incorporate their stories of the Virgin of Guadalupe into a patriotic history.[26] Yet, the seventeenth-century narrative history of the Virgin of Guadalupe reveals a heterogeneous historiographical process. Many of the authors associated with the Guadalupe texts were nahuatlato priests, immersed in both the Indian and Hispanic cultural spheres. Laso de la Vega wrote in Nahuatl. Becerra Tanco wrote extensively of his growing up in a Nahuatl-speaking community, and his ability to speak and understand the language is central to his establishing authority in matters related to Guadalupe's apparition. Sigüenza was not a native speaker of Nahuatl but indicates that he did understand the language. Florencia was also conversant in Nahuatl. By the mid-seventeenth century there were many Hispanic priests who were nahuatlatos, conversant in the spoken language and also familiar with the more stylized classical form conserved in such texts as the *Cantares mexicanos* and the *Romances de los señores de la Nueva España*. There was a shared cultural context where the native expressive traditions were known and studied by both native and Hispanic intellectuals, sometimes in collaboration. The Guadalupe cult is in that sense a direct outgrowth of the kinds of relationships I have labeled "the colonial economy of letters," in which knowledge and authority were constructed through a complex series of interactions among diverse but not always divergent intellectual communities.

There is no evidence that Fernando de Alva Ixtlilxochitl himself was responsible for any of the narrative history related to the Virgin of Guadalupe. But looking at the question of his involvement in the history of the apparition and miracles associated with the Virgin allows us to focus on his role as a touchstone within the colonial economy of letters.[27] The twentieth-century and early twenty-first-century scholarship on the authorship of the Guadalupe legend has attempted to fix on singular figures who created different versions of the narrative. Yet, both within the seventeenth-century texts and in the context of their production we find evidence of a collective and collaborative enterprise. Becerra Tanco used his knowledge of Nahuatl to seek out stories of the Virgin of Guadalupe that had been maintained in oral tradition and written texts. His searching brought him into contact with Nahuatl-speaking creole priests and Alva Ixtlilxochtil himself. Sigüenza famously, and from his perspective regrettably, shared the materials related to Guadalupe that he had inherited from Alva Ixtlilxochitl with Florencia. Though there is no overt indication of collaboration in *Huei tlamahuiçoltica*, at a minimum Laso de la Vega was knowledgeable of the tradition of elevated Nahuatl discourse through sermons or religious treatises produced by other Nahuatl-speaking priests. These interpersonal connections provide the basis for a new way of approaching the question of cultural production and authorship of the seventeenth-century story of the Virgin of Guadalupe and the genealogy of the Guadalupe legend.

Conclusion

Fernando de Alva Ixtlilxochtil worked, as we have seen, in an elegiac mode. His recovery of historical memory related to his indigenous family's community of origin represented for him an effort in a struggle against erasure and oblivion that began with the burning of the archives in Tetzcoco. What is more, the context of demographic collapse that surrounded his generation and the generation before him meant that he was among the last double-cultured mestizo writers in central Mexico capable of spanning in one person a past that ran through the pre-Columbian pictorial traditions to oral histories in Nahuatl and postconquest legal struggles in order to convert that knowledge into written accounts measured against the dominant Spanish historiography. While his posthumous fame has in many ways eclipsed that of Alva Ixtlilxochitl, Sigüenza was himself by no means a person of great social station in New Spain. Read against the panorama of indigenous leaders laid out for the contemplation of a new viceroy, Sigüenza's later self-depiction as the heroic savior of the viceregal archives during the 1692 corn riots can perhaps lead us to understand him as well as a figure engaged in a project of recovery for which the

preservation of historical memory was part and parcel of a proper order-
ing of society. As a result of all the complex relationships he maintained
through the colonial economy of letters, Sigüenza became the last cus-
todian of Alva Ixtlilxochitl's symbolically powerful native archive. After
Sigüenza, the materials so painstakingly assembled by Alva Ixtlilxochitl
would be dispersed and end up in places as distant from each other and
from Mexico as the Cambridge University Library in the United Kingdom or the Benson Library at the University of Texas at Austin. Between
these two figures, then, we can intuit a trajectory for this body of learning which was to prove so crucial for the self-conception of Mexico as a
society possessed of its own unique past. Nowhere are the stakes for that
past higher than in the formation of the Guadalupe cult and its association with native culture.

As has been definitively shown, the Guadalupe cult, even in its native-
language source materials, was the creation of creole writers who were in
contact with creole priests who worked in the evangelization of Nahua
communities. While Sigüenza was not directly involved in generating
the foundational Guadalupan texts, his writings related to the apparition
helped perform what we can now understand as a critical historical task.
By suggesting a tie between the Guadalupe cult and Alva Ixtlilxochitl's
manuscript collection, Sigüenza and those who have used his texts to
support a certain historiography of the apparition have relied on a line of
authority rooted in the native archive. But in the absence of a continued
dialogue with active indigenous or mestizo *letrados*, without figures like
Fernando de Alva Ixtlilxochitl, the native archive from which they drew
their legitimacy no longer belonged to native communities. Given the
subsequent dispersion of Alva Ixtlilxochitl's library after Sigüenza's death,
we might even say that subsequent generations of scholars have had only
the rhetorical image of a native archive, which has been available for a
multitude of uses, none of which can really be supported or questioned.
The development of the Guadalupe cult in the second half of the seventeenth century can be marked as the moment when the native archive
ceased to be a native archive and became an emblem of authority within
a new series of social and cultural processes.

Native Knowledge and Colonial Networks

In a symbolic ceremony occasioned by the seventy-fifth anniversary of the National Institute of Anthropology and History (INAH) and the fifty years of the National Museum of Anthropology, the secretary of public education, Emilio Chuayffet Chemor, representing the president of the republic, Enrique Peña Nieto, delivered to the people of Mexico the *Códice Chimalpahin*, a foundational document for the nation, repatriated by the Mexican state in an historic act.

[En una ceremonia simbólica con motivo del 75 aniversario del Instituto Nacional de Antropología e Historia (INAH) y los 50 años del Museo Nacional de Antropología, el secretario de Educación Pública, Emilio Chuayffet Chemor, en representación del Presidente de la República, Enrique Peña Nieto, entregó al pueblo de México el *Códice Chimalpahin*, documento fundacional de la nación, repatriado por el Estado mexicano en un hecho histórico.]
—INAH, "El gobierno de México recupera el Códice Chimalpahin"

On September 17, 2014—just one day after *16 de septiembre* and the commemoration of Mexican independence—in a grand ceremony linked to two historic celebrations, three volumes of colonial-era manuscripts were officially returned to Mexican soil. In the press release from INAH cited above (2014), these materials are tightly linked to a tradition of patriotic historiography and the construction of national identity in the twenty-first century. As numerous scholars have noted, the histories written by Alva Ixtlilxochitl provide a basis for Mexican national consciousness and history (O'Gorman 1975, 1:218; Brading 1991, 273–75; García Loaeza 2009). The excitement around the repatriation of the three volumes containing Alva Ixtlilxochitl's original manuscripts shows that the role these texts have played in the emergence and growth of patriotic history in Mexico is ongoing. Undeniably important, the movement of the manuscripts from Alva Ixtlilxochitl to Sigüenza, the transcription of those materials by the eighteenth-century historians Boturini and Echeverría y Veytia, and their early publication by the nineteenth-century scholars Bustamante and Chavero all provide a window into the ever-growing and strengthening discourse of Mexican nationalism that came to be associated with this collection of texts. However, when we focus solely on the teleological advance from one generation to another along the same path toward nationalist historiography, we miss an opportunity to appreciate the connections that were key to Alva Ixtlilxochitl in his own time as he developed his project in the seventeenth century.

In an editorial published soon after the repatriation of the "Códice Chimalpahin," titled "The Government Buys 'Its' Past" [Gobierno compra 'su' pasado], Mexican writer Heriberto Yépez gives voice to some of the discomfort surrounding Indian intellectuals and their role in the writing of Mexico's history. First expressing a conflicted sort of relief that the documents were not purchased by a US institution, which would have represented "yet another academic-imperial trophy" [un trofeo académico-imperial más], Yépez then says: "Moreover, the documents that are included are very problematic. They are visions of *letrados* (Chimalpahin and Ixtlilxochitl) in whom there exist elements that are at once a defense of the indigenous corpus and of the successful colonization of its being" [Los documentos ahí incluidos, además, son bastante problemáticos. Son visiones de letrados (Chimalpahin e Ixtlilxóchitl) en quienes habitan elementos tanto de defensa del corpus indígena como de la exitosa colonización de su ser] (2014). Perhaps in the spirit of polemic, Yépez goes on to argue that "these texts are registers of the colonial period, in all its meanings" [esos textos son registros de la Colonia definiéndolo todo]. There is boundless truth in that sentence. The three volumes of manuscripts register the colonial experience in myriad ways: (1) the writing of native histories in alphabetic script; (2) the incorporation of native histories into patriotic narratives; and (3) the continued relevance of those native histories from the colonial period to contemporary cultural and political discourses. We can inflect our study of the three volumes of manuscripts in each of these ways to offer fresh perspectives on indigenous writings and the colonial world. Yépez's intervention is, however, likely intended to underline the way in which native knowledge and stories have been stolen from the native communities over a period of many centuries, both before and after Alva Ixtlilxochitl's time. In this sense, the discussions around the repatriation of the "Códice Chimalpahin" highlight the relevance and resonance of Rolena Adorno's insights into the "polemics of possession" (2007). The debates over the right of Spanish conquest and treatment of native inhabitants of the Americas that Adorno so elegantly unfolds extend thus to related and also lingering questions over the rights to native knowledge.

Facing the destruction of historical memory, as the elders died and the remaining sources for native history were lost to the ravages of time, Alva Ixtlilxochitl salvaged knowledge of the native past in the language of the colonial elite. His project four hundred years ago was closely tied to his efforts to save local knowledge for the benefit of his family and community and even his own professional aspirations. Susan Schroeder has noted the impulse toward micropatriotic histories by Indian and mestizo authors at the turn of the seventeenth century, which she says was motivated by "a keen sense of urgency to keep to tradition while securing vestigial positions of high status within the colonial system" (1997, 1:6). In her efforts to situate the intellectual production of Chimalpahin, Schroeder has suggested that the church of San Francisco in Mexico City could have served as a magnet to attract Nahua intellectuals (2010). Drawn by the great library and the chapel of San Josef de los Naturales, she has speculated that Chimalpahin, Alva Ixtlilxochitl, and Alvarado Tezozomoc could have made connections with other lettered Nahuas who were eager to share "sources and stories about their respective histories" (106). Alva Ixtlilxochitl's histories attest to his drive to seek knowledge of the native past in a diverse range of places and contexts. It would be natural to assume that he was also eager to find interlocutors with whom he could share that knowledge. If Alva Ixtlilxochitl's work reflects the totality of colonial experience, he was not alone in the effort to pass knowledge between generations and between communities.

In this book I have reapproached the study of Alva Ixtlilxochitl's works with a keen eye toward the social networks that undergirded their preparation, production, and circulation. The nodes of intersection between Alva Ixtlilxochitl and his environs were diverse: they included the community of native elders from Tetzcoco and other Nahua cities and towns, such as Gabriel de Segovia; Indian intellectuals who were also at work on their own historiographical projects, such as Huitzimengari; and Spanish religious, such as Torquemada. All these contexts and connections influenced the way in which Alva Ixtlilxochitl interpreted and documented native history. While the movement of Alva Ixtlilxochitl's collection of native pictorial and alphabetic writings to Sigüenza is hugely symbolic, it also should be registered as significant in terms of the social connection that brought it about. Alva Ixtlilxochitl participated in intellectual activities and production that were part of numerous circuits within and beyond the Indian communities, and Sigüenza was likewise engaged with contemporary creoles, Spaniards, and members of families from the native elite. Sigüenza's inheritance of Alva Ixtlilxochitl's archive was not simply a fortunate (or unfortunate) happenstance, but rather a gift precipitated by his enduring personal connection and commitment to Alva Ixtlilxochitl's older son. In this way, the importance of Alva Ixtlilxochitl and Sigüenza as Mexican intellectuals can be traced not simply in a linear fashion, as predecessors to the eighteenth-century patriotic historians, but more intriguingly as part of diverse networks of intellectuals connected to various segments of colonial society. As we examine Alva Ixtlilxochitl's and Sigüenza's social networks, we not only gain insight into the various connections and sources that influence their works, but we are also able to reevaluate the relationships between indigenous, mestizo, and creole intellectual spheres in colonial Mexico. In the process we gain a richer and more complete sense of the real structures of power and influence in this society.

NOTES

Introduction

Epigraph. Carson opens *Economy of the Unlost,* her study of the twentieth-century German-language poet Paul Celan and the ancient Greek poet Simonides, with a discussion of the gift. Describing her method for thinking and writing about the two poets from two very different contexts and time periods, she says that working on them within the same analytical framework kept both in motion: "Moving and not settling, they are side by side in conversation and yet no conversation takes place" (vii–viii). Though the overlap between the two subjects of my book is much more evident and relevant, I too will attempt to look at Alva Ixtlilxochitl and Sigüenza dynamically, side by side, in order to bring them into a new focus.

1. In an early essay on the topic, José Juan Arrom noted three divisions in colonial populations: those of Old World (be it African or European) stock born in the New World, inhabitants of the New World born in the Old World, and Indians with ancestral ties to the New World. Within this division, the term "creole" refers to an individual who is not Indian but was born in the Indies (1971). In his influential treatment of the topic, David Brading consistently combines the term "creole" with the term "patriot" when speaking of early nationalist sentiments and thought. Brading's genealogy traces a notion of ideological independence from the Spanish Crown, beginning with the conquistadors (1991).

2. My quotes of Mauss are taken from the translation by Ian Cunnison.

3. Mauss famously focused on the Northwestern Native North American tradition of "potlatch" as "more than a legal phenomenon; it is one of those phenomena we propose to call 'total.' It is religious, mythological and shamanistic. . . . It is economic; and one has to assess the value, importance, causes and effects of transactions which are enormous even when reckoned by European standards. The potlatch is also a phenome-non of social morphology; the reunion of tribes, clans, families and nations produces great excitement. . . . Finally, from the jural point of

view, we have already noted the contractual forms and what we might call the human element of the contract, and the legal status of the contracting parties. . . . To this we now add that the material objects of the contracts have a virtue of their own which causes them to be given and compels the making of counter-gifts" (1967, 36–37).

4. In his well-received study, Cañizares-Esguerra condenses the dominant scholarly approach to the relationship between creoles and natives when he announces at the beginning of *How to Write the History of the New World* that "Spanish American authors, by and large, were Creole clerics who came to regard the precolonial and early colonial Amerindian upper classes as their own ancestors, but concomitantly despised plebeian mestizos and Amerindians" (2001, 8–9). In a similar vein, though over a decade earlier, Florescano wrote, "At the end of the seventeenth century, the Creoles found in the pre-Hispanic past and the exuberant American nature two distinctive elements that separated them from the Spaniards and affirmed their identity with the land that protected them" (1994 [1987], 187). See also Lafaye (1987 [1974]) and Brading (1991).

5. "In the last resort, Sigüenza's role was to act as a vital, indispensable link between Ixtlilxochitl and the historians of the eighteenth century" (Brading 1991, 371)

6. The image has been the object of scholarly interventions, at times confirming and at others disputing de Certeau's analysis. For example, in the opening chapter of *Inventing America* (1994), José Rabasa offers a close reading of the image and the way in which "America" captures the ideological intent of European accounts of the discovery (6). For a fuller development of this argument, see the chapter "The Nakedness of America?" (23–48). In *Reading Columbus* (1993), Margarita Zamora draws our attention to the critical issue of gender in the "America" engraving, when she notes that "de Certeau's seminal erotic interpretation of Van der Straet's drawing seems to have missed the most obvious point of all—when the conqueror arrives on 'America's' shores, 'the body of the other,' *her* body, has already been inscribed in the feminine mode. Van der Straet's allegory does not invent but translates the signs of a discourse already in existence" (154).

7. These are just a few examples of the trailblazing scholarship on colonial Indians and their traditions from recent decades: Rolena Adorno, *Guaman Poma: Writing and Resistance in Colonial Peru* (1986); Louise Burkhart, *The Slippery Earth: Nahua-Christian Moral Dialogue in Sixteenth-Century Mexico* (1989); James Lockhart, *The Nahuas after the Conquest: A Social*

and Cultural History of the Indians of Central Mexico, Sixteenth through Eighteenth Centuries (1992); Elizabeth Hill Boone, *Stories in Red and Black: Pictorial Histories of the Aztecs and Mixtecs* (2000); *The Huarochirí Manuscript: A Testament of Ancient and Colonial Andean Religion* (1991), translated by Frank Salomon and George L. Urioste, with annotations by Salomon; and Salomon, *The Cord Keepers: Khipus and Cultural Life in a Peruvian Village* (2004).

8. Borah and Cook allow that the estimate of 25.2 for the total population of central Mexico on the eve of the Spanish Conquest should be understood within a "wide margin of error." They go on to suggest that their evidence could support ranges of 20 to 28 million or 18.8 to 26.3 million, depending on how the average family number is calculated and the regularity of tribute payments (1963, 88). Their extensive study of population history during the colonial period was published in three volumes as *Essays in Population History: Mexico and the Caribbean* (Cook and Borah 1979). Their research centered around three years—1568, 1595, and 1646.

9. For an overview of New Conquest History, see Matthew Restall, "The New Conquest History" (2012). Some examples of scholarship in this vein include: Matthew Restall, *Maya Conquistador* (1998); Matthew Restall and Florine Asselbergs, *Invading Guatemala: Spanish, Nahua, and Maya Accounts of the Conquest Wars* (2007); *Indian Conquistadors: Indigenous Allies in the Conquest of Mesoamerica* (2007), edited by Laura Matthew and Michel Oudijk; and Laura Matthew, *Memories of Conquest: Becoming Mexicano in Colonial Guatemala* (2012).

10. Recent studies of natives in colonial Mexico and the Andes by scholars from history, art history, anthropology, and literature include: Yanna Yannakakis, *The Art of Being In-Between: Native Intermediaries, Indian Identity, and Local Rule in Colonial Oaxaca* (2008); Kathryn Burns, *Into the Archive: Writing and Power in Colonial Peru* (2010); John Charles, *Allies at Odds: The Andean Church and Its Indigenous Agents, 1583–1671* (2010); David Tavárez, *The Invisible War: Indigenous Devotions, Discipline, and Dissent in Colonial Mexico* (2011); Peter Villella, "Indian Lords, Hispanic Gentlemen: The Salazars of Colonial Tlaxcala" (2012); *Indigenous Intellectuals: Knowledge, Power, and Colonial Culture in Mexico and the Andes*, edited by Gabriela Ramos and Yanna Yannakakis (2014); Alessandra Russo, *The Untranslatable Image: A Mestizo History of the Arts in New Spain, 1500–1600* (2014); and Kelly McDonough, *The Learned Ones: Nahua Intellectuals in Postconquest Mexico* (2014).

11. Here I refer explicitly to Miguel León-Portilla's edition of native texts that addressed the conquest, *Visión de los vencidos: Relaciones indígenas de la conquista* (1959). The influential text has been widely translated and published; the twenty-ninth Spanish edition was published in 2008.

12. In recent years, scholars in literature, history, anthropology, linguistics, and art history have continued to engage with Rama's provocative model, especially in Andean studies. In *Esclavos de la ciudad letrada: Esclavitud, escritura y colonialismo en Lima* (1650–1700), José Ramón Jouve Martín studies the interaction between the African community and lettered culture in seventeenth-century Lima (2005). Alcira Dueñas looks at Indians and mestizos as transformative agents in the Andes in *Indians and Mestizos in the "Lettered City": Reshaping Justice, Social Hierarchy, and Political Culture in Colonial Peru* (2010). As Stephanie Merrim promises in the introduction to *The Spectacular City, Mexico, and Colonial Hispanic Literary Culture*, her "Spectacular City both intersects with and exceeds Angel Rama's 'ciudad letrada'" (2010, 3). Frank Salomon and Mercedes Niño-Murcia move the study of the impact of lettered culture to the rural regions of Peru in *The Lettered Mountain: A Peruvian Village's Way with Writing* (2011). As do the other studies, Joanne Rappaport and Tom Cummins's *Beyond the Lettered City: Indigenous Literacies in the Andes* (2012) critically extends Rama's discussion of the lettered city. Ramón de la Campa presents an insightful analysis of the enduring relevance of Rama's essay in "El desafío inesperado de *La ciudad letrada*" (1997).

13. Translations are my own, unless otherwise noted.

14. Gemelli Careri traveled from his home in Naples across Europe, Africa, and Asia, and then on to Mexico and the Philippines. His travels and discoveries were documented in his six-part account *Giro del mondo*, first published in 1699.

15. Though *México* in the colonial period referred only to Mexico City, "New Spain" is not an easy substitute for "colonial Mexico." New Spain included a much greater expanse of territories—e.g., the Philippines, portions of the United States, and Central America—that are not part of my study. I have opted to use "Mexico," and more specifically "colonial Mexico," to bring our attention to the region marked by today's political geography.

16. Here I follow the titles used by Edmundo O'Gorman in his Spanish edition of Alva Ixtlilxochitl's complete works (1975–1977).

Chapter 1

1. Lot 14 of Christie's sale 1550 from May 21, 2014, is labeled in the catalog as "The Codex Chimalpahin and Historical Works by Fernando de Alva Ixtlilxochitl." The initial bidding price for the three volumes is listed as $500,000–830,000 (18–19).
2. Though ultimately private, the sale was facilitated by Christie's. According to the press release put out by Christie's on September 18, 2014, "INAH (Instituto Nacional de Antropología e Historia) contacted Christie's in May of this year, prior to the London auction in which the Codex was originally consigned, to make a private offer. The manuscripts had long been part of the archives of the British and Foreign Bible Society who were very supportive in helping facilitate the return of this historic object to Mexico" (2014b).
3. When referring to the manuscript volumes that were purchased from the Bible Society and are now housed in INAH's library, the Biblioteca Nacional de Antropología e Historia, I shall use the newly adopted name for the three volumes, "Códice Chimalphahin." Christie's borrowed the title "Codex Chimalpahin" from the two-volume edition of the third manuscript volume, translated and edited by Susan Schroeder and Arthur Anderson, *Codex Chimalpahin*, which includes the *Historia o chronica mexicana* by Chimalpahin (1997). This is also the name, though in Spanish, that is being used for all three volumes of the manuscripts since their repatriation to Mexico.
4. "ARCHIVE, 1490. Taken from the late-Latin *archivum*, and that taken from the Greek *arkheion* 'residency of the magistrates,' 'archive,' derived from *arkhe* 'command,' 'office of magistrate'" [ARCHIVO, 1490. Tom. del lat. tardío *archivum*, y éste del gr. *arkheion* "residencia de los magistrados," "archivo," deriv. de *arkhe* "mando," "magistratura"] (Corominas 1961, 59).
5. In recent decades, historians have also revisited the topic of archives and the documents they hold. In *Fiction in the Archives: Pardon Tales and Their Tellers in Sixteenth-Century France* (1987), Natalie Zemon Davis opened a new critical approach to archives. She began to read archival documents and the stories they held as "fictional," invoking "the broader sense of the root word *fingere*" and the texts' "forming, shaping, and molding elements: the crafting of a narrative" (3). Other key studies that attempt to reevaluate the historian's relationships with the archive are Carolyn Steedman's *Dust: The Archive and Cultural History* (2002) and Ann Laura Stoler's *Along the Archival Grain: Epistemic Anxieties and Colonial Common Sense* (2009). In *Into the Archive: Writing and Power in Colonial Peru*

(2010), Kathryn Burns studies notarial practices and sheds light on the individuals whose labor formed the archive in colonial Cuzco. Each of these innovative and provocative works attempts to tease out new stories from administrative archives by both finding new historical information and reassessing the way historical experience was created.

6. Gabriel López de Sigüenza announced in the opening line of his prefatory letter to Antonio de Aunzibai that his uncle composed the poem when he was twenty-three years old (Sigüenza 2008 [1700], 81).

7. The passage is taken from the preface by Gabriel López de Sigüenza to Carlos de Sigüenza y Góngora's posthumously published *Oriental planeta evangélico: Epopeya sacro-panegyrica al apostol grande de las Indias, S. Francisco Xavier* (1700). Antonio Lorente Medina published a new edition of *Oriental planeta evangélico* in 2008; his source was a copy of the original published text that is now part of the Genaro García Collection in the Nettie Lee Benson Library at the University of Texas at Austin. The complete copy from the Benson Library is available for reading through Google Books (*books.google.com*).

8. Schroeder discusses in great detail the professional relationship and friendship between Mora and Thomson in "Father José María Luis Mora, Liberalism, and the British and Foreign Bible Society in Nineteenth-Century Mexico" (1994).

9. As part of his extensive study of the Boturini collection, John B. Glass offers an analysis of the legal proceedings against Boturini, along with a transcription of the case itself (1979). Jorge Cañizares-Esguerra provides an informative study of Boturini in his study of eighteenth-century historiography on the New World, *How to Write the History of the New World* (2001). See especially "Historiography and Patriotism in Spain" (130–203), in which Cañizares-Esguerra focuses on Boturini's position vis-à-vis the European historians.

10. Glass studies the influence of Boturini's manuscript copies of Alva Ixtlilxochitl's texts on later copies and published editions (1979, 2:101–78; 1981). O'Gorman enumerates the extant copies of Alva Ixtlilxochitl's texts in "Inventario de manuscritos" (1975–1977, 2:237–43).

11. Ayer Ms. 1109 at the Newberry Library in Chicago contains Boturini's manuscript copy of *Sumaria relación de todas las cosas que han sucedido en la Nueva España, Relación sucinta en forma de memorial,* and *Sumaria relación de la historia general de esta Nueva España.* Ayer Ms. 1109 also contains the three documents that are found in volume 2 of Códice Chimalpahin.

12. Notably, the one image of the manuscripts that appears in *Historical Catalogue of the Manuscripts of Bible House Library* is clearly in Chimalpahin's hand and comes from the *Historia o chronica mexicana* (Jesson 1982, 191). The *Chronica mexicana* has come to be known as the *Crónica mexicayotl* and for centuries has been attributed to don Fernando de Alvarado Tezozomoc (1525–1610). In "The Truth about the *Crónica mexicayotl*," Susan Schroeder offers a reassessment of the authorship of *Chronica mexicana* in which she names Chimalpahin as the author (2011).

13. Ruwet contributed a carefully prepared description of the contents of all three volumes to *Codex Chimalpahin*. Volumes 1 and 2 contain the manuscripts of Alva Ixtlilxochitl's five historical texts. Bracketing off the titles of texts that have been renamed over the centuries, Ruwet lists in volume 1: [*Historia de la nación chichimeca*] (folios 1–143) and [*Compendio histórico del reino de Texcoco*] (folios 147–214r); and, in volume 2: *Sumaria relación de las cosas de Nueva España* (folios 1–17r), *Sumaria relación de la historia de esta Nueva España* (folios 17v–81v), and [*Relación sucinta en forma de memorial*] (folios 161–75). The most developed and well known of Alva Ixtlilxochitl's works, *Historia de la nación chichimeca*, was named thus in the eighteenth century by Mariano Fernández de Echeverría y Veytia (Alva Ixtlilxochitl 1975–1977, 1:214–15; Glass 1981, 158–60). In the manuscript, the text is titled "Sumaria relación." As with volume 3, there are numerous unrelated texts included in the first two volumes, among them the autograph manuscript of *Suma y epíloga de toda la descripción de Tlaxcala* by Diego Muñoz Camargo (ca. 1529–1599) (Ruwet 1997, 17–24). In 1994, Andrea Martínez Baracs and Carlos Sempat Assadourian published an edition of *Suma epíloga de toda la descripción de Tlaxcala* for which Wayne Ruwet wrote the prologue.

14. For a discussion of the original Alva Ixtlilxochitl manuscripts found in the "Códice Chimalpahin," see Brian (2014). Published months before the sale of the Bible Society volumes to INAH, the essay refers to the materials as BSMS 374.

15. This document is mentioned in Ruwet's "Physical Description of the Manuscripts," but he does not name the author (1997, 20–21).

16. As with the notes in the *Sumaria relación*, Ruwet simply mentions "two unfoliated pages of notes (loose)" but does not name Sigüenza as the author of them (1997, 20).

17. James Lockhart provides the following definition of the Nahuatl term *altepetl*: "Any sovereign state; in central Mexico, generally the local ethnic

states the Spaniards were to call pueblos. They became municipalities after the conquest and are sometimes called towns in this book" (1992, 607).

18. The handwriting used in the *Relación de Tetzcoco* manuscript matches that known to be Alva Ixtlilxochitl's in his autograph manuscripts and in signed legal documents. In his edition of *Relación de Tetzcoco*, René Acuña arrived at the same conclusion (Pomar 1986).

19. This text, titled *Testimonio que dan el gobernador, alcaldes, regidores del pueblo de San Salvador Quatlacinco del año de mil seiscientos ocho, el día diez y ocho de noviembre, a don Fernando de Alva Cortés*, is not present in the original Alva Ixtlilxochitl manuscripts. It was apparently copied by Boturini and then again by Veytia, who includes the testimony from the local leaders after his transcription of the *Compendio*. Veytia's manuscript copy, cataloged as Ayer Ms. 1108 (folios 260v–274r), is now located at the Newberry Library in Chicago.

20. There are many variants in colonial documents for the spelling of the Purépecha leader's title: *Cazonci* is the most common, but also found are *Caltzontzin* and *Casulci* (López Sarrelangue 1999 [1965], 31). The leader is exclusively referred to by his title in the document found in the "Códice Chimalpahin," and this is in keeping with most documentation related to the Caçolçi (Cazonci). Krippner-Martínez offers an insightful study of the court records related to the Nuño de Guzmán trial (2001).

21. Stephanie Wood, in discussing Indian women historians, mentions that there is an image of doña Bartola in the Codex Cardona (Wood 2003, 153n10).

22. Miguel Sánchez Lamego published an edition of the map and its history in *El primer mapa general de México elaborado por un mexicano* (1955). For an updated analysis of Sigüenza's maps, see Trabulse (1988).

23. Ernest J. Burrus (1959) outlined the eighteenth- and nineteenth-century sources that make reference to Sigüenza's collection of native-authored manuscripts.

24. Citing León y Gama, Trabulse also indicates that the *Códice Ixtlilxochitl* carried the label "Fragmentos de historia mexicana" (Trabulse 1988, 31).

25. While exiled in Italy, Clavijero first wrote the text in Spanish and then in Italian, the language in which it was first published in 1780. Working from the original Spanish manuscript, Mariano Cuevas published an edition of the Spanish text in 1964.

26. Clavijero explicitly asserts his authority against that of the European authors in several passages like this one: "Neither Buffon, nor Pauw, nor

Robertson, nor many other European authors know how to understand the founding of those nations from Anahuac, from which many centuries before they had had in the northern countries of the New World" [Ni Buffon, ni Paw, ni Robertson, ni otros muchos autores europeos saben distinguir el establecimiento de aquellas naciones de Anáhuac, del que muchos siglos antes habían tenido en los países septentrionales del Nuevo Mundo] (1964 [1780], 459).

27. Guillermo Bonfil Batalla suggests a provocative definition of *indio* in his article "El concepto del indio en América: Una categoría de la situación colonial," where he argues that the most important factor in subsuming the many types of native people under the single category of Indian is not race, ethnicity, or class but their subordinate position in colonial society: "The category of Indian, in effect, is a supraethnic category that does not denote any specific content about the groups that it covers, but rather a particular relationship between them and other sectors in the global colonial system of which the Indians form a part. The category of Indian denotes the condition of colonized and makes necessary reference to the colonial relationship" [La categoría de indio, en efecto, es una categoría supraétnica que no denota ningún contenido específico de los grupos que abarca, sino una particular relación entre ellos y otros sectores del sistema social global del que los indios forman parte. La categoría de indio denota la condición de colonizado y hace referencia necesaria a la relación colonial] (1972, 110). In *Peru's Indian Peoples and the Challenge of Spanish Conquest*, Steve Stern offers a similar analysis: "This book tells how conquest transformed vigorous native peoples of the Andean sierra into an inferior cast of 'Indians' subordinated to Spanish colonizers and Europe's creation of a world market" (1993, xvii).

Chapter 2

Epigraph. Sigüenza (1684), 128v.

1. Edmundo O'Gorman suggests that don Juan de Alva Cortés died between 1680 and 1682 (1975–1977, 1:41), while Guido Munch gives 1684 as the date of his death (1976, 52). The permissions for the publication of *Parayso occidental* (1684) were secured in 1682, which suggests that O'Gorman's earlier range of dates is most likely more accurate, since it would seem that Sigüenza wrote, or at least completed, *Parayso occidental* after don Juan's death.

2. See Borah for a discussion of the cacique as a *señor natural*, who "as counterpart to European feudal seigneurs were to continue governing and judging the natives" (1983, 18). The term *señor natural* has roots in Spain. Robert Chamberlain has defined the *señor natural* "as a lord who, by inherent nature of superior qualities, goodness, and virtue, and by birth of superior station, attains power legitimately and exercises dominion over all within his lands justly and in accord with divine, natural, and human law and reason, being universally accepted, recognized, and obeyed by his vassals and subjects and acknowledged by other lords and their peoples as one who rightfully possesses his office and rightfully wields authority within his territory" (1939, 130).

3. Published documents related to the cacicazgo of San Juan Teotihuacan can be found in Fernández de Recas (1961, 113–25), O'Gorman's two-volume edition of Alva Ixtlilxochitl's works (Alva Ixtlilxochitl 1975–1977, 2:279–402), Munch (1976), and Pérez-Rocha and Tena (2000, 201–10; 261–79; 379–404). Many of these publications are drawn from Archivo General de la Nación (Mexico City) Vínculos y Mayorazgos (AGN-V), volume 232. This volume is in poor condition and its original organization is difficult to follow, as the folios have been shifted around throughout the centuries. There are multiple foliations found on individual sheets: some are marked in pen and some in pencil. When possible I shall cite from the published editions that contain these documents; when I do cite directly from the archival documents, I shall cite the foliation in pen.

4. In a law from February 27, 1538, the Crown expressly prohibited the use of *señor* by elite natives: "We prohibit caciques from using the title *señor of the town*, because this pleases us and our royal authority. We ask of the viceroys, audiencia, and governors that they not allow or permit it, but rather they can only call themselves *caciques* or *principales*" [Prohibimos a los caciques que se puedan llamar o intitular señores de los pueblos, porque así conviene a nuestro servicio y preeminencia real. Y mandamos a los virreyes, audiencia y gobernadores, que no le consienten, ni permitan y solamente puedan llamarse caciques o principales] (*Recopilación* 1681, volume 2, folio 220r). Though presumably this mandate was an attempt to make clear the distinction between the nobility of the Old World and the native nobility of the New World, *señor* and *cacique* as well as *señorío* and *cacicazgo* were used interchangeably. For additional studies of cacicazgos, see Fernández de Recas (1961), Chance (1994), and Menegus Bornemann and Aguirre Salvador (2005).

5. Don Fernando de Alva Ixtlilxochitl wrote a lengthy treatment of Ixtlilxo-chitl's activities during the conquest in his "Thirteenth Relation" of the *Compendio histórico* (ca. 1608), where he described Ixtlilxochitl as "the greatest and most loyal ally [Cortés] had in this land and whose aid in winning this land was second only to God's" (Alva Ixtlilxochitl 2015, 45).

6. As part of a petition for a coat of arms, don Francisco Verdugo Quetzal-mamalitzin Huetzin stated that his father and other relatives had served Cortés in the conquest of New Spain and that he himself had served in the conquest and pacification of Nueva Galicia with Nuño de Guzmán (Alva Ixtlilxochitl 1975–1977, 2:279). These deeds are also addressed in a letter to King Philip II (Pérez-Rocha and Tena 2000, 201).

7. For studies on Indians and the law in colonial Mexico see the following: Borah (1983); Kellogg (1995); Owensby (2008); Ruiz Medrano (2010); Yannakakis (2013); and van Deusen (2015).

8. As Brian Owensby has remarked, "in calling them *indios*, Spaniards were not merely recognizing and naming an existing difference between themselves and these New World others, so much as they were creating new categories: they were 'inventing' the Indians and thus themselves in relation to the Indians" (2008, 24).

9. Upon invoking this term, Woodrow Borah cites a lengthy passage from the sixteenth-century audiencia judge Alonso de Zorita that describes and laments the rise in suits brought by Indians (1983, 40–42).

10. The portrait of doña Ana Ixtlilxochitl, drawn on the back side of a legal document that carries a seal from 1684, has been inserted among eighteenth-century documents related to the cacicazgo of San Juan Teotihuacan. It is likely that a later petitioner submitted the portrait as part of a request to the court of the king. There is a clue as to the original location of the portrait in AGN-V volume 232, where there is a compan-ion portrait of a man, drawn with the same pen and ink and in the same style. A twentieth-century reader, using a blue ballpoint pen, inscribed on the portrait "portrait of don Diego de Alva" [retrato de don Diego de Alva], though there is no evidence to support that claim.

11. Doña Josefa Antonia de Alva y Cortés, an eighteenth-century female descendant of doña Ana Cortés Ixtlilxochitl, claimed her right to inherit the role of cacica by citing doña Ana as an earlier example of a female leader of the cacicazgo (AGN-V volume 232, folio 659).

12. For studies of the role of women in Alva Ixtlilxochitl's texts, see Kellogg (2013) and Townsend (2014). For a very instructive biographical sketch

of Alva Ixtlilxochitl, with details about his parents and grandparents, see Townsend (2014).

13. Doña Ana Cortés Ixtlilxochitl named two executors in her will: don Fernando de Alva Ixtlilxochitl and one of his younger brothers, don Bartolomé de Alva (Munch 1976, 50). These two were her most educated and literate children, and perhaps for that reason she named them as executors. Doña Ana herself was unable to read or write (Munch 1976, 50).

14. Some of these documents have been published previously (Alva Ixtlilxochitl 1975–1977, 2:371–402; Munch 1976, 44–57). I shall cite additional archival documents that confirm Sigüenza's involvement and provide further insights into his role in the cacicazgo struggles.

15. Martínez's study has direct bearing on the case of the San Juan Teotihuacan cacicazgo. In fact, she takes up the institution of the cacicazgo and in her estimation, the "cacicazgo, which established the legal framework for the entailment of indigenous estates and thus also for the perpetuation of native wealth, property, and status, fused pre-Hispanic and Castilian traditions" (2008, 108). She briefly addresses the cacicazgo of Alva Ixtlilxochitl's family as well as his historical writings (114–15).

16. Martínez (2008) explores these topics in two complementary book chapters, titled "Nobility and Purity in the *República de Indios*" (91–122) and "Nobility and Purity in the *República de Españoles*" (123–41). In the first of these chapters, she focuses on the case of don Fernando de Alva Ixtlilxochitl, among those of other privileged Indian and mestizo figures from sixteenth- and seventeenth-century New Spain.

17. The *Recopilación de las leyes de los reynos de las Indias* (1681) has a section dedicated to laws related to caciques; it describes seventeen laws dating from 1537 to 1628 (2:219v–221v).

18. Mörner cites Woodrow Borah's monumental study of the demographic changes in New Spain, which indicates that between 1565 and 1650 the population of Indians in Central Mexico dropped precipitously from 4,409,000 to 1,500,000 (Mörner 1967, 98).

19. Cope illustrates this observation with the following remark about the capital of New Spain: "A spatial analysis of central Mexico City thus reveals a vertically segregated society, divided primarily along class rather than racial lines" (1994, 32).

20. Borah and Cook's *The Aboriginal Population of Central Mexico on the Eve of the Spanish Conquest* suggests that the native population of Mexico in 1519 was twenty-five million (1963, 88–90).

21. "To the viceroy and the *Audiencia* [High Court] in Mexico City, may justice be upheld in reference to the petition by don Juan de Alvarado and the rest of the natives from the city of Tetzcoco, who are descendants of Nezahualpilli; they ask that lands within the city limits that are now held by many Spaniards be returned and restored to them" [Al virrey y Audiencia de México, que hagan justicia cerca de lo que don Joan de Alvarado y los demás naturales de la ciudad de Tezcuco, descendientes de Nezahualpilcintli, piden sobre que se les vuelvan y restituyan las tierras que dejó en término de la dicha ciudad, que poseen muchos españoles] (Alva Ixtlilxochitl 1975–1977, 2:293).

22. O'Gorman suggested in his "Hipótesis de una cronología" that the *Sumaria relación de todas las cosas que han sucedido en esta Nueva España* was written prior to the *Compendio histórico del reino de Texcoco* (1975–1977, 1:229–33). Since it is generally accepted that the *Compendio* was finished by 1608, it would be unlikely that the *Sumaria relación* predated it, given the clues provided to its date of production by the coincidence of Gabriel de Segovia in the legal document from 1611, just a year before his name appeared in the *Sumaria relación*. It would now appear more likely that the *Sumaria relación* was written after the *Compendio histórico*.

23. Edmundo O'Gorman published this document in the second of his two-volume edition of don Fernando de Alva Ixtlilxochitl's works. The decree is directed at the viceroy of New Spain, the Marqués de Guadal-cázar. In it the king names Alva Ixtlilxochitl and records the deeds of his family that will earn him a royal dispensation: "Don Fernando de Alva Ixtlilxochitl is . . . the great-great-grandson of don Fernando Ixtlilxochitl and Nezahualpilli, who were lords of the city of Tetzcoco, one of the three capitals of this New Spain. . . . When don Hernando Cortés, Marqués del Valle, went there, the said great-great-grandfather went out to receive him peacefully and offer him his loyalty, receiving baptism . . . and at his expense he helped the said marqués in the conquest and pacification of Mexico City with many of his vassals. . . . Taking into consideration the above, my wish is that the said don Fernando de Alva Ixtlilxochitl receive grace and favor" [Don Fernando de Alva Ixtilsúchil es . . . bisnieto de don Fernando Ixtilsúchil, y Mesagalpilzintli [*sic*], que fueron señores naturales de la ciudad de Texcuco, una de las tres cabeceras, de esa Nueva España. . . . Cuando fue a ella don Hernando Cortés, marqués del Valle, el dicho su bisabuelo le salió a recibir de paz y le dio la obediencia, recibi-endo el santo bautismo . . . y a su costa y mención ayudó al dicho marqués

en la conquista y pacificación de esa ciudad de México con muchos de sus
vasallos. . . . Teniendo en consideración a lo sobre dicho, mi voluntad es
que el dicho don Fernando de Alva Ixtilsúchil reciba merced y favor] (Alva
Ixtlilxochitl 1975–1977, 2:343).

24. For an analysis of the *relación de méritos y servicios*, see Macleod (1998)
and Adorno (1997).

25. The names of the five Spaniards were Damián Pérez Delgadillo, Martín
Delgadillo, Diego Gómez, Francisco Díaz Calderón, and Andrés de las
Nabas. The petitions and decrees associated with the legal proceedings
from 1643 can be found in Alva Ixtlilxochitl (1975–1977, 2:344–69).

26. Sigüenza's will was published with other assorted documents as an
appendix to the biography written by Francisco Pérez Salazar, *Biografía de
don Carlos de Sigüenza y Góngora* (1928).

27. Munch includes a summary of these complaints and excerpts from some
of the petitions (1976, 30–31).

28. This passage from Sigüenza has been influential on the assessment of Aztec
vestal virgins by art historian James Córdova (2009). Pilar Alberti Manzanares (1994) engages with Sigüenza's representation of *cihuatlamacazque*,
specifically in the context of two unpublished manuscripts that drew from
the discussion of the topic in his *Parayso occidental*.

29. See 1 Timothy 1:17.

30. Alva Ixtlilxochitl described his informants and their access to historical
knowledge within the text (1975–1977, 1:285–88).

31. Brading's emphasis on the importance of Alva Ixtlilxochitl's collection to
later creole scholars is eloquently taken up in recent studies by literary
critic Anna More, in *Baroque Sovereignty: Carlos de Sigüenza y Góngora
and the Creole Archive of Colonial Mexico* (2013). As with Brading, More's
focus is on the symbolic function of Sigüenza's access to and use of the
native materials that were in large part inherited from Alva Ixtlilxochitl in
the emergence of creole patriotism in seventeenth-century Mexico.

Chapter 3

1. *The Historian's Craft* was unfinished when Bloch was captured and
murdered by the Gestapo outside Lyon in the summer of 1944. *Apologie
pour l'Histoire, ou Métier d'Historien* was published in 1949 and in English
translation by Peter Putnam as *The Historian's Craft* in 1954. The epigraph
is taken from chapter 2, "Historical observation," where Bloch emphasizes

that knowledge of the past is indirect and thus he makes the point that it is essential for historians to be transparent in their use of sources (71).

2. O'Gorman's edition was based on copies of Alva Ixtlilxochitl's original works, as he did not have access to the original manuscripts, because their location was not widely known until a decade after the publication of his edition. Lorenzo Boturini Benaduci was the first to copy Alva Ixtlilxochitl's manuscripts, and he mentions them in *Catalogo del Musèo Indiano*, which follows Boturini's *Idea de una nueva historia* in the 1746 edition of that work.

3. In his edition of Alva Ixtlilxochitl's complete works, Edmundo O'Gorman includes a list of cited texts and authors (1975–1977, 1:78–85).

4. At the end of the *Sumaria relación de las cosas de la Nueva España*, Alva Ixtlilxochitl provides the names and other vital information of some of his informants (1975–1977, 1:286).

5. Pomar's *Relación de Tetzcoco* is an example of a *relación geográfica*. In 1577, Juan López de Velasco, the lead cosmographer and chronicler of the Council of the Indies, sent out to towns and villages throughout the Indies a three-page questionnaire whose fifty questions aimed to gather all manner of information about the lands of the New World. The responses, known as *relaciones geográficas*, were produced in the form of texts and maps. For studies of these materials, see Acuña (1982–1988, volumes 1–10) and Mundy (1996).

6. In the opening of the *Relación de Tetzcoco*, Pomar says that soon after Cortés arrived "they burned Nezahualpilli's royal houses, where there was a large room that was the general archive of their papers on which were painted all the ancient things; now his descendants cry with great emotion for having been left in the dark without news or memory of the deeds of their ancestors. . . . They burned them for fear of Fray Juan de Zumárraga, the first archbishop of Mexico, so that he would not interpret them as idolatrous" [se las q[ue]maron en las casas reales de NEZAHUALPILTZ-INTLI, en un gran aposento q[ue] era el archivo general de sus papeles, en que estaban pintadas todas sus cosas antiguas, que hoy día lloran sus descendientes con mucho sentimiento, por haber q[ue]dado como a oscuras sin noticia ni memoria de los hechos de sus pasados. . . . Los q[ue]maron de temor de D[ON] FRAY JUAN DE ZUMARRAGA, primer arzobispo de *México*, por[que] no los atribuyese a cosas de idolatría] (1986, 46).

7. "Time changed all of this. With the fall of the kings and the nobles mentioned above, the travails and persecutions of their descendants and

the calamity suffered by their underlings and vassals" [todo lo cual mudó el tiempo con la caída de los reyes y señores, y [con] los trabajos y persecuciones de sus descendientes y la calamidad de sus súbditos y vasallos] (Alva Ixtlilxochitl 1975–1977, 1:527).

8. Covarrubias concludes the entry on *tradución* (translation) with these words: "About this, Horace, in his *Art of Poetry*, cautioned emphatically, saying: Faithful interpreter, take care not to translate word for word" [Esto advirtió bien Horacio, en su Arte poética, diziendo: *Nec verbum verbo curabis reddere fidus Interpres*] (1943 [1611], 972).

9. Here we may recall the impact of Barbara Cassin's *Dictionary of Untranslatables: A Philosophical Lexicon* (2014), a project on presumably untranslatable philosophical terms, which has resulted in a multidisciplinary collaboration by scholars based in Europe and the United States. Cassin's delineation of the term "untranslatable" had a direct impact on the study of colonial Mexico in Alessandra Russo's *The Untranslatable Image: A Mestizo History of the Arts in New Spain, 1500–1600* (2014), which addresses the merging of European and native artistic and visual traditions.

10. Trouillot has emphasized that the past can be silenced at four points in the process of writing history: "the moment of fact creation (the making of *sources*); the moment of fact assembly (the making of *archives*); the moment of fact retrieval (the making of *narratives*); and the moment of retrospective significance (the making of *history* in the final instance)" (1995, 26).

11. In his section on historical literature in *Historia de la literatura náhuatl*, Garibay discusses the works of Fray Diego Durán, don Fernando Alvarado Tezozomoc, Diego Muñoz Camargo, Fray Juan Tovar, and don Fernando de Alva Ixtlilxochitl (1971, 2:291–313). He emphasizes that his interest is in the "literary value" of their texts rather than their "documentary or historical value" (2:292).

12. Adorno's work on Alva Ixtlilxochitl first started to take shape in the late 1980s. In two articles published in 1989, she demonstrated how Alva Ixtlilxochitl engaged with the European discourse of Christian militancy (*la milicia cristiana*) in order to incorporate his own ancestors into the prevailing historical narrative of the conquest (1989a and 1989b). These two articles are also very significant because they represent early attempts to incorporate Alva Ixtlilxochitl into a critical and scholarly discussion of intellectual production by native or mestizo writers. In *The Polemics of Possession in Spanish American Narrative* Adorno again takes up the works

of Alva Ixtlilxochitl, though more explicitly in relation to her overall analysis of struggles for sovereignty in colonial texts (2007, 137–46).

13. "The 'letters' from Titu Cusi and Guaman Poma or, in Mexico, the 'Historical Compendium of the Kingdom of Tetzcoco' by Ixtlilxochitl, constitute the true beginning of an Indian-Hispanic writing. . . . These texts offer, articulated in an unedited fashion, two contributions, the European and the indigenous, a new point of view, initially 'subjective,' about the world" [Las "cartas" de Titu Cusi y de Guaman Poma o, en México, el "Compendio histórico del reino de Texcoco" de Ixtlilxóchitl, constituyen el verdadero comienzo de una escritura indo-hispánica. . . . Estos textos ofrecen, articulando de modo inédito los dos aportes, el europeo y el indígena, un punto de vista nuevo, incipientemente "subjetivo," sobre el mundo] (Lienhard 1991, 52).

14. "[They] affirmed to the Spaniards the Indian blood that ran in their veins, taking care to point out that it was noble blood. But culturally they were not nor did they feel like Indians" (Florescano 1994 [1987], 126) [Asumieron ante los españoles la sangre india que corría por sus venas, cuidando de señalar que era sangre noble. Pero culturalmente no eran ni se sentían indios] (382–83).

15. In the second part of the *Comentarios reales*, known as the *Historia general del Perú*, Garcilaso de la Vega, "El Inca," proudly announces himself to the reader as a mestizo: "Full-throated, I call myself [mestizo] and I am honored to be so" [Me lo llamo yo a boca llena y me honro con él] (2007, 253).

16. Alva Ixtlilxochitl has garnered significant critical attention recently from scholars in history, literature, and anthropology, and this work has tended to rely less heavily on the descriptor "mestizo," instead locating his written work and his professional activities in a specific historical, social, political and discursive context. The 2014 special issue on don Fernando de Alva Ixtlilxochitl published by *Colonial Latin American Review* offers examples of recent approaches to his work (Benton 2014; Brian 2014; García Loaeza 2014; Kauffman 2014; Townsend 2014; Villella 2014). An interdisciplinary volume of essays focused on Alva Ixtlilxochitl and his work and impact, coedited by Jongsoo Lee and Galen Brokaw, is forthcoming. Lee and Brokaw also published a volume dedicated to Tetzcoco, in which Alva Ixtlilxochitl is regularly discussed (2014). Additionally, Bradley Benton, Pablo García Loaeza, and I have produced a scholarly edition and translation of Alva Ixtlilxochitl's "Thirteenth Relation" (Alva

Ixtlilxochitl 2015), and this group with Peter Villella is undertaking a translation and scholarly edition of Alva Ixtlilxochitl's *Historia de la nación chichimeca*, with support from a National Endowment for the Humanities Scholarly Editions and Translations Grant. Benton, Villella, and Leisa Kauffmann are also in the process of completing and publishing monographs that address aspects of Alva Ixtlilxochitl's life and works.

17. As I have noted in an essay that addresses Alva Ixtlilxochitl's original manuscripts, this dedication and the following prologue precede the *Historia de la nación chichimeca* in the original (Brian 2014, 99). Recognizing that earlier transcriptions and editions had placed the dedication and prologue before the *Historia de la nación chichimeca*, O'Gorman asserted in a footnote that he believed the introductory pieces belonged with the *Sumaria relación de la historia general de esta Nueva España* (1975–1977, 1:525). As the dedication is addressed to 'Illmo. Señor,' a form of address generally reserved for the archbishop, O'Gorman concludes that the text was intended for Archbishop don Juan Pérez de la Serna and that we can then date the text to 1625, the last year of his service (1:232). Since the dedication and prologue clearly accompany the *Historia de la nación chichimeca* in the original manuscripts, the dating of both texts and the significance of the prefatory pieces will need to be revisited.

18. John Frederick Schwaller doubts the claim that Alva Ixtlilxochitl studied at the Colegio de Santa Cruz de Santiago Tlatelolco since he was not "a full-blooded native" (Sell and Schwaller 1999, 5). See also Townsend (2014). Rocío Cortés places Alva Ixtlilxochitl along with Tezozomoc and Chimalpahin in the "post-Colegio generation" that was "connected to the intellectual Franciscan-Jesuit circle on native research" (2008, 98).

19. At the beginning of each volume, Torquemada included a list of authors cited.

20. In his study *Xenophon's Imperial Fiction*, James Tatum states that "Xenophon provided humanists with a crucial text for princes and their tutors, just as he already had instructed the dynasts of ancient Greece and Rome" (1989, 8–9). According to Xenophon, through the course of his childhood and early adulthood, Cyrus develops the essential characteristics of an effective leader and with these he successfully conquers vast territories, including Media, the lands controlled by his grandfather Astyages, the king of the Medes. For extended discussions of Xenophon's *Education of Cyrus* and the mirror of princes genre, see Nadon (2001) and Gray (2011).

21. Though Machiavelli wrote *The Prince* in 1513, the text was not published until 1531, four years after the author's death. Robert Bireley attests to the popularity of *The Prince* by enumerating the fifteen editions of it that were published between 1531 and 1559, the year the text was placed on the *Index librorum prohibitorum* (Bireley 1990, 5).

22. Emblematic literature was a fashionable current in baroque prose across Europe. All emblem literature from the sixteenth and seventeenth centuries was composed of three elements—the image, the motto, and the exposition on the theme. Andrea Alciati's *Emblematum Libellus* (1531) was influential for Saavedra Fajardo and other emblematists from the Hispanic world. For more on Alciati, see Mario Praz (1964).

23. In *Ballads of the Lords of New Spain*, John Bierhorst's translation of the *Romances de los Señores de la Nueva España*, Bierhorst comments on Alva Ixtlilxochitl's portrayal of Nezahualcoyotl as a poet and a humanist. In this context he offers an alternate transcription of the Nahuatl phrase quoted in Alva Ixtlilxochitl (*Ipan in chiucnauhtlamanpan mitztica in tloque nahuaque ipalnemohuani teyocoyani icelteotl oquiyocox in ixquich quexquich mitta in amotta*), as well as an English translation of that passage: "He who dwells above the nine levels [of the other world], the Ever Present, the Ever New, Life Giver, Creator, Only Spirit, who created all that is seen and is not seen." Bierhorst then comments that "the passage is not from the *Cantares* or the *Romances*; it bears the stamp of Christian influence and is possibly from a now-lost literary composition inspired by the *netotiliztli* [a specific form of Nahuatl song]" (2009, 22n62).

24. A facsimile edition of Fray Alonso de Molina's *Vocabulario en lengua castellana y mexicana y mexicana y castellana* was published by Porrúa in 1992.

25. León-Portilla gives the following etymological explanation of this term: "*In Tloque in Nahuaque* derives from the two base words, *tloc* and *náhuac*. *Tloc* means 'near' . . . *Náhuac* is, literally, 'in the circuit of' or 'in the ring.' . . . The personal possessive suffix *e*, which is appended to both these adverbial forms (*tloqu-e* and *Nahuaqu-e*), connotes that 'being near' and the 'circuit' or 'ring' are 'of him.' . . . Garibay, bringing Nahuatl thought closer to our own mental atmosphere, rendered it as 'the one who is near to everything and to whom everything is near'" (1963, 92–93).

26. For detailed studies of the provenance of the *Codex Ixtlilxochitl*, see Durand-Forest (1976) and Boone (1983).

Chapter 4

Epigraph. Sigüenza 1995 [1684], c2.

1. I thank Kenneth Ward for sharing with me his transcription of this document from the AGN that illuminates Sigüenza's role in the Inquisition at the end of his life.

2. Leonard begins to develop this analysis of Sigüenza in his 1929 biography, *Don Carlos de Sigüenza y Góngora: A Mexican Savant of the Seventeenth Century.* Leonard offers a more fully developed depiction of this period in his now classic 1959 text, *Baroque Times in Old Mexico.*

3. Leonard's translation can be found in *Don Carlos de Sigüenza y Góngora* under the heading "Appendix B," with the caption "Letter of Don Carlos de Sigüenza to Admiral Pez Recounting the Incidents of the Corn Riot in Mexico City, June 8, 1692" (1929, 210–77). In 1932, Leonard published the first Spanish edition under the title *Alboroto y motín de los indios de México.* The copy of Sigüenza's letter that Leonard worked with for his translation and edition is housed at the Bancroft Library at the University of California, Berkeley (Bancroft Mss M-M 226). On the first folio, under the title, *Alboroto y motin de los Indios de Mexco*, we find a note in Sigüenza's hand: "Copy of the letter of don Carlos de Sigüenza y Góngora, cosmographer of the king in New Spain, professor of mathematics at the Royal University and chaplain at the Hospital Amor de Dios in the city. In which he explains to Admiral don Andrés de Pez about the uprising" [Copia de la carta de D. Carlos de Sigüenza y Góngora, cosmographo del Rey en la N. España. Cathedratico de Mathematicas en la R^l Universi^d y capellan mayor del Hospital Rl de Amor de Dios de la ciudad en q le da razon al Almirante Don Andres de Pez del tumulto].

4. Leonard generally follows Sigüenza's explanation, which states that the riot was incited because of a severe corn shortage. Basing his summation on archival materials, Cope asserts that "plebeian participants, in contrast, show little concern for the causes of the riot, which they viewed as largely inexplicable" (1994, 160).

5. *Alboroto y motín* has been the object of various incisive literary analyses. In his study of the text, Cogdell (1994) emphasizes a paradox in Sigüenza's writings, where the ancient indigenous figures are treated with great admiration while the living native inhabitants of New Spain are despised. Rabasa (1994b) performs a subaltern reading of the letter and finds evidence of insurgency in what he views as Sigüenza's counterinsurgent rant. Extending the counterreading in another direction, Moraña (2000)

salvages a resistant voice from what she reads as Sigüenza's hegemonic representation of the events. Recent scholarship has begun to complicate these binary readings where affiliations appear to be clear and clearly opposed. More (2013) teases out a subtle reading of the shifts in creole ideas of communities, while Nemser (2014) uses the text as a point of entry into a study of the physicality and materiality of Mexico City.

6. Tavárez offers an insightful discussion of the works and efforts of Villavicencio in *The Invisible War: Indigenous Devotions, Discipline, and Dissent in Colonial Mexico*, his study of native spiritual practices in the postconquest period (2011, 179–83).

7. One group of graduate students who read this text with me went so far as to dub him "Super Sigüenza" for the actions he claims to have taken during the riots to save Mexico's cultural patrimony. Among this group, I especially thank Pablo Balbontín, Braeden Jones, Leda Lozier, and Sergio Salazar for focusing our collective attention on Sigüenza's unusual self-representation.

8. For a study of this ritual, see Mañé (1955). Octavio Paz relies heavily on Mañé in his description of the triumphal arch and the viceregal entrée into the capital in "Ritos políticos," a chapter in *Sor Juana Inés de la Cruz, o Las trampas de la fe* (1982). Paz published an earlier version of the chapter as an essay, "Ritos políticos en la Nueva España" (1979).

9. For more extensive studies of *Teatro de virtudes*, see Paz (1982), Lorente Medina (1996), García Loaeza (2009), More (2013), and Adorno (2014). Essays by Jones (1979) and Merkl (1992) address the arches designed by Sigüenza and Sor Juana and their accompanying texts.

10. Sigüenza undertook two projects before *Teatro de virtudes* that also aim to represent pre-Hispanic native leaders as model Christian princes. *Glorias de Querétaro* (1945 [1680]), published three months before the triumphal arch, celebrates the founding of a church dedicated to the Virgin of Guadalupe in Querétaro, the first outside of Mexico City. In it, Sigüenza documents the history of Querétaro and he recounts a celebratory pageant (*máscara*) of Indians dressed in traditional costume who paraded through the city. The *Noticia chronológica* is a peculiar text consisting of eight printed pages and fourteen manuscript folios. The printed text provides a brief description of pre-Hispanic Mexica leaders through the Marqués de la Laguna, who ruled as viceroy of New Spain from 1680 until 1686. The original copy of *Noticia chronológica* is housed at the Lilly Library at Indiana University. José Porrúa published

a limited edition of thirty copies of the text in 1948 and William Bryant cites selections of the text in his edition of *Teatro de virtudes* (1984c). I thank Wayne Ruwet for sharing his copy of the published edition of *Noticia chronológica* with me. For a discussion of the relation between *Teatro de virtudes*, *Glorias de Querétaro*, and *Noticia chronológica* see More (2013) and Adorno (2014).

11. The characterization of Juan Diego as a native man of humble origins wearing a distinctively indigenous item of clothing is central to the narrative of the Guadalupe apparition story. *Macehual* is the hispanized form of the Nahuatl *macehualli*, meaning "subject, commoner," and *tilma* is the hispanized form of the Nahuatl *tilmahtli*, meaning "cloak, blanket, an indigenous man's garment fastened on one shoulder" (Karttunen 1992, 127; 241).

12. Louise Burkhart clearly and succinctly debunks the connection between the Virgin of Guadalupe and a pre-Hispanic goddess by asserting that "Tonantzin is Mary; Mary is Tonantzin. That Indians used this title for Mary indicates that they viewed her as a maternal figure personally connected with them. To understand what a figure like Our Lady of Guadalupe could mean to them, connections must be sought not to ancient goddesses but to the religious life of Christianized Nahua Indians in the Mexico City area during the second half of the sixteenth century" (2001, 209).

13. There is a deep subfield of Guadalupe studies. Among the many examples of influential studies are Edmundo O'Gorman's *Destierro de sombras: Luz en el origen y culto de Nuestra Señora de Guadalupe de Tepeyac* (1986) and David Brading's *Mexican Phoenix, Our Lady of Guadalupe: Image and Tradition across Five Centuries* (2001).

14. Lisa Sousa, Stafford Poole, and James Lockhart open their introduction to *The Story of Guadalupe: Luis Laso de la Vega's "Huei tlamahuiçoltica" of 1649* with this sentence: "The devotion of Our Lady of Guadalupe is one of the most important elements in the development of a specifically Mexican tradition of religion and nationality over the centuries" (1998, 1).

15. Though there is no evidence of a written version of the apparition story until the middle of the seventeenth century, scholars have found evidence of an indigenous shrine associated with the Virgin from the middle of the sixteenth century (Martínez Baracs 2000)

16. Miguel León-Portilla's *Tonantzin Guadalupe* (2000), a translation and critical edition of the *Nican mopohua* (the apparition story from the *Huei*

tlamahuiçoltica), unequivocally names Antonio Valeriano as the original author. Valeriano is also cited as the true author of the *Nican mopohua* in popular histories oriented to Guadalupe devotees, such as *Our Lady of Guadalupe, Mother of the Civilization of Love* (Anderson and Chávez 2009, 171).

17. The role of the image of Guadalupe in the apparition story is a seventeenth-century innovation, according to Stafford Poole. Of the beliefs around the *tilma* image in the mid-sixteenth century, Poole states: "Whatever the image may have been, it was regarded as miraculous in the sense that it worked miracles, not that it was miraculous in origin" (1995, 63). In an essay on the image, Jeanette Favrot Peterson meticulously explains that the *tilma* painting was produced by the native artist Marcos Cipac de Aquino, who had been educated under the auspices of the Franciscan order at San José de los Naturales. Citing Spanish and Nahuatl texts from the period, Peterson makes the well-grounded argument that the now sacred and iconic *tilma* image was produced by Cipac de Aquino and put on display at Tepeyacac in 1555 or 1556 (2005). For further analysis of the image of Guadalupe, see Peterson (2014).

18. Stafford Poole carefully teases out the essential arguments and sources used in the seventeenth-century Guadalupan narratives (1995, 127–70). Though Becerra Tanco, Florencia, and Sigüenza each argued for a native connection to the Guadalupe story, Poole explains that they do not present Valeriano and Alva Ixtlilxochitl as the authors of the *Huei tlamahuiçoltica*.

19. Sousa, Poole, and Lockhart offer these translations of the titles from the 1649 Nahuatl text (1998).

20. Sousa, Poole, and Lockhart conducted a careful philological analysis and concluded that there is a close relationship between the *Imagen de la Virgen* and the *Huei tlamahuiçoltica* and "a very strong role of Laso de la Vega himself in the composition of the Nahuatl work, going against our expectation that the person primarily responsible for the final version of an ecclesiastical text in older Nahuatl would have been an indigenous aide (or aides)" (1998, 3).

21. Becerra Tanco's 1666 text was given the title *Origen milagroso del Sanuartio de Nuestra Señora de Guadalupe* and that is the title offered for the version of the text found in Torre Villar and Navarro de Anda's *Testimonios históricos guadalupanos* (1982), though they in fact include the 1675 edition. A facsimile edition of *Felicidad de México* (1675) was published in 1979 by Editorial Jus. As Poole has explained, there are significant

differences between the 1666 and 1675 versions (1995, 144–49), which he summarizes as follows: "Becerra Tanco added the identification of the Indian as a graduate of Santa Cruz and suppressed the identification of his Nahuatl 'Relación' with the *Nican mopohua*" (147).

22. "The well-known scholar and historian Carlos de Sigüenza y Góngora offers testimony in which he attributes authorship of the *Nican mopohua* not to Laso de la Vega whose publication he was familiar with, but rather to an Indian of considerable prestige. Regarding this, Sigüenza y Góngora wrote in one of his books: 'I say and I swear that I found this relation [the *Nican mopohua*] among don Fernando de Alva's papers'" [Se debe al conocido erudito e historiador Carlos de Sigüenza y Góngora un testimonio en que atribuye la autoría del *Nican mopohua*, no a Lasso de la Vega cuya publicación conocía, sino a un indígena de considerable prestigio. Acerca de esto Sigüenza y Góngora escribió en uno de sus libros: Digo y juro que esta relación [el *Nican mopohua*] que hallé entre los papeles de don Fernando de Alva] (León-Portilla 2000, 24)

23. "It is important to note that Sigüenza y Góngora did not identify this account with the *Nican mopohua*. He identified it as the original of the Spanish paraphrase that he lent to Florencia, which the latter said had also been used by Becerra Tanco. As has been mentioned, the quotations given by Florencia show that the 'Relación' and the *Nican mopohua* were two different accounts and that the 'Relación' also differed from Becerra Tanco's account" (Poole 1995, 167).

24. On this point Stafford Poole says: "Florencia and Sigüenza y Góngora are two of the most influential writers in the history of the Guadalupe tradition. In particular, they laid the foundation for Valeriano's authorship of the *Nican mopohua*, an authorship that is widely accepted today. Yet careful analysis shows that this is not the case. Like Sánchez and others before them they had a maddening propensity for referring to documents that only they had seen and that they did not see fit to describe in detail or reproduce. Their testimonies were not clear and in the long run only added to the confusion that surrounds most Guadalupan documentation" (1995, 170). David Brading makes a similar statement about the lost documents, and concludes by saying, "All that survived was the arguments of Becerra Tanco, the confused ruminations of Florencia and the stark affirmations of Sigüenza y Góngora" (2001, 118).

25. For more on Alva Ixtlilxochitl's relation to the Guadalupe narrative, see Brian (forthcoming).

26. The creole identity of the seventeenth-century authors of the Guadalupe story is foregrounded in foundational analyses of the patriotic motivations behind Guadalupan texts, such as Francisco de la Maza's *Guadalupanismo mexicano* (1953) and Jacques Lafaye's *Quetzalcóatl et Guadalupe* (1974).

27. Jeanette Favrot Peterson has described the context of the production of the iconic painting of the Virgin of Guadalupe as "kaleidoscopic," where the painter "was immersed in an array of iconographic, stylistic, and material sources as well as biblical and theological texts" (2005, 609). Peterson's focus on the influence of multiple and diverse traditions in the painting is a potentially fruitful model for studying the writing of the narrative story of Guadalupe.

BIBLIOGRAPHY

AGN   Archivo General de la Nación, Mexico City
AGN-C   Capellanías
AGN-H   Historia
AGN-I   Inquisición
AGN-T   Tierras
AGN-V   Vínculos y Mayorazgos
CC   "Códice Chimalpahin," INAH, Mexico City.

Acosta, Joseph de. 1985. *Historia natural y moral de las Indias* [1590]. Mexico
    City: Fondo de Cultura Económica.
Acuña, René, editor. 1982–1988. *Relaciones geográfics del siglo XVI.* 10 vols.
    Mexico City: Universidad Nacional Autónoma de México, Instituto de
    Investigaciones Antropológicas.
Adorno, Rolena. 1986. *Guaman Poma: Writing and Resistance in Colonial Peru.*
    Austin: University of Texas Press.
———. 1987. "La *ciudad letrada* y los discursos coloniales." *Hispamérica* 16
    (48): 3–24.
———. 1989a. "Arms, Letters, and the Native Historian in Early Colonial
    Mexico." In *1492–1992: Re/Discovering Colonial Writing*, edited by René
    Jara and Nicholas Spadaccini, 201–24. Hispanic Issues 4. Minneapolis:
    Prisma Institute.
———. 1989b. "The Warrior and the War Community: Constructions of the
    Civil Order in Mexican Conquest History." *Dispositio* 14:225–46.
———. 1994. "The Indigenous Ethnographer: The 'Indio ladino' as historian
    and cultural mediator." In *Implicit Understandings: Observing, Reporting, and
    Reflecting on the Encounters between Europeans and Other Peoples in the Early
    Modern Era*, edited by Stuart Schwartz, 378–402. Cambridge: Cambridge
    University Press.
———. 1997. "History, Law, and the Eyewitness Protocols of Authority in
    Bernal Díaz del Castillo's *Historia verdadera de la conquista de la Nueva
    España*." In *The Project of Prose in Early Modern Europe*, edited by Elizabeth

Fowler and Roland Greene, 154–75. New York: Cambridge University Press.

————. 2007. *The Polemics of Possession in Spanish American Narrative*. New Haven, CT: Yale University Press.

————. 2012. "Court and Chronicle: A Native Andean's Engagement with Spanish Colonial Law." In *Native Claims: Indigenous Law against Empire, 1500–1920*, edited by Saliha Belmessous, 63–84. New York: Oxford University Press.

————. 2014. "Carlos de Sigüenza y Góngora (1645–1700): 'El amante más fino de nuestra patria.'" *Hispanófila* 171:11–27.

Alberti Manzanares, Pilar. 1994. "Mujeres sacerdotisas aztecas: Las cihuatlamacazque mencionadas en dos manuscritos inéditos" *Estudios de cultura náhuatl* 24:171–217.

Alva Ixtlilxochitl, Fernando de. *Historia de la nación chichimeca; Compendio histórico del reino de Tezcuco; Sumaria relación de las cosas de la Nueva España; Sumaria relación de la historia de esta Nueva España;* and *Relación sucinta en forma de memorial*. In CC, volumes 1 and 2.

————. *Sumaria relación de todas las cosas que han sucedido en la Nueva España; Relación sucinta en forma de memorial;* and *Sumaria relación de la historia general de esta Nueva España*. Manuscript transcription by Lorenzo Boturini Benaduci. Ayer Ms. 1109. Newberry Library, Chicago.

————. 1755. *Sumaria relación de todas las cosas que han sucedido en la Nueva España; Compendio histórico de los reyes de Tescuco;* and *Relación sucinta en forma de memorial*. Manuscript copy by Mariano Fernández de Echeverría y Veytia. 1755. Ayer Ms. 1108. Newberry Library, Chicago.

————. 1891–1892. *Obras históricas de don Fernando de Alva Ixtlilxochitl*. Edited by Alfredo Chavero. Mexico City: Oficina tip. de la Secretaria de Fomento.

————. 1975–1977. *Obras históricas*. Edited by Edmundo O'Gorman. 2 vols. Mexico City: Universidad Nacional Autónoma de México.

————. 2015. *The Native Conquistador: Alva Ixtlilxochitl's Account of the Conquest of New Spain*. Edited and translated by Amber Brian, Bradley Benton, and Pablo García Loaeza. University Park: Pennsylvania State University Press.

Anderson, Carl, and Eduardo Chávez. 2009. *Our Lady of Guadalupe, Mother of the Civilization of Love*. New York: Doubleday.

Arrom, José Juan. 1971. "Criollo: Definición y matices de un concepto." In *Certidumbre de América: Estudios de letras, folklore y cultura*, 11–26. Madrid: Editorial Gredos.

Bauer, Ralph, and José Antonio Mazzotti, editors. 2009. *Creole Subjects in the Colonial Americas*. Chapel Hill: University of North Carolina Press.

Becerra Tanco, Luis. 1979. *Felicidad de México en el principio, y milagroso origen, que tubo el Santuario de la Virgen Maria N. Señora de Guadalupe* [1675]. Facsimile edition. Edited by Miguel Civeira Taboada. Mexico City: Editorial Jus.

————. 1982. *Origen milagroso del santuario de Nuestra Señora de Guadalupe* [1675, with printed date of 1666]. In Torre Villar and Navarro de Anda 1982, 309–33.

Benjamin, Walter. 1996. "The Task of the Translator" [1923]. In *Selected Writings*, vol. 1: *1913–1926*, edited by Michael W. Jennings, 253–63. Cambridge, MA: Belknap Press of Harvard University Press.

Benton, Bradley. 2014. "The Outsider: Alva Ixtlilxochitl's Tenuous Ties to the City of Tetzcoco." *Colonial Latin American Review* 23 (1): 37–52.

Benton, Lauren. 2002. *Law and Colonial Cultures: Legal Regimes in World History, 1400–1900*. Cambridge: Cambridge University Press.

Beristáin y Souza, José Mariano. 1883. *Biblioteca Hispano Americana Septentrional*. 3 vols. Amecameca, Mexico: Tipografía del Colegio Católico.

Bierhorst, John, translator and editor. 2009. *Ballads of the Lords of New Spain: The Codex "Romances de los señores de la Nueva España."* Austin: University of Texas Press.

Bireley, Robert. 1990. *The Counter-Reformation Prince: Anti-Machiavellianism or Catholic Statecraft in Early Modern Europe*. Chapel Hill: University of North Carolina Press.

Bloch, Marc. 1954. *The Historian's Craft*. Translated by Peter Putnam. Manchester: Manchester University Press; New York: Alfred A. Knopf.

Bonfil Batalla, Guillermo. 1972. "El concepto del indio en América: una categoría de la situación colonial." *Anales de antropología* 9:105–24.

Boone, Elizabeth Hill. 1983. *The Codex Magliabechiano and the Lost Prototype of the Magliabechiano Group*. Berkeley: University of California Press.

————. 1998. "Pictorial Documents and Visual Thinking in Postconquest Mexico." In *Native Traditions in the Postconquest World*, edited by Elizabeth Hill Boone and Tom Cummins, 149–99. Washington, DC: Dumbarton Oaks Research Library and Collection. Available at *www.doaks.org*.

————. 2000. *Stories in Red and Black: Pictorial Histories of the Aztecs and Mixtecs*. Austin: University of Texas Press.

————. 2014. "Foreword." In *Indigenous Intellectuals: Knowledge, Power, and Colonial Culture in Mexico and the Andes*, edited by Gabriela Ramos and Yanna Yannakakis, ix–xiv. Durham, NC: Duke University Press.

Borah, Woodrow. 1983. *Justice by Insurance: The General Indian Court of Colonial Mexico and the Legal Aides of the Half-Real*. Berkeley: University of California Press.

Borah, Woodrow, and Sherburne F. Cook. 1963. *The Aboriginal Population on the Eve of the Spanish Conquest*. Ibero-Americana 45. Berkeley: University of California Press.

Boruchoff, David. 2004. "The Poetry of History." *Colonial Latin American Review* 13 (2): 275–82.

Boturini Benaduci, Lorenzo. 1999. *Idea de una nueva historia general de la América Septentrional* [1746]. Facsimile edition. Mexico City: INAH, Consejo Nacional Para la Cultura y las Artes. The edition includes *Catalogo del Musèo Indiano*.

Brading, D. A. 1991. *The First America: The Spanish Monarchy, Creole Patriots, and the Liberal State, 1492–1867*. New York: Cambridge University Press.

———. 2001. *Mexican Phoenix, Our Lady of Guadalupe: Image and Tradition across Five Centuries*. New York: Cambridge University Press.

Brian, Amber. 2014. "The Original Alva Ixtlilxochitl Manuscripts at Cambridge University." *Colonial Latin American Review* 23 (1): 84–101.

———. Forthcoming. "Alva Ixtlilxochitl and the Guadalupe Legend: The Question of Authorship." In *Fernando de Alva Ixtlilxochitl and His Legacy*, edited by Jongsoo Lee and Galen Brokaw. Tucson: University of Arizona Press.

Brubaker, Rogers, and Frederick Cooper. 2000. "Beyond 'Identity.'" *Theory and Society* 29:1–47.

Burkhart, Louise. 1989. *The Slippery Earth: Nahua-Christian Moral Dialogue in Sixteenth-Century Mexico*. Tucson: University of Arizona Press.

———. 1993. "The Cult of the Virgin of Guadalupe in Mexico." In *World Spirituality: An Encyclopedic History of the Religious Quest*. Volume 4, *South and Meso-American Native Spirituality*, edited by Gary Gossen and Miguel León-Portilla, 198–227. New York: Crossroad Publishing Company.

———. 2001. *Before Guadalupe: The Virgin Mary in Early Colonial Nahuatl Literature*. Albany: Institute for Mesoamerican Studies, University at Albany.

Burns, Kathryn. 2010. *Into the Archive: Writing and Power in Colonial Peru*. Durham, NC: Duke University Press.

Burrus, Ernest J. 1959. "Clavijero and the Lost Sigüenza y Góngora Manuscripts." *Estudios de cultura náhuatl* 1:59–90.

Bustamante, Carlos María de. 1829. *Horribles crueldades de los conquistadores de México*. Mexico City: A. Valdés.

Campa, Ramón de la. 1997. "El desafío inesperado de La ciudad letrada." In *Angel Rama y los estudios latinoamericanos*, edited by Mabel Moraña, 29–53. Pittsburgh: Instituto Internacional de Literatura Iberoamericana.

Cañizares-Esguerra, Jorge. 2001. *How to Write the History of the New World: Histories, Epistemologies, and Identities in the Eighteenth-Century Atlantic World*. Stanford, CA: Stanford University Press.

Carson, Anne. 1999. *Economy of the Unlost (Reading Simonides with Paul Celan)*. Princeton, NJ: Princeton University Press.

Cassin, Barbara, editor. 2014. *Dictionary of Untranslatables: A Philosophical Lexicon*. Princeton, NJ: Princeton University Press.

Chamberlain, Robert S. 1939. "The Concept of the '*Señor Natural*' as Revealed by Castilian Law and Administrative Documents." *Hispanic American Historical Review* 19 (2): 130–37.

Chance, John. 1994. "Indian Elites in Late Colonial Mesoamerica." In *Caciques and Their People: A Volume in Honor of Ronald Spores*, edited by Joyce Marcus and Judith Francis Zeitlin, 45–65. Ann Arbor: Museum of Anthropology, University of Michigan.

Charles, John. 2010. *Allies at Odds: The Andean Church and Its Indigenous Agents, 1583–1671*. Albuquerque: University of New Mexico Press.

Chimalpahin Quauhtlehuanitzin, Domingo de San Antón Muñón. 1997. *Codex Chimalpahin: Society and Politics in Mexico Tenochtitlan, Tlatelolco, Texcoco, Culhuacan, and Other Nahua Altepetl in Central Mexico*. Translated and edited by Arthur J. O. Anderson and Susan Schroeder. 2 vols. Norman: University of Oklahoma.

Christie's. 2014a. *Valuable Manuscripts and Printed Books, Wednesday 21 May 2014*. London: Christie, Manson & Woods.

———. 2014b. "Release: 17th Century Manuscript Detailing Early History of Aztec Nation Makes a Celebrated Return to Mexico," *christies.com*. September 18.

Clavijero, Francisco Javier. 1964. *Historia antigua de México* [1780]. Edited by Mariano Cuevas. Mexico City: Porrúa.

Cline, Howard F., editor. 1975. *Handbook of Middle American Indians*. Vol. 15, *Guide to Ethnohistorical Sources, Part 4*. Austin: University of Texas Press.

Cogdell, Sam. 1994. "Criollos, gachupines, y 'plebe tan en extremo plebe': Retórica e ideología criollas en *Alboroto y motín de México* de Sigüenza y Góngora." In *Relecturas del Barroco de Indias*, edited by Mabel Moraña, 245–79. Hanover, NH: Ediciones del Norte.

Cook, Sherburne F., and Woodrow Borah. 1960. *The Indian Population of Central Mexico, 1531–1610*. Ibero-Americana 44. Berkeley: University of California Press.

———. 1979. *Essays in Population History: Mexico and California*. Vol. 3. Berkeley: University of California Press.

Cooper, Frederick. 2005. *Colonialism in Question: Theory, Knowledge, History*. Berkeley: University of California Press.

Cope, R. Douglas. 1994. *The Limits of Racial Domination: Plebeian Society in Colonial Mexico City, 1524–1730*. Madison: University of Wisconsin Press.

Córdova, James. 2009. "Aztec Vestal Virgins and the Brides of Christ: The Mixed Heritage of New Spain's *Monjas Coronadas*." *Colonial Latin American Review* 18 (2): 189–218.

Corominas, Joan. 1961. *Breve diccionario etimológico de la lengua castellana*. Madrid: Editorial Gredos.

Cortés, Rocío. 2008. "The Colegio Imperial de Santa Cruz de Tlatelolco and Its Aftermath: Nahua Intellectuals and the Spiritual Conquest of Mexico." In *A Companion to Latin American Literature and Culture*, edited by Sara Castro-Klarén, 86–105. Malden, MA: Blackwell.

Covarrubias, Sebastián de. 1943. *Tesoro de la lengua castellana o española* [1611]. Barcelona: S. A. Horta.

Davis, Natalie Zemon. 1987. *Fiction in the Archives: Pardon Tales and Their Tellers in Sixteenth-Century France*. Stanford, CA: Stanford University Press.

de Certeau, Michel. 1988. *The Writing of History* [1975]. Translated by Tom Conley. New York: Columbia University Press.

de la Cadena, Marisol. 2005. "Are 'Mestizos' Hybrids? The Conceptual Politics of Andean Identities." *Journal of Latin American Studies*. 37 (2): 259–84.

Díaz, Mónica. 2010. *Indigenous Writings from the Convent: Negotiating Ethnic Autonomy in Colonial Mexico*. Tucson: University of Arizona Press.

Douglas, Eduardo de J. 2010. *In the Palace of Nezahualcoyotl: Painting Manuscripts, Writing the Pre-Hispanic Past in Early Colonial Period Tetzcoco, Mexico*. Austin: University of Texas Press.

Dueñas, Alcira. 2010. *Indians and Mestizos in the "Lettered City": Reshaping Justice, Social Hierarchy, and Political Culture in Colonial Peru*. Boulder: University Press of Colorado.

Durand-Forest, Jacqueline de. 1976. "Commentaire." In *Codex Ixtlilxochitl (Bibliothèque nationale, Paris, MS mexicain 65–71)*, edited by Ferdinand Anders. Facsimile edition. Fontes rerum mexicanarum, volume 9. Graz, Austria: Akademische Druck- und Verlagsanstalt.

Escalante Gonzalbo, Pablo. 2004. "Portrait of Moctezuma (Motecuhzoma II, Xocoyotzin)." In *Painting a New World: Mexican Art and Life, 1521–1821,* edited by Donna Pierce, Rogelio Ruiz Gomar, and Clara Bargellini, 171–77. Denver: Denver Art Museum.

Fernández de Recas, Guillermo S. 1961. *Cacicazgos y nobiliario indígeba de la Nueva España.* Mexico City: Universidad Nacional Autónoma de México.

Fisher, Andrew B., and Matthew D. O'Hara, editors. 2009a. *Imperial Subjects: Race and Identity in Colonial Latin America.* Durham, NC: Duke University Press.

————. 2009b. "Introduction: Racial Identities and Their Interpreters in Colonial Latin America." In Fisher and O'Hara 2009a, 1–38.

Florencia, Francisco de. 1982. "La estrella del norte de México" [1688]. In Torre Villar and Navarro de Anda 1982, 359–99.

Florescano, Enrique. 1994. *Memory, Myth, and Time in Mexico: From the Aztecs to Independence* [1987]. Translated by Albert Bork and Kathryn Bork. Austin: University of Texas Press.

Foucault, Michel. 1972. *The Archaeology of Knowledge and The Discourse of Language* [1969]. Translated by A. M. Sheridan Smith. New York: Pantheon Books.

García Loaeza, Pablo. 2009. "Saldos del criollismo: El *Teatro de virtudes políticas* de Carlos de Sigüenza y Góngora a la luz de la historiografía de Fernando de Alva Ixtlilxóchitl." *Colonial Latin American Review* 18 (2): 219–35.

————. 2014. "Deeds to Be Praised for All Time: Alva Ixtlilxochitl's *Historia de la nación chichimeca* and Geoffrey of Monmouth's *History of the Kings of Britain.*" *Colonial Latin American Review.* 23 (1): 53–69.

Garibay K., Ángel María. 1971. *Historia de la literatura náhuatl* [1954]. 2 vols. Mexico City: Porrúa.

Gemelli Careri, Giovanni Francesco. 1955. *Viaje a la Nueva España.* Translated into Spanish by José María Agreda y Sánchez. 2 vols. Mexico City: Editora Ibero-Mexicana. Originally published as *Giro del mondo* (1699).

Gerhard, Peter. 1993. *A Guide to the Historical Geography of New Spain.* Norman: University of Oklahoma Press.

Gibson, Charles. 1975. "A Survey of Middle American Prose Manuscripts in the Native Historical Tradition." In Cline 1975, 311–21.

Gibson, Charles, and John B. Glass. 1975. "A Census of Middle American Prose Manuscripts in the Native Historical Traditions." In Cline 1975, 322–400.

Glass, John B. 1979. *The Boturini Collection and the Text of the Legal Proceedings in Mexico, 1742–1743*. Lincoln Center, MA: Conemex Associates.

———. 1981. *The Boturini Collection: Documents Numbers 1743-1-1 through 1743-2-6*. Lincoln Center, MA: Conemex Associates.

González Echevarría, Roberto. 1998. *Myth and Archive: A Theory of Latin American Narrative* [1990]. Durham, NC: Duke University Press.

Gray, Vivienne. 2011. *Xenophon's Mirror of Princes: Reading the Reflections*. Oxford: Oxford University Press.

Greenblatt, Stephen. 2010. "Cultural Mobility: An Introduction." In *Cultural Mobility: A Manifesto*, edited by Greenblatt, 1–23. Cambridge: Cambridge University Press.

Higgins, Antony. 2000. *Constructing the Criollo Archive: Subjects of Knowledge in the* Bibliotheca mexicana *and the* Rusticatio mexicana. West Lafayette, IN: Purdue University Press.

INAH. 2014. "El gobierno de México recupera el Códice Chimalpahin." *inah.gob.mex*. September 17.

Jesson, Alan F., editor. 1982. *Historical Catalogue of the Manuscripts of Bible House Library*. Comp. M. Rosaria Falivene. London: British and Foreign Bible Society.

Jiménez, Nora. 2002. "Príncipe indígena y latino: Una compra de libros de Antonio Huitziméngari (1559)." *Relaciones* 23:91.

Jones, Joseph. 1979. "La erudición elegante: Observations on the Emblematic Tradition in Sor Juana's *Neptuno alegórico* and Sigüenza's *Teatro de virtudes políticas*." *Hispanófila* 65:43–58.

Jouve Martín, José Ramón. 2005. *Esclavos de la ciudad letrada: Esclavitud, escritura y colonialismo en Lima (1650–1700)*. Lima: Instituto de Estudios Peruanos.

Karttunen, Frances. 1992. *An Analytical Dictionary of Nahuatl*. Norman: University of Oklahoma Press.

Kauffmann, Leisa. 2014. "Alva Ixtlilxochitl's Colonial Mexican Trickster Tale: Nezahualcoyotl and Tezcatlipoca in the *Historia de la nación chichimeca*." *Colonial Latin American Review* 23 (1): 70–83.

Keen, Benjamin. 1971. *The Aztec Image in Western Thought*. New Brunswick, NJ: Rutgers University Press.

Kellogg, Susan. 1995. *Law and the Transformation of Aztec Culture, 1500–1700*. Norman: University of Oklahoma Press.

———. 2013. "The Mysterious Mothers of Alva Ixtlilxochitl: Women, Kings, and Power in Late Prehispanic and Conquest Tetzcoco." In *Género y arqueología en Mesoamérica: Homenaje a Rosemary Joyce*, edited by María Rodríguez-Shadow and Susan Kellogg, 153–76. Mexico City: Centro de Estudios de Antropología y la Mujer.

Kingsborough, Lord [Edward King]. 1848. *Antiquities of Mexico*. Vol. 9. London: Robert Havell and Conaghi.

Krippner-Martínez, James. 2001. *Rereading the Conquest: Power, Politics, and the History of Early Colonial Michoacán, Mexico, 1521–1565*. University Park: Pennsylvania State University Press.

Lafaye, Jacques. 1987. *Quetzalcoatl and Guadalupe: The Formation of Mexican National Consciousness, 1531–1813* [1974]. Translated by Benjamin Keen. Chicago: University of Chicago Press.

Laso de la Vega, Luis. 1998. *The Story of Guadalupe: Luis Laso de la Vega's "Huei tlamahuiçoltica" of 1649*. Edited and translated by Lisa Sousa, Stafford Poole, and James Lockhart. Stanford, CA: Stanford University Press; Los Angeles: UCLA Latin American Center Publications, University of California, Los Angeles.

Lavrín, Asunción. 2008. *Brides of Christ: Conventual Life in Colonial Mexico*. Stanford, CA: Stanford University Press.

Lee, Jongsoo. 2008. *The Allure of Nezahualcoyotl: Pre-Hispanic History, Religion, and Nahua Poetics*. Albuquerque: University of New Mexico Press.

———. 2014. "Mestizaje and the Creation of Mexican National Literature: Ángel María Garibary Kintana's Nahuatl Project." *Bulletin of Spanish Studies* 91:1–24.

Lee, Jongsoo, and Galen Brokaw, editors. 2014. *Texcoco: Prehispanic and Colonial Perspectives*. Boulder: University Press of Colorado.

Leonard, Irving. 1929. *Don Carlos de Sigüenza y Góngora: A Mexican Savant in the Seventeenth Century*. Berkeley: University of California Press.

———. 1959. *Baroque Times in Old Mexico*. Ann Arbor: University of Michigan Press.

León-Portilla, Miguel. 1963. *Aztec Thought and Culture*. Translated by Jack Emory Davis. Norman: University of Oklahoma Press.

———. 2000. *Tonantzin Guadalupe: Pensamiento náhuatl y mensaje cristiano en el "Nican mopohua."* Mexico City: Fondo de Cultura Económica.

———. 2008. *Visión de los vencidos: Relaciones indígenas de la conquista* [1959]. Mexico City: Biblioteca del Estudiante Universitario, Universidad Nacional Autónoma de México.

Lezama Lima, José. 1993. *La expresión americana*. Mexico City: Fondo de Cultura Económica.

Lienhard, Martin. 1991. *La voz y su huella: Escritura y conflicto étnico-cultural en América Latina, 1492–1988*. Hanover, NH: Ediciones del Norte.

Lockhart, James. 1992. *The Nahuas after the Conquest: A Social and Cultural History of the Indians of Central Mexico, Sixteenth through Eighteenth Centuries*. Stanford, CA: Stanford University Press.

———. 1999. *Of Things of the Indies: Essays Old and New in Early Latin American History*. Stanford, CA: Stanford University Press.

López Sarrelangue, Delfina Esmeralda. 1999. *La nobleza indígena de Pátzcuaro en la época virreinal* [1965]. Morelia, Michoacán: Morevallado Editores.

Lorente Medina, Antonio. 1996. *La prosa de Sigüenza y Góngora y la formación de la conciencia criolla mexicana*. Mexico City: Fondo de Cultura Económica.

MacCormack, Sabine. 2007. *On the Wings of Time: Rome, the Incas, Spain, and Peru*. Princeton, NJ: Princeton University Press.

Macleod, Murdo. 1998. "Self-Promotion: The *Relaciones de méritos y servicios* and Their Historical and Political Interpretation." *Colonial Latin American Historical Review* 7 (1): 25–42.

Mañé, Jorge Ignacio. 1955. *Introducción al estudio de los Virreyes de Nueva España, 1535–1746*. Mexico City: Ediciones Selectas.

Maravall, José Antonio. 1984. "Maquiavelo y maquiavelismo en España." In *Estudios de historia del pensamiento español*, 39–72. Madrid: Ediciones Cultura Hispánica.

Martínez, María Elena. 2008. *Genealogical Fictions: Limpieza de Sangre, Religion, and Gender in Colonial Mexico*. Stanford: Stanford University Press.

Martínez Baracs, Rodrigo. 2000. "Tepeyac en la conquista de México: Problemas historiográficos." In *Tepeyac: Estudios históricos*, edited by Carmen Aguilera and Ismael Arturo Montero García, 55–118. Mexico City: Editorial de Tepeyac.

Matthew, Laura. 2012. *Memories of Conquest: Becoming Mexicano in Colonial Guatemala*. Chapel Hill: University of North Carolina Press.

Matthew, Laura, and Michel Oudijk, editors. 2007. *Indian Conquistadors: Indigenous Allies in the Conquest of Mesoamerica*. Norman: University of Oklahoma Press.

Mauss, Marcel. 1967. *The Gift: Forms and Functions of Exchange in Archaic Societies*. Translated by Ian Cunnison. New York: Norton. Originally published as *Essai sur le don, forme archaïque de l'echange* (1925).

Maza, Francisco de la. 1981. *El guadalupanismo mexicano* [1953]. Mexico City: Fondo de Cultura Económica.

Mazzotti, José Antonio, editor. 2000. *Agencias criollas: La ambigüedad "colonial" en las letras hispanoamericanas*. Pittsburgh: Biblioteca de América, Instituto Internacional de Literatura Iberoamericana.

McDonough, Kelly. 2014. *The Learned Ones: Nahua Intellectuals in Postconquest Mexico*. Tucson: University of Arizona Press.

Mendieta, Gerónimo de. 1971. *Historia eclesiástica indiana*. Mexico City: Editorial Porrúa.

Menegus Bornemann, Margarita, and Rodolfo Aguirre Salvador. 2005. *El cacicazgo en Nueva España y Filipinas*. Mexico City: Plaza y Valdés; Universidad Nacional Autónoma de México; Centro de Estudios Sobre la Universidad.

Merkl, Heinrich. 1992. "Juana Inés de la Cruz y Carlos de Sigüenza y Góngora en 1680." *Iberoromania* 36:21–37.

Merrim, Stephanie. 2010. *The Spectacular City, Mexico, and Colonial Hispanic Literary Culture*. Austin: University of Texas Press.

Mignolo, Walter. 1995. *The Darker Side of the Renaissance: Literacy, Territoriality, and Colonization*. Ann Arbor: University of Michigan Press.

Molina, Alonso de. 1992. *Vocabulario en lengua castellana y mexicana y mexicana y castellana* [1571]. Facsimile edition. Mexico City: Editorial Porrúa.

Moraña, Mabel. 2000. "El 'tumulto de indios' de 1692 en los pliegues de la fiesta barroca: Historiografía, subversión popular y agencia criolla en el México colonial." In Mazzotti 2000, 161–75.

More, Anna. 2013. *Baroque Sovereignty: Carlos de Sigüenza y Góngora and the Creole Archive of Colonial Mexico*. Philadelphia: University of Pennsylvania Press.

Mörner, Magnus. 1967. *Race Mixture in the History of Latin America*. Boston: Little, Brown.

———. 1970. *La corona española y los foráneos en los pueblos de indios de América*. Stockholm: Instituto de Estudios Iberoamericanos.

Mumford, Jeremy. 2009. "Aristocracy on the Auction Block: Race, Lords, and the Perpetuity Controversy of Sixteenth-Century Peru." In Fisher and O'Hara 2009a, 39–59.

Munch, Guido. 1976. *El cacicazgo de San Juan Teotihuacán durante la colonia (1521–1821)*. Mexico City: Instituto Nacional de Antropología e Historia.

Mundy, Barbara. 1996. *The Mapping of New Spain: Indigenous Cartography and the Maps of the Relaciones Geográficas*. Chicago: University of Chicago Press.

Muñoz Camargo, Diego. 1994. *Suma y epíloga de toda la descripción de Tlaxcala*. Edited by Andrea Martínez Baracs and Carlos Sempat Assadourian. Tlaxcala, Mexico: Universidad Autónoma de Tlaxcala.

Nadon, Christopher. 2001. *Xenophon's Prince: Republic and Empire in the Cyropaedia*. Berkeley: University of California Press.

Nemser, Daniel. 2014. "Archaeology in the Lettered City." *Colonial Latin American Review* 23 (2): 197–223.

O'Gorman, Edmundo, editor. 1975–1977. *Obras históricas: Fernando de Alva Ixtlilxochitl*. 2 vols. Mexico City: Universidad Nacional Autónoma de México.

———. 1986. *Destierro de sombras: Luz en el origen y culto de Nuestra Señora de Guadalupe de Tepeyac*. Mexico City: Universidad Nacional Autónoma de México.

Offner, Jerome. 1983. *Law and Politics in Aztec Texcoco*. New York: Cambridge University Press.

Owensby, Brian P. 2008. *Empire of Law and Indian Justice in Colonial Mexico*. Stanford, CA: Stanford University Press.

Pagden, Anthony. 1987. "Identity Formation in Spanish America." In *Colonial Identity in the Atlantic World: 1500–1800*, edited by Nicholas Canny and Anthony Pagden, 51–93. Princeton, NJ: Princeton University Press.

———. 1995. *Lords of All the World: Ideologies of Empire in Spain, Britain, and France, c. 1500–c. 1800*. New Haven, CT: Yale University Press.

Paz, Octavio. 1979. "Ritos políticos en la Nueva España." *Vuelta* 35:4–10.

———. 1982. *Sor Juana Inés de la Cruz, o Las trampas de la fe*. Mexico City: Fondo de Cultura Económica.

Pérez-Rocha, Emma, and Rafael Tena, editors. 2000. *La nobleza indígena del centro de México después de la conquista*. Mexico City: Institutio Nacional de Antropología e Historia.

Pérez Salazar, Francisco. 1928. *Biografía de D. Carlos de Sigüenza y Góngora*. Mexico City: Antigua Imprenta de Murguia.

Peterson, Jeanette Favrot. 2005. "Creating the Virgin of Guadalupe: The Cloth, the Artist, and Sources in Sixteenth-Century New Spain." *Americas* 61 (4): 571–610.

———. 2014. *Visualizing Guadalupe: From Black Madonna to Queen of the Americas*. Austin: University of Texas Press.

Pomar, Juan Bautista. *Relación de Texcoco, instrucción y memoria, romances de los señores de la Nueva España*. Ms. G57–G59. Benson Library. University of Texas at Austin.

———. 1986. *Relación de la ciudad y provincia de Tezcoco*. Edited by René Acuña. Volume 3 of Acuña 1982–1988.

Poole, Stafford. 1995. *Our Lady of Guadalupe: The Origins and Sources of a Mexican National Symbol, 1531–1797*. Tucson: University of Arizona Press.

———. 2006. *The Guadalupan Controversies in Mexico*. Stanford, CA: Stanford University Press.

Praz, Mario. 1964. *Studies in Seventeenth-Century Imagery*. Rome: Edizioni de Storia e Letteratura.

Rabasa, José. 1994a. *Inventing America: Spanish Historiography and the Formation of Eurocentrism*. Norman: University of Oklahoma Press.

———. 1994b. "Pre-Columbian Pasts and Indian Presents in Mexican History." *Dispositio* 19 (46): 245–70.

———. 2010. *Without History: Subaltern Studies, the Zapatista Insurgency, and the Specter of History*. Pittsburgh: University of Pittsburgh Press.

Rama, Ángel, 1996. *The Lettered City* [1984]. Translated by John Charles Chasteen. Durham, NC: Duke University Press.

Ramos, Gabriela, and Yanna Yannakakis, editors. 2014. *Indigenous Intellectuals: Knowledge, Power, and Colonial Culture in Mexico and the Andes*. Durham, NC: Duke University Press.

Rappaport, Joanne. 2014. *The Disappearing Mestizo: Configuring Difference in the Colonial New Kingdom of Granada*. Durham, NC: Duke University Press.

Rappaport, Joanne, and Tom Cummins. 2012. *Beyond the Lettered City: Indigenous Literacies in the Andes*. Durham, NC: Duke University Press.

Recopilación de las leyes de los reynos de las Indias, 1681. 4 vols. Madrid: Julián Paredes.

Restall, Matthew. 1998. *Maya Conquistador*. Boston: Beacon Press.

———. 2012. "The New Conquest History." *History Compass* 10 (2): 151–60.

Restall, Matthew, and Florine Asselbergs. 2007. *Invading Guatemala: Spanish, Nahua, and Maya Accounts of the Conquest Wars*. University Park: Pennsylvania State University Press.

Ricard, Robert. 1966. *The Spiritual Conquest of Mexico* [1933]. Translated by Lesley Byrd Simpson. Berkeley: University of California Press.

Rivadeneira, Pedro de. 1868. *Obras escogidas*. Volume 60. Biblioteca de autores españoles. Madrid: M. Rivadeneira.

Ross, Kathleen. 1993. *The Baroque Narrative of Carlos de Sigüenza y Góngora: A New World Paradise*. Cambridge: Cambridge University Press.

Ruiz Medrano, Ethelia. 2010. *Mexico's Indigenous Communities: Their Lands and Histories, 1500–2010*. Boulder: University Press of Colorado.

Russo, Alessandra. 2014. *The Untranslatable Image: A Mestizo History of the Arts in New Spain, 1500–1600*. Austin: University of Texas Press.

Ruwet, Wayne. 1997. "Physical Description of the Manuscripts." In Chimalpahin 1997, 1:17–24.

Saavedra Fajardo, Diego de. 1927–1930. *Idea de un príncipe político-cristiano* [1640]. Edited by Vicente García de Diego. 4 vols. Madrid: Ediciones de La Lectura.

Salomon, Frank. 1982. "Chronicles of the Impossible: Notes on Three Peruvian Indigenous Historians." In *From Oral to Written Expression: Native Andean Chronicles of the Early Colonial Period*, edited by Rolena Adorno, 9–39. Syracuse, NY: Maxwell School of Citizenship and Public Affairs, Syracuse University.

———. 1991. *The Huarochirí Manuscript: A Testament of Ancient and Colonial Andean Religion*. Austin: University of Texas Press.

———. 2004. *The Cord Keepers: Khipus and Cultural Life in a Peruvian Village*. Durham, NC: Duke University Press.

Salomon, Frank, and Mercedes Niño-Murcia. 2011. *The Lettered Mountain: A Peruvian Village's Way with Writing*. Durham, NC: Duke University Press.

Salomon, Frank, and George L. Urioste, translators. 1991. *The Huarochirí Manuscript: A Testament of Ancient and Colonial Andean Religion*. Annotations and introductory essay by Salomon. Austin: University of Texas Press.

Sánchez, Miguel. 1982. *Imagen de la Virgen María Madre de Dios de Guadalupe* [1648]. In Torre Villar and Navarro de Anda 1982, 152–281. Mexico City: Fondo de Cultura Económica.

Sánchez Lamego, Miguel. 1955. *El primer mapa general de México elaborado por un mexicano*. Mexico City: Instituto de Geografía e Historia.

Schroeder, Susan. 1991. *Chimalpahin and the Kingdoms of Chalco*. Tucson: University of Arizona Press.

———. 1994. "Father José María Luis Mora, Liberalism, and the British and Foreign Bible Society in Nineteenth-Century Mexico." *Americas* 50 (3): 377–97.

———. 1997. "Introduction." In Chimalpahin 1997, 1:3–13.

———. 2007. "Introduction: The Genre of Conquest Studies." In Matthew and Oudijk 2007, 5–27.

———. 2010. "Chimalpahin Rewrites the Conquest: Yet Another Epic History?" In *The Conquest All over Again: Nahuas and Zapotecs Thinking, Writing, and Painting Spanish Colonialism*, edited by Schroeder, 101–23. Brighton: Sussex Academic Press.

———. 2011. "The Truth about the *Crónica mexicayotl*." *Colonial Latin American Review* 20 (2): 233–47.

Schwaller, John Frederick. 1994. "Nahuatl Studies and the 'Circle' of Horacio Carochi." *Estudios de Cultura Náhuatl* 24:387–98.

————. 2011. *The History of the Catholic Church in Latin America: From Conquest to Revolution and Beyond*. New York: New York University Press.

Sell, Barry D., and John Frederick Schwaller, editors and translators. 1999. *A Guide to Confession Large and Small in the Mexican Language, 1634*, by Bartolomé de Alva. Critical edition. With Lu Ann Homza. Norman: University of Oklahoma Press.

Sigüenza y Góngora, Carlos de. 1929. "Letter to Admiral Pez" [ca. 1692]. Edited and translated by Irving Leonard. In Leonard 1929, 210–77.

————. 1945. *Glorias de Querétaro* [1680]. Querétaro, Mexico: Ediciones Cimatario.

————. 1948. *Noticia chronológica de los reyes, emperadores, governadores, presidentes y vi-reyes de esta nobilíssima ciudad de México*. Mexico City: José Porrúa.

————. 1960. *Piedad heroyca de Don Fernando Cortés* [ca. 1689]. Edited by Jaime Delgado. Madrid: José Porrúa Turanzas.

————. 1963. *Documentos inéditos de don Carlos de Sigüenza y Góngora*. Edited by Irving Leonard. Mexico City: Centro Bibliográfico Juan José de Eguiara y Eguren.

————. 1984a. *Seis obras*. Edited by William Bryant. Caracas: Biblioteca Ayacucho.

————. 1984b. *Alboroto y motín*. In 1984a, 93–144.

————. 1984c. *Teatro de virtudes políticas*. In 1984a, 165–240.

————. 1995. *Parayso occidental: Plantado y cultivado por la liberal benefica mano* [1684]. Facsimile edition. Mexico: Universidad Nacional Autónoma de México/Condumex.

————. 2008. *Oriental planeta evangélico: Epopeya sacro-panegyrica al apostol grande de las Indias, S. Francisco Xavier* [1700]. Edited by Antonio Lorente Medina. Pamplona, Spain: University of Navarra; Madrid: Iberoamericana; Frankfurt: Vervuet.

Solano, Francisco de. 1984. "Fiestas en la ciudad de México." In *La ville en Amerique Espagnole Coloniale*, edited by André Saint-Lu, 243–332. Paris: Universite de la Sorbonne Nouvelle Paris III.

Sousa, Lisa, Stafford Poole, and James Lockhart. 1998. "Introduction." In *The Story of Guadalupe: Luis Laso de la Vega's "Huei tlamahuiçoltica" of 1649*, edited and translated by Sousa, Poole, and Lockhart, 1–47. Stanford, CA: Stanford University Press; Los Angeles: UCLA Latin American Center Publications, University of California, Los Angeles.

Steedman, Carolyn. 2002. *Dust: The Archive and Cultural History*. New Brunswick, NJ: Rutgers University Press.

Stern, Steve. 1993. *Peru's Indian Peoples and the Challenge of Spanish Conquest: Huamanga to 1640*. Madison: University of Wisconsin Press.

Stoler, Ann Laura. 2009. *Along the Archival Grain: Epistemic Anxieties and Colonial Common Sense*. Princeton, NJ: Princeton University Press.

Stoler, Ann Laura, and Frederick Cooper. 1997. "Between Metropole and Colony: Rethinking a Research Agenda." In *Tensions of Empire: Colonial Cultures in a Bourgeois World*, edited by Stoler and Cooper, 1–56. Berkeley: University of California Press.

Tatum, James. 1989. *Xenophon's Imperial Fiction: On the Education of Cyrus*. Princeton, NJ: Princeton University Press.

Tavárez, David. 2011. *The Invisible War: Indigenous Devotions, Discipline, and Dissent in Colonial Mexico*. Stanford, CA: Stanford University Press.

Thompson, John Eric S. 1941. "The Missing Illustrations of the Pomar Relación." *Notes on Middle American Archaeology and Ethnology* (Carnegie Institution of Washington) 1 (4): 15–21.

Torquemada, Juan de. 1969. *Monarquía indiana* [1615]. 3 vols. Facsimile of second edition [1723]. Mexico City: Editorial Porrúa.

Torre Villar, Ernesto de la, and Ramiro Navarro de Anda, editors. 1982. *Testimonios histórico guadalupanos*. Mexico City: Fondo de Cultura Económica.

Townsend, Camilla. 2010. *Here in This Year: Seventeenth-Century Nahuatl Annals of the Tlaxcala-Puebla Valley*. Stanford, CA: Stanford University Press.

———. 2014. "Introduction: The Evolution of Alva Ixtlilxochitl's Scholarly Life." *Colonial Latin American Review* 23 (1): 1–17.

Trabulse, Elías. 1988. *Los manuscritos perdidos de Sigüenza y Góngora*. Mexico City: El Colegio de México.

Trouillot, Michel-Rolph. 1995. *Silencing the Past: Power and the Production of History*. Boston: Beacon Press.

van Deusen, Nancy. 2015. *Global Indios: The Indigenous Struggle for Justice in Sixteenth-Century Spain*. Durham, NC: Duke University Press.

Vega, Garcilaso de la [El Inca]. 1999. *Comentarios reales (selección)*. Second edition. Edited by Enrique Pupo-Walker. Madrid: Ediciones Cátedra.

Velazco, Salvador. 2003. *Visiones de Anáhuac, reconstrucciones historiográficas y etnicidades emergentes en el México colonial: Fernando de Alva Ixtlilxóchitl, Diego Muñoz Camargo y Hernando Alvarado Tezozómoc*. Guadalajara, Mexico: Universidad de Guadalajara.

Venuti, Lawrence. 2012. *Translation Changes Everything: Theory and Practice.* New York: Routledge.

Villavicencio, Diego Jaime Ricardo. 1692. *Luz, y methodo, de confesar idolatras, y destierro de idolatrias, debajo del tratado siguiente.* Puebla de los Ángeles, Mexico: Imprenta de Diego Fernández de León.

Villella, Peter. 2012. "Indian Lords, Hispanic Gentlemen: The Salazars of Colonial Tlaxcala." *Americas* 69 (1): 1–36.

———. 2014. "The Last Acolhua: Alva Ixtlilxochitl and Elite Native Historiography in Early New Spain." *Colonial Latin American Review* 23 (1): 18–36.

Vitulli, Juan M., and David M. Solodkow, editors. 2009. *Poéticas de lo criollo: La transformación del concepto "criollo" en las letras hispanoamericanas (siglo XVI al XIX).* Buenos Aires: Ediciones Corregidor.

Voigt, Lisa. 2006. "Peregrine Peregrinations: Rewriting Travel and Discovery in Mestizo Chronicles of New Spain." *Revista de Estudios Hispánicos* 40 (1): 1–22.

von Wobeser, Gisela. 1998. "Las capellanías de misas: Su función religiosa, social y económica en la Nueva España." In *Cofradías, capellanías y obras pías en la América colonial,* edited by Pilar Martínez López-Cano, Gisela von Wobeser, and Juan Guillermo Muñoz, 119–30. Mexico City: Universidad Nacional Autónoma de México.

Wood, Stephanie. 2003. *Transcending Conquest: Nahua Views of Spanish Colonial Mexico.* Norman: University of Oklahoma Press.

Xenophon. 2001. *The Education of Cyrus.* Translated and annotated by Wayne Ambler. Ithaca, NY: Cornell University Press.

Yannakakis, Yanna. 2008. *The Art of Being In-Between: Native Intermediaries, Indian Identity, and Local Rule in Colonial Oaxaca.* Durham, NC: Duke University Press.

———. 2013. "Indigenous People and Legal Culture in Spanish America." *History Compass* 11 (11): 931–47.

Yépez, Heriberto. 2014. "Gobierno compra 'su' pasado." *Milenio.com.* September 20.

Zamora, Margarita. 1988. *Language, Authority, and Indigenous History in the "Comentarios reales de los incas."* New York: Cambridge University Press.

———. 1993. *Reading Columbus.* Berkeley: University of California Press.

INDEX

Numbers in italic refer to figures.